REVELATION
Pray Always to Escape
All These Things
That Will Come Upon the Earth

By
Robert Lee Drumheller

Cover Art
Alena Harrold

Layout, Design, Printing
Commercial Printing Brokerage

First Edition   August, 2017

REVELATION
Pray Always to Escape All These Things
That Will Come Upon the Earth

Copyright ©2017 by Robert Lee Drumheller

All rights reserved. No part of this publication may be reproduced, stored in a retrieval system, or transmitted in any form or by any means electronic, photocopying, recording or otherwise, without prior permission in writing from the copyright owner.

Library of Congress Control Number: 2017912446
Trade Edition
ISBN 978-0-692-91173-0 (soft cover)
ISBN 978-0-692-91174-7 (epub)

ACKNOWLEDGMENTS

I want to thank my lovely wife, Jadwiga, for her support and assistance with my manuscript. This book would not be possible without her support and encouragement. I appreciate all the many hours she spent editing and giving advice—more than you will ever know.

I want to thank my daughter, Jennifer James, and her husband, Joseph James, for their support in proofreading my manuscript and for the wisdom with which the Lord has blessed them both.

Scriptures taken from the King James Version (public domain) unless otherwise noted.

The New King James Version, and English Standard Version, are taken from Bible Gateway (www.biblegateway.com). Used by Permission.

Table of Contents

Acknowledgments...3
Index of Illustrations..6
Glossary of Terms..7
Introduction..9
Chapter 1 – The Revelation of Jesus Christ.......................................15
Chapter 2 – Letters to the Churches – Part One................................23
Chapter 3 – Letters to the Churches – Part Two................................41
Chapter 4 – The Heavenly Scene...51
Chapter 5 – The Lion and the Book..63
Chapter 6 – Opening of the Seals..73
Chapter 7 – Multitude of Witnesses..99
Chapter 8 – Trumpet Judgments – Part One...................................105
Chapter 9 – Trumpet Judgments – Part Two...................................117
Chapter 10 – The Mighty Angel and the Book.................................125
Chapter 11 – The Two Witnesses...129
Chapter 12 – War in Heaven...141
Chapter 13 – The Two Beasts..149
Chapter 14 – The *Thumos* of God...165
Chapter 15 – Preparation for the Seven Last Plagues......................175
Chapter 16 – The Vials of Wrath..179
Chapter 17 – The Destruction of Religious Babylon........................191
Chapter 18 – The Destruction of Commercial Babylon...................211
Chapter 19 – The Return of Jesus Christ...225
Chapter 20 – The Kingdom Age and the Final Judgment...............237
Chapter 21 – The New Heaven and New Earth................................253
Chapter 22 – He is Coming Quickly..259
Final Thoughts...265
Appendix A...273
Appendix B...275
Appendix C...277
Bibliography...279
Index..281
About the Author..287

Illustrations

Pre-Tribulation Rapture View	58
Before the First Seal is Opened View	58
Sixth Seal Rapture View	91
Intra-Seal Rapture View	94
Pre-Wrath Rapture View	95
Mid-Tribulation Rapture View	97
Post-Tribulation Rapture View	106
The Two Witnesses	138

GLOSSARY OF TERMS

Day of Christ - refers to the event where the Lord Jesus comes for His church and takes His church home to heaven. This event is also known as the rapture.

Day of the Lord - refers to the events and time period that follows the rapture of the church. The Day of the Lord will be a time of judgment. It will be a time of great trouble for those who dwell on the earth.

Wrath of God - there are two different Greek words for wrath used in the Book of Revelation. One Greek word is *orge* which means anger, judgment. The other Greek word is *thumos* which means fierce anger, indignation. Similar to the Wrath of the Lamb.

Seventieth Week of Daniel - a seven year period that commences with the antichrist signing a covenant with the nation of Israel and ending when the Lord Jesus Christ returns to the earth.

Harpazo - the Greek word for caught is harpazo which means to seize, catch up, snatch away by force. Used in I Thessalonians 4:16-17 when the Lord descends from heaven for His church and those who are alive will be **caught** up to meet the Lord in the air. This event is known most commonly as the rapture of the church.

Received Text - also referred to as the "Textus Receptus." Of the 5,255 Greek manuscripts, 90 percent make up the Received Text. The earliest complete copies are from the 5th century with the majority dated much later. Writings from the early church fathers from the 1st and 2nd century contain quotations from the Received Text. They are the group of Greek manuscripts that are in agreement with one another.

Alexandrian Manuscripts - the group of Greek manuscripts that can be traced to Alexandria, Egypt, and represent 10 percent of the 5,255 Greek manuscripts. These manuscripts are not in agreement with the Received Text nor are they in agreement with each other. The two most famous of the Alexandrian manuscripts are the Codex Vaticanus and the Codex Sinaiticus.

Codex Vaticanus – the oldest complete Greek manuscript which is dated at AD 300. It was discovered in the Vatican library.

Codex Sinaiticus – the second oldest complete Greek manuscript which is dated at AD 400. It was discovered in 1859 in a monastery at Mount Sinai by Constantin von Tischendorf.

Kingdom of Antichrist – a one world religious system that will be established by the antichrist. All nations and races will be commanded to worship the antichrist as he declares himself to be God.

Kingdom of the Antichrist – the political system that will rule the world with the antichrist as the ruler.

King James Version (KJV).
New King James Version (NKJV).
English Standard Version (ESV).
New International Version (NIV).

Introduction

WHEN STUDYING BIBLE prophecy, such as the Book of Revelation, it is important to study the Bible as a whole and not to pick out a few Scriptures, build a teaching around those Scriptures, and ignore the rest of the Bible. The author has learned that studying Bible prophecy is like building a puzzle. It is not possible to obtain a complete picture of the puzzle with only a few puzzle pieces in place. It is important to attach all the pieces of the puzzle to reveal the true picture of the puzzle. When studying Bible prophecy it is important to find all the puzzle pieces in order to obtain a true picture of what will transpire in the future.

Studying the Book of Revelation by itself will not provide a true picture of End Time Prophecy. The Lord has concealed many puzzle pieces of the future in various books of the Bible. There are puzzle pieces throughout the Old Testament and the New Testament. Therefore, studying the Book of Revelation by itself will not present the reader with a true and complete picture of the future of this planet. The Lord requires us to dig into the Scriptures and to find these hidden puzzle pieces. This is one of the reasons why the author has endeavored to write this book. The author has included many of the Scriptures directly in the book to assist the reader.

A second reason for the writing of this book is based upon our Lord's exhortation to the believer found in Luke 21:36:

[36] *Watch ye therefore, and pray always, that ye may be accounted worthy to escape all these things that shall come to pass, and to stand before the Son of man.* (Luke 21:36)

Revelation

The Lord Jesus is exhorting His disciples to watch and pray. The follower of Jesus is to study End Time Prophecy to be aware of the events that will come upon the earth in the last days. It is possible, just as the apostles were sleeping in the garden (Matthew 26:36-46) and required a sudden awakening that the true and faithful church will need to be awakened when Jesus makes His Glorious Appearance as recorded in Matthew 25:1-13. The Lord Jesus taught His disciples the story of the ten virgins, where five were wise, but five were foolish. One common trait for all ten virgins is that they were sleeping. Five of the ten were true believers and five were not. The true believers had oil in their lamps which is symbolic of the Holy Spirit. Another common trait is that all ten virgins believed in the Lord Jesus Christ, but five had head knowledge of the Lord Jesus and five were filled with the Holy Spirit and had a personal relationship with the Lord Jesus, and were following Him as true and faithful disciples. The five true and faithful disciples went into the marriage supper despite being asleep. The five foolish virgins had head knowledge of Jesus, but lacked true commitment and were left behind when the Bridegroom (Jesus) appeared. The foolish virgins are oblivious to what has taken place and now it is too late for them as the Bridegroom has come and has departed back to heaven.

Another example of watching and being ready for the coming of the Bridegroom is recorded in the Song of Solomon. The Song of Solomon hinges around two dreams found in chapters 3 and 5. In chapter 3 the bride is ready for the bridegroom and it is her best dream. In chapter 5 the bride is not ready, she misses the bridegroom and now it is too late for her. Therefore, our Lord is encouraging us to watch and pray always as no man knows the day or the hour when Jesus will come for His church.

When studying Bible prophecy and obtaining the puzzle pieces contained in the Old Testament, we see that some prophecies were not totally fulfilled in the Old Testament and have a fulfillment in the future. In addition, there are prophecies that happened in the past and will occur again in the future. Jacob Prasch, founder of Moriel Ministries, has written about these events and has identified them as Midrash and Pesher Midrash in his books. He has done an excellent job of using Midrash and Pesher Midrash when it comes to Bible prophecy.

Midrash: By definition it is an ancient commentary on part of the Hebrew Scriptures, attached to the biblical text. Midrash is used to show what happened in the past will happen again in the future. Midrash can be used as Doctrine because there are clear meanings of multiple fulfillments

Introduction

of prophecies. There are many prophecies in the Scriptures that have dual fulfillments. Examples are:
- Abomination of desolation as recorded in Matthew 24:15, Daniel 8:8-13, 9:27, Daniel 12:11. Jesus is declaring that what happened in the past is going to happen again in the future. Just as Antiochus Epiphanes had defiled the temple by placing an idol in the most Holy Place, the coming antichrist will do the same by placing an idol in the rebuilt Temple;
- Elijah – He prophesied during his own time, and he prophesied again during the first coming of the Messiah, and he will prophecy again before the second coming of the Messiah as recorded in Malachi 4:5;
- Babylon – not all the prophecies against Babylon that the prophet Jeremiah prophesied in chapters 50 and 51 have been fulfilled. These chapters describe the utter destruction of Babylon indicating that the land will endure a perpetual desolation and that no man would live there. Today there are people living in Babylon which signifies that the prophecy against Babylon has not been completely fulfilled.

Midrash is a key to understanding Bible prophecy. If Midrash is not followed, one can easily develop a skewed interpretation of Bible prophecy and the Book of Revelation. The principle of Midrash allows for multiple fulfillments, when applicable. Whatever happened in the past will occur again in the future is the application.

Pesher: By definition Pesher means "interpretation" in the sense of "solution." It is an interpretive commentary on Scripture, especially one in Hebrew. These are types in the Scriptures that are used to illustrate a truth. A key to understanding prophecy is understanding history because what happened in the past is a clue as to what shall happen in the future and this is consistent with Pesher interpretation. Pesher interpretation is never used and should never be used as Doctrine. For Example, Antiochus Epiphanes is a type of the antichrist. The antichrist will desecrate the Jewish Temple by placing an idol in the most Holy Place. This is a typology of what the antichrist will do, just as Antiochus had done. It is wrong to state that Antiochus is going to rise from the dead and be the antichrist. That is not scriptural. It is equally wrong to say that Judas Iscariot will rise from the dead and be the antichrist, even though Judas Iscariot and the antichrist are both called the sons of perdition in the Scriptures.

There are four main views of end-time prophecies. They are:

Revelation

- Preterism – The belief that the Bible is primarily intended to teach moral principles, and therefore those who adhere to that belief assert that these things have already happened. The belief that the events of the Olivet Discourse (Matthew 24, Mark 13, and Luke 21) were totally fulfilled in AD 70 along with the dismissal of the prophetic predictions of the Book of Revelation.
- Historicism – The belief that the events in the Book of Revelation were events prophesied for the future, but they have already been completely fulfilled during the early church era.
- Poemicism – The belief that prophecy is designed to encourage Christians at any time in history, particularly in times of persecution.
- Futurism – The belief that all things have yet to be fulfilled in the future.

Jacob Prasch has pointed out that there is a fifth viewpoint concerning End Time Prophecy and that is the Jewish way of looking at the Scriptures, which allows all four approaches to be true simultaneously and complimenting each other. An example of the fifth view would be the destruction of Jerusalem in AD 70. There is another future event to come upon the nation of Israel and Jerusalem during the reign of the antichrist that will be similar to the judgment that occurred in AD 70.

In I Thessalonians 4:17, the Greek word for caught is "harpazo" which means to seize, catch up, snatch away by force. This event to be "caught up" to meet the Lord Jesus in the air is commonly referred to as the rapture among many Christians today. The timing of the harpazo is another reason why the author is writing this book.

The author has discovered ten different viewpoints as to the timing of when Jesus will return to remove His church from the earth at the time of this writing. There has been much division of the churches over the timing of the harpazo. As true believers in the body of Christ, we are not to be divided on future biblical events, but we are to disagree agreeably. In this book, the author will attempt to show the Scriptures each side uses in support of their view of the timing of the harpazo. The intent of the author is to refrain from taking a position within the contents of this book of which view he supports in the appearance of the Lord Jesus for His church. When there is no scriptural support for a given view this will also be declared in the book.

When studying the timing of the harpazo and Bible prophecy, the phrase "tribulation period" always comes up. We know from the Book of Daniel that there is a tribulation period coming upon the earth. The word tribulation appears in the King James Version 25 times and nowhere does

Introduction

it refer to a seven-year tribulation. The correct interpretation appears to be in reference to the seventieth week of Daniel as noted in chapter 9:

²⁴ *"Seventy weeks are determined For your people and for your holy city, To finish the transgression, To make an end of sins, To make reconciliation for iniquity, To bring in everlasting righteousness, To seal up vision and prophecy, And to anoint the Most Holy.* ²⁵ *"Know therefore and understand, That from the going forth of the command To restore and build Jerusalem Until Messiah the Prince, There shall be seven weeks and sixty-two weeks; The street shall be built again, and the wall, Even in troublesome times.* ²⁶ *"And after the sixty-two weeks Messiah shall be cut off, but not for Himself; and the people of the prince who is to come shall destroy the city and the sanctuary. The end of it shall be with a flood, and till the end of the war desolations are determined.* ²⁷ *Then he shall confirm a covenant with many for one week; but in the middle of the week He shall bring an end to sacrifice and offering. And on the wing of abominations shall be one who makes desolate, even until the consummation, which is determined, is poured out on the desolate."* (Daniel 9:24-27 NKJV).

Here in Daniel 9:24-27 we have a classic Midrash or multiple fulfillments of prophecies:
- Prophecy of Jerusalem to be rebuilt. At Daniel's time the city was in ruins;
- Prophecy of the coming of the Messiah;
- Prophecy of the death of the Messiah. This is an example of dual Midrash as ministry of Jesus lasted three-and-a-half years and Jesus was crucified three and a half days after He made His triumphant entry;
- Prophecy of one seven-year period that is yet to come in the future.

The ten views of the rapture (harpazo) that will be covered in the book are:
- **Pre-Tribulation View** – the belief that Jesus Christ will come for His church before the seven year tribulation period or before the seventieth week from Daniel 9:24-27;
- **Before the First Seal is opened View** – the belief that the church will see the beginning of the seventieth week from Daniel 9:24-27 and the revealing of the antichrist when he makes a covenant with the Jews before Jesus comes for His church, which would be before the First Seal is opened;

- **Mid-Tribulational View** – the belief that Jesus will return for the church age believers in the middle of the seven-year tribulation. This would be the mid-point of the seventieth week from Daniel 9:24-27 and at the start of the Great Tribulation when the abomination of desolation is set up in the rebuilt Temple;
- **The Sixth Seal View** – the belief that the coming of Christ for His church coincides with the announcement of the Sixth Seal;
- **The Intra-Seal View** – the belief that the coming of Christ for His church will be after the announcement of the Sixth Seal but before the Seventh Seal is opened. There is a pause after the announcement of the Sixth Seal before the plagues of the Sixth Seal are unleashed upon the earth. Before the pause is over, Christ comes for His church and the awful plagues of the Sixth Seal are unleashed;
- **Pre-Wrath View** – the view that the rapture of the church will occur when the Seventh Seal is opened. The wrath of God will begin with the Trumpet judgments;
- **Post-Tribulation View but Earlier** – the view that the rapture of the church will occur before the Bowl Judgments;
- **Post-Tribulational View** – the view that the rapture and second coming of Jesus Christ are the same event. This would be at the conclusion of the seventieth week from Daniel 9:24-27;
- **Partial Rapture View** – only the spirit-filled believers will be raptured. The carnal believers and the unsaved will go through the entire seven-year tribulation (seventieth week of Daniel). This would represent the parable of the ten virgins as recorded in Matthew 25:1-13.
- **A-Tribulational View** – there is no literal period of time in the future known as the tribulation period. This view denies that there is to be a rapture of the church.

We will cover these ten views of the rapture of the church in chapters 4 through 8.

Chapter 1

The Revelation of Jesus Christ

Revelation 1:1-3

The Revelation of Jesus Christ, which God gave unto him, to shew unto his servants things which must shortly come to pass; and he sent and signified it by his angel unto his servant John: Who bare record of the word of God, and of the testimony of Jesus Christ, and of all things that he saw. Blessed is he that readeth, and they that hear the words of this prophecy, and keep those things which are written therein: for the time is at hand.

THIS IS THE revelation of Jesus Christ which God the Father gave unto Jesus, to show unto His servants those things which must shortly come to pass. The Lord Jesus chose an angel as the instrument, to show unto John what must shortly come to pass. This chapter and the entire Book of Revelation are about Jesus Christ. The Lord Jesus is the head over the churches, and as the head He has the authority to encourage and to exhort the members in the churches. The Lord Jesus has the authority to reveal to the churches what they are doing wrong and what they need to do to make the necessary corrections. In the Book of Genesis we see the beginning of man, and in the Book of Revelation the judgment upon the men of this world that choose to rebel against their Creator and to follow after the lusts of their own hearts.

John was an eye witness of the Lord Jesus Christ as He walked upon the earth. John declared what he heard and saw. He writes the same in his epistle:

Revelation

¹That which was from the beginning, which we have heard, which we have seen with our eyes, which we have looked upon, and our hands have handled, of the Word of life; ² (For the life was manifested, and we have seen it, and bear witness, and shew unto you that eternal life, which was with the Father, and was manifested unto us;) ³ That which we have seen and heard declare we unto you, that ye also may have fellowship with us: and truly our fellowship is with the Father, and with his Son Jesus Christ. (I John 1:1-3)

John declares what he had heard, seen and touched. He heard the words of the Lord Jesus and he remembered them. John puts the emphasis upon the words of Jesus first, above those things that he saw Jesus do. Salvation begins by hearing and believing the words of the Almighty God. The Greek words for "looked upon" are more intense than just seeing with observation. These words mean to study or to gaze upon. These words show that the apostles were gazing intently when they observed everything that Jesus said and did. Lastly, John declares that he touched the Lord Jesus when He was upon the earth, which shows that Jesus was reachable by those who reached out to Him. It also dispels the stories that were being declared at the time of the apostle John that Jesus did not have a physical body when He walked upon the earth and therefore could not have been crucified. John quickly dispels these stories as he declares that he was an eye witness of the Lord Jesus when He walked upon the earth.

The Book of Revelation is about Jesus and of the kingdom that is soon to come upon the earth. Those who read and study this book will have the knowledge of God's plan for the end of man's rule upon the earth and the great promise of Christ's return to reign as King of Kings and Lord of Lords. There is a blessing for those that read, hear, and take heed to those words of this prophecy.

Revelation 1:4-8
John's Address to the Seven Churches in Asia

John to the seven churches which are in Asia: Grace be unto you, and peace, from him which is, and which was, and which is to come; and from the seven Spirits which are before his throne; And from Jesus Christ, who is the faithful witness, and the first begotten of the dead, and the prince of the kings of the earth. Unto him that loved us, and washed us from our sins in his own blood, and hath made us kings and priests unto God and his Father; to him be glory and dominion for ever and ever. Amen. Behold, he cometh with clouds; and every eye shall see him, and they also which pierced him: and all kindreds of the earth shall wail because of him. Even so,

Amen. *I am Alpha and Omega, the beginning and the ending, saith the Lord, which is, and which was, and which is to come, the Almighty.*

John is instructed to write to seven churches which were located in Asia, and existed at the time of John's writing. Why seven churches and only these ones? In the Scriptures the number seven represents completeness—as declared by the prophet Isaiah, one spirit in sevenfold perfection (Isaiah 11:2). The seven churches represent the seven stages of church history and reveal their spiritual condition for the last 2,000 years. The seven churches will also represent the seven types of churches that will exist throughout the church age until the Lord Jesus appears.

The Father is described as He who is, and who was, and who is to come. Past, present and future—the eternal God, with no beginning or end—He has always existed. We also have a description of the Lord Jesus. In His first coming, Jesus dealt with sin, and in His second coming He will deal with sinners. The Book of Revelation portrays a complete picture of the Lord Jesus, something that we do not see in the Gospels. Jesus is described as:

- The faithful witness;
- The first born of the dead;
- The ruler of the kings of the earth;
- He loved us;
- He washed away our sins;
- He made us kings and priests;
- To Him be glory and dominion forever and ever.

When Jesus appears to remove His church, every eye shall see Him. It will not be a secret coming when the Lord Jesus comes to take His church home to heaven. Instead this will be a visible event for the world to witness as Revelation 1:7 suggests: "Behold, He comes with clouds; and every eye shall see Him." For example, there are verses in Matthew and Daniel that declare that the Lord Jesus will come with the clouds of heaven. Matthew declares that this will be a visible event for all who are alive on the earth when He comes for His church and when He returns to reign as King of Kings and Lord of Lords:

[13] *I saw in the night visions, and, behold, one like the Son of man came with the clouds of heaven, and came to the Ancient of days, and they brought him near before him.* (Daniel 7:13)

Revelation

²⁹ *Immediately after the tribulation of those days shall the sun be darkened, and the moon shall not give her light, and the stars shall fall from heaven, and the powers of the heavens shall be shaken:* ³⁰ *And then shall appear the sign of the Son of man in heaven: and then shall all the tribes of the earth mourn, and they shall see the Son of man coming in the clouds of heaven with power and great glory.* ³¹ *And he shall send his angels with a great sound of a trumpet, and they shall gather together his elect from the four winds, from one end of heaven to the other.* (Matthew 24:29-31)

The above verses reveal that every eye shall see Him when He appears to gather His church and to take His church home to heaven, and everyone shall see Him when He returns to reign as King of Kings and Lord of Lords. There are some Bible scholars that use John 14:1-3 to show that Jesus will come secretly when He comes for His church and that the harpazo will not be a physical event for all to witness. The text that these scholars use is John 14:1-3, however this is not a good text to use to support that theory as there is no mention of a secret coming:

¹*Let not your heart be troubled: ye believe in God, believe also in me.* ² *In my Father's house are many mansions: if it were not so, I would have told you. I go to prepare a place for you.* ³ *And if I go and prepare a place for you, I will come again, and receive you unto myself; that where I am, there ye may be also.* (John 14:1-3)

Revelation 1:9-20
The Commission of John

I John, who also am your brother, and companion in tribulation, and in the kingdom and patience of Jesus Christ, was in the isle that is called Patmos, for the word of God, and for the testimony of Jesus Christ. I was in the Spirit on the Lord's day, and heard behind me a great voice, as of a trumpet, Saying, I am Alpha and Omega, the first and the last: and, What thou seest, write in a book, and send it unto the seven churches which are in Asia; unto Ephesus, and unto Smyrna, and unto Pergamos, and unto Thyatira, and unto Sardis, and unto Philadelphia, and unto Laodicea. And I turned to see the voice that spake with me. And being turned, I saw seven golden candlesticks; And in the midst of the seven candlesticks one like unto the Son of man, clothed with a garment down to the foot, and girt about the paps with a golden girdle. His head and his hairs were white like wool, as white as snow; and his eyes were as a flame of fire; And his feet like unto fine brass, as if they burned in a furnace; and his voice as the sound of many waters. And he had in his right hand seven stars: and out of his mouth went a sharp twoedged sword: and his countenance was as the sun shineth in his strength. And when I saw him, I fell at his feet as dead. And he laid his right hand upon me, saying unto me, Fear not; I am the first and the last: [18] *I am he that liveth, and was dead; and, behold, I am alive for evermore, Amen; and have the keys of hell and of death.* [19] *Write the things which thou hast seen, and the things which are, and the things which shall be hereafter;* [20] *the mystery of the seven stars which thou sawest in my right hand, and the seven golden candlesticks. The seven stars are the angels of the seven churches: and the seven candlesticks which thou sawest are the seven churches.*

John calls himself a brother in Christ, not elevating himself as the last living apostle. We are all one in God's eyes and God is not a respecter of persons. John declares that he was located on the island of Patmos and that he was sent there for the Word of God. Tradition declares that Rome attempted to martyr him by boiling him in oil, but the Lord spared him as he spared the three Hebrew men from the burning fiery furnace in Daniel 3. When Rome was unable to kill John, he was exiled to Patmos. We can see from history that the Lord preserved John because his ministry was not complete as he was called to write the Book of Revelation. It is believed that John wrote the Book of Revelation sometime after the year AD 90.

John sees the Lord Jesus walking in the midst of the seven lamp stands, which represent the church, and John is overwhelmed with Jesus' glory.

John was commanded to write the things that he saw, the things which are, and the things that will take place after these things. In other words, John is to write about the things that he sees (in chapter 1); the things that are, which is the church age (in chapters 2 and 3); and the things to come after these things—things that come after the church age (in chapters 4 through 22). This outline is the key to studying the Book of Revelation as the book is divided into three sections: the things that John sees in chapter 1, the message of Christ to His churches in chapters 2 and 3, and those things that come after the church things, which is in the future starting in chapter 4. The same Greek words for "after these things" (*meta tauta*) are also used in Revelation 4:1. Some Bible scholars believe that the things that concern the church are over at the start of chapter 4 when John is taken up into heaven. With this background they believe the harpazo will take place at the same time as the event in Revelation 4:1.

There are two views of the harpazo as they relate to Revelation 1:19 and Revelation 4:1:

- Pre-Tribulation view
- Before the First Seal is opened view

Revelation

¹⁹*Write the things which thou hast seen, and the things which are, and the things which shall be hereafter.* (Revelation 1:19)

¹*After this I looked, and, behold, a door was opened in heaven: and the first voice which I heard was as it were of a trumpet talking with me; which said, Come up hither, and I will shew thee things which must be hereafter.* (Revelation 4:1)

Those scholars who adhere to the Pre-Tribulation view will use Revelation 1:19 and Revelation 4:1 as their proof texts. However, the starting point of the seventieth week of Daniel is when the antichrist signs a covenant with the nation of Israel for seven years. The Pre-Tribulation view is based on the assumption that the antichrist has been revealed to the true and faithful church before the covenant is signed with the nation of Israel, but there is no Scripture to support this viewpoint. The first indication of the identity of the antichrist that is recorded in the Scriptures is when he makes a covenant with the nation of Israel.

Those scholars who adhere to the view that the harpazo occurs Before the First Seal is opened will also use these same verses as their proof texts. The Scripture in Daniel 9:27 is also used as the proof text alongside these Scriptures showing the antichrist has been identified as he signs a covenant with the nation of Israel for seven years. The seventieth week of Daniel would then start at this point and the church will be raptured after the covenant is signed with Israel but Before the First Seal is opened. Paul was very specific that the church would need to recognize the antichrist before the harpazo:

¹*Now we beseech you, brethren, by the coming of our Lord Jesus Christ, and by our gathering together unto him,* ²*that ye be not soon shaken in mind, or be troubled, neither by spirit, nor by word, nor by letter as from us, as that the day of Christ is at hand.* ³*Let no man deceive you by any means: for that day shall not come, except there come a falling away first, and that man of sin be revealed, the son of perdition.* (II Thessalonians 2:1-3)

What is omitted is the length of time that will take place from the day that the antichrist signs a covenant with the nation of Israel, which signals the start of the seventieth week of Daniel, and the day on the earth when the First Seal is opened in heaven. The Scriptures are silent as to the length of time that takes place after the covenant is signed and the opening of the First Seal. Some scholars believe that there is a period of time between these two events as the antichrist is seen with a crown on his head when he goes forth in his conquests.

Finally, to close out chapter 1, we see that Jesus has the keys of hell and death. He is the door to heaven and all who desire to go to heaven will have to come through Him. Pope Innocent III declared that the Catholic Church has the keys of heaven and hell during the time that he was pope from AD 1198 to AD 1216. This would be a contradiction to what Jesus is declaring in chapter 1, that He alone has the keys to heaven and hell.

Chapter 2

Letters to the Churches - Part One

Revelation 2:1-7
Letter to the Church of Ephesus – Time Period: AD 30 to AD 100
(In Greek meaning "Not Lasting")

Unto the angel of the church of Ephesus write; These things saith he that holdeth the seven stars in his right hand, who walketh in the midst of the seven golden candlesticks; I know thy works, and thy labour, and thy patience, and how thou canst not bear them which are evil: and thou hast tried them which say they are apostles, and are not, and hast found them liars: And hast borne, and hast patience, and for my name's sake hast laboured, and hast not fainted. Nevertheless I have somewhat against thee, because thou hast left thy first love. Remember therefore from whence thou art fallen, and repent, and do the first works; or else I will come unto thee quickly, and will remove thy candlestick out of his place, except thou repent. But this thou hast, that thou hatest the deeds of the Nicolaitanes, which I also hate. He that hath an ear, let him hear what the Spirit saith unto the churches; to him that overcometh will I give to eat of the tree of life, which is in the midst of the paradise of God.

AS THE HEAD of the church, Jesus has the right to tell us what the church is doing right and what the church is doing wrong, and what the church needs to do to make the necessary corrections. The Lord does not want to see anyone perish but that all should come to Jesus and walk in the truth. It is the goal of every believer to make it to heaven and take as many persons along with us as possible. We want to hear those words: "Well done good and faithful servant; enter into the joy of thy Lord."

Revelation

Jesus holds the churches in His hand and walks in the midst them. His words to the churches consist of judicial verdicts, warning, and promises. The apostle Paul, when he addressed the elders of the Ephesian church, warned them that in the future wolves in sheep's clothing will infiltrate the church (Acts 20:17-38).

The church of Ephesus had many good qualities. They had works (labor and toil), and they knew their Bible. They had discernment as they recognized false doctrine and false teachers because they held to the truth. The church at Ephesus tested the false teachers and found them to be liars, which showed their discernment. To have discernment, one needs to know their Bible, and the church at Ephesus knew the Scriptures.

Discernment is a characteristic that is lacking in the churches today. There are teachers today who preach sermons to attract people to them and not to Jesus. True teachers will bring a person closer to the Lord Jesus; false teachers will draw people closer to an individual other than Jesus. True teaching is others-centered and looks to bless others, and to help them to be all that they can be in Christ Jesus. False teaching is seeking the possessions of others to gratify their own self-centered lusts. The apostle John warns of the false teachers in his epistle:

[1] Beloved, believe not every spirit, but try the spirits whether they are of God: because many false prophets are gone out into the world. (I John 4:1)

The church of Ephesus followed the teaching of John in his first epistle as they examined the teachings of those men who were coming to Ephesus. Today this discernment is needed as there are liars in the churches spreading their false teachings. There are teachers holding counterfeit revivals like those that took place in Toronto, Canada, and Pensacola, Florida. True revivals have always started with prayer and fasting, confession of sin, and repentance. Counterfeit revivals are centered on signs and wonders and not on the leading of the Holy Spirit. The Holy Spirit will always draw men to Jesus and not to signs and wonders. Signs and wonders were used in the Book of Acts as evidence of the power and authority of the Lord Jesus Christ and to draw men to the Lord Jesus. Counterfeit revivals lack intercessory prayer and fasting, confession of sin and repentance from sin. In some cases a genuine revival can take place, however the motives of the preacher may not be pure. For example, the heart of the preacher may be filled with pride as he seeks to take credit for the genuine revival that is taking place. Just as Charles Spurgeon predicted what would happen to the church, it has happened. The church leaders have ceased feeding the sheep and are now entertaining the goats. This will be apparent when we get to the church of Laodicea in chapter 3.

Other qualities that the church of Ephesus possessed are their perseverance and patience when they were tested and tempted. They were not weary in laboring for Jesus. They remained steadfast in their perseverance and patience. They were growing in the Lord, but their love for the Lord Jesus was growing cold. The love for Him is always tied toward the love that we have for one another. Jesus commanded His disciples to love one another as Peter and John wrote in their epistles:

5 And beside this, giving all diligence, add to your faith virtue; and to virtue knowledge; 6 and to knowledge temperance; and to temperance patience; and to patience godliness; 7 and to godliness brotherly kindness; and to brotherly kindness charity. 8 For if these things be in you, and abound, they make you that ye shall neither be barren nor unfruitful in the knowledge of our Lord Jesus Christ. 9 But he that lacketh these things is blind, and cannot see afar off, and hath forgotten that he was purged from his old sins. (II Peter 1:5-9)

23 And this is his commandment, that we should believe on the name of his Son Jesus Christ, and love one another, as he gave us commandment. (I John 3:23)

The Christian cannot say that he loves God, but hates his brothers and sisters in Christ. When we truly love God then we will love our brothers and sisters in Christ, and that love will be in the open for all to see. This is the love that the church of Ephesus had, but lost. The Greek word for Ephesus means "not lasting" and indeed the church of Ephesus was a church that ceased to exist. The Lord Jesus will not stay in a church that lacks love, and today there are very few churches at Ephesus; most have ceased to exist. The church of Ephesus refers historically to the time period of AD 30 to AD 100.

The church at Ephesus had truth, but they forgot that early Christians may err because they are still learning and growing in faith. Christians who have been recently saved are learning and will make many mistakes. The Lord is patient with them as He is with all of us. Christians who have walked with the Lord for many years need to be just as patient and loving as the Lord Jesus. No one expects an infant to be perfect, and we need to have the same attitude toward our brothers and sisters in Christ. Everyone wants to be loved, and Christ requires His children to love one another.

The only concern the Lord Jesus had for the church of Ephesus was that they had lost their love for Him—the love that they once had when they had first believed on Him. We can also ask ourselves the following questions as we have walked with the Lord Jesus for many years: Do we love the Lord Jesus with the same love as when we first fell in love with Him? Have we taken Him for granted? Have we lost our joy? The first love that budded in our hearts when we received Jesus into our hearts—that pure and intense love—is the love that we should have for the Lord Himself. Everything else flows from our love for Jesus. The priority of the church is a sincere and intense love for the Lord and for our brothers and sisters in Christ. Do you remember when your love for the Lord was the most important love in your life? King David knew what this meant. He prayed, "Restore unto me the joy of thy salvation" (Psalm 51:12).

In his epistle to Timothy, Paul expressed his concern about the waning love within the Ephesian church:

3 As I besought thee to abide still at Ephesus, when I went into Macedonia, that thou mightest charge some that they teach no other doctrine, 4 Neither give heed to fables and endless genealogies, which minister questions, rather than godly edifying which is in faith: so do. 5 Now the end of the commandment is charity out of a pure heart, and of a good conscience, and of faith unfeigned: 6 from which some having swerved have turned aside unto vain jangling; 7 desiring to be teachers of the law; understanding neither what they say, nor whereof they affirm. (I Timothy 1:3-7)

There are two things that happen when people begin to lose their first love: The quality and quantity of their prayer life begins to decrease and they begin to lose their evangelistic zeal. These are red flags that we need to apply and to be conscience of. As it happened to the church at Ephesus, a church which had truth and knew their Bible, it can happen to us. When Jesus is continuously loved the way He was loved the day He was first believed upon, our relationship with Him will be strong and secure.

The Lord Jesus commended the church of Ephesus for hating the deeds of the Nicolaitanes. Nicolaitanism in the Greek is the exaltation of the clergy over the laity—the suppression of the people. The church at Ephesus knew that they had direct access to the Father and could come to the Father in boldness and confidence as Paul wrote in Ephesians and as revealed in the Book of Hebrews:

18 For through him we both have access by one Spirit unto the Father. (Ephesians 2:18)

12 In whom we have boldness and access with confidence by the faith of him. (Ephesians 3:12)

19 Having therefore, brethren, boldness to enter into the holiest by the blood of Jesus, 20 By a new and living way, which he hath consecrated for us, through the veil, that is to say, his flesh; 21 And having an high priest over the house of God; 22 Let us draw near with a true heart in full assurance of faith, having our hearts sprinkled from an evil conscience, and our bodies washed with pure water. (Hebrews 10:19-22)

As Christians, we have direct access to the presence of God; we do not need to go through any man to approach God on our behalf. This was the direct teaching of Paul. Those who teach otherwise are teaching as the Nicolaitanes had taught. Again, the church of Ephesus was strong in the Word of God and they knew that one can approach the Father directly in confidence and in boldness. They knew that it was an error to believe that anyone needed to go to a priest and then have the priest go to the Father on behalf of the one coming to the priest. Jesus declared that He hates this (Revelation 2:6). All believers in Jesus have direct access to the Father, and all believers can come boldly in prayer to the Father with confidence that our prayers will be heard.

Those who overcome have the privilege of eating from the tree of life (Revelation 2:7).

Those who overcome are believers, and those who do not overcome are not believers, as John wrote in his first epistle (I John 5:4-5).

Revelation 2:8-11
Letter to the Church of Smyrna – Time Period: AD 100 – AD 313
(In Greek meaning "Anointed for Burial")

And unto the angel of the church in Smyrna write; these things saith the first and the last, which was dead, and is alive; I know thy works, and tribulation, and poverty, (but thou art rich) and I know the blasphemy of them which say they are Jews, and are not, but are the synagogue of Satan. Fear none of those things which thou shalt suffer: behold, the devil shall cast some of you into prison, that ye may be tried; and ye shall have tribulation ten days: be thou faithful unto death, and I will give thee a crown of life. He that hath an ear, let him hear what the Spirit saith unto the churches; He that overcometh shall not be hurt of the second death.

Today, Smyrna is a beautiful city on the western shore of Turkey. The Greek word for Smyrna means "anointed for burial." Smyrna is symbolic of the persecuted church and the church that did not deny their faith in time of persecution. The church of Smyrna represents the persecuted church age from AD 100 to AD 313.

Revelation

Smyrna relates approximately to the pre-Nicaean period of church history after the apostles in the 2nd and 3rd centuries until the time of Constantine (AD 321) and the Council of Nicaea (AD 325). These were some of the hardest times as there was great persecution of the churches during this period. Indeed, some years after John's death, the Jewish leadership along with some Gentiles formed a mob and called for the death of the local bishop Polycarp, who was a disciple of the apostle John. All those who live godly lives will suffer persecution, as Paul and John wrote:

^{12} *Yea, and all that will live godly in Christ Jesus shall suffer persecution.* (II Timothy 3:12)

^{33} *These things I have spoken unto you, that in me ye might have peace. In the world ye shall have tribulation: but be of good cheer; I have overcome the world.* (John 16:33)

"Be fearless and faithful" is a message that we all need to hear in the midst of a godless and hostile society that seeks to eliminate the Christian witness and remove God's standards from public life. Persecution is growing in the Unites States and is a common occurrence in Africa, the Middle East, and the Far East where many of our brothers and sisters in Christ are being martyred for their faith. The promise that Christ gives to those who remain faithful is that they will have the peace of God that passes all understanding; and as Jesus overcame, He will provide the same power that we too may overcome.

In church history, there were ten great persecutions from the Roman Empire, spanning the years from AD 64 to about AD 305. It was not easy to be a Christian and live in Smyrna, the seat of emperor worship. In the book, "Foxes Book of Martyrs," it is estimated that about five million Christians were put to death during this time period. The Greek word for Smyrna means "anointed for burial" as Smyrna represents the persecuted church. Below are the ten emperors who brought about the greatest persecution of the church during this time:

- Nero: 64 - 68 (before John wrote to the seven churches)
- Domitian: 81 - 96
- Trajan: 98 - 117
- Hadrian: 117 - 138
- Antonius Pius: 138 - 161
- Marcus Aurelius: 161 - 180

- Commodus: 177 - 192
- Septimus Severitus: 192 - 211
- Decius: 249 - 257
- Valerian: 257 - 303
- Diocletian: 303 - 305

Christians have a promise that when they die they will be present with the Lord as recorded in II Corinthians 5:6-9. There is also the promise of a resurrection that is found in Revelation 20:6.

6 Therefore we are always confident, knowing that, whilst we are at home in the body, we are absent from the Lord: 7 (For we walk by faith, not by sight:) 8 We are confident, I say, and willing rather to be absent from the body, and to be present with the Lord. 9 Wherefore we labour, that, whether present or absent, we may be accepted of him. (II Corinthians 5:6-9)

6 Blessed and holy is he that hath part in the first resurrection: on such the second death hath no power, but they shall be priests of God and of Christ, and shall reign with him a thousand years. (Revelation 20:6)

The child of God has many promises that are comforting during times of persecution. When the child of God has his eyes on heavenly things and is filled and empowered by the Holy Spirit, he has the victory in overcoming the world and things of the world.

There is a great promise that death will not separate the believer from the Lord Jesus. The child of God is automatically in the presence of the Lord after he dies. Paul even considered that being in the presence of the Lord is a greater blessing than living here on the earth in our earthly body.

There is a second death as the Lord declared to the church of Smyrna. The second death is a spiritual death and is described in Revelation 20. Those who remain true and faithful to Jesus will not take part in the second death which will be spending eternity in the lake of fire. The faithful church of Smyrna has a promise that they will receive a crown of life. James mentions that a crown of life is reserved for those who love the Lord Jesus (James 1:12). The church of Smyrna will live and reign with the Lord Jesus when He returns to set up His kingdom on the earth.

Unlike the church of Ephesus that had truth but did not have love, the church of Smyrna possessed truth and love. They had truth because the Christians during this church age would choose death rather than deny that Jesus is Lord. There were no hypocrites in the church of Smyrna. During times of persecution the hypocrites will leave the church. The church of

Revelation

Smyrna also had love. As declared in I John 5, those who love the Lord Jesus will also love all of the saints who believe in the Lord Jesus. One cannot love God and hate the members of the church, as John declares in his first epistle. The final words of the Lord Jesus to His disciples were that they should love one another (John 13:34-35). Jesus declared that the world will recognize His true disciples because of their love for one another. The greatest work of evangelism that the church can perform today is to love one another. This is the sign of the Christian that the Lord Jesus Himself has commanded the people of this lost world to look for. It is not the invention of man's programs to grow the church, but it is the love, the true love toward one another. It is love that propels true biblical church growth, and it is truth that keeps the church pure.

The church of Smyrna had works, trials, and poverty, but they were rich toward God. There were false teachers proclaiming that they were something that they were not. Jesus instructs the saints not to fear, but to be faithful, even unto death. Men have a choice: two births and one death, or one birth and two deaths. The second death, which is recorded in Revelation 20:14-15, is a spiritual death—separation from the Lord for all eternity. The second death is to be avoided at all costs. Dear reader, if you do not know Jesus as your Lord and Savior, consider receiving Him as your Lord and Savior right now. To be with Jesus in heaven for all eternity should be the desire of all men. There is a glorious future for those who believe that Jesus Christ is the Son of God, and confess their sins and share their faith with others that they may be saved. The goal of every believer should be to make it to heaven and to take as many people as they can with them.

Revelation 2:12-17
Letter to the church of Pergamos – Time Period: AD 313 – AD 590
(In Greek meaning "Divorced, Spiritual Adultery" Birth of State Church)

And to the angel of the church in Pergamos write; These things saith he which hath the sharp sword with two edges; I know thy works, and where thou dwellest, even where Satan's seat is: and thou holdest fast my name, and hast not denied my faith, even in those days wherein Antipas was my faithful martyr, who was slain among you, where Satan dwelleth. But I have a few things against thee, because thou hast there them that hold the doctrine of Balaam, who taught Balak to cast a stumblingblock before the children of Israel, to eat things sacrificed unto idols, and to commit fornication. So hast thou also them that hold the doctrine of the Nicolaitanes, which thing I hate. Repent; or else I will come unto thee quickly, and

Letters to the Churches - Part One

will fight against them with the sword of my mouth. He that hath an ear, let him hear what the Spirit saith unto the churches; to him that overcometh will I give to eat of the hidden manna, and will give him a white stone, and in the stone a new name written, which no man knoweth saving he that receiveth it.

The church at Pergamos was commended for its works. It was a church planted in an evil region; similar to church planting in a wicked place today. The church of Pergamos was to be a light in a dark place. They held fast to the name of Jesus and did not deny the Lord Jesus in this wicked place. They even chose to suffer martyrdom rather than deny the Lord Jesus Christ.

In 29 BC Pergamos was given permission to erect and dedicate a temple to Augustus. Pergamos also contained an altar to Zeus. A short distance from the altar to Zeus was a temple to the goddess Athena. Also, Asklepios, the god of healing, was honored with a great medical school whose college of medical priests was associated with the worship of this god. The idol of Asklepios was shaped like a serpent, a symbol still used by the medical profession today.

For a city that had many temples to other gods, it was at Pergamos that we see the birth of the priesthood in the church, which is referred to as the deeds of the Nicolaitanes. Idols, rituals, and relics began at this time in church history. Idols and relics are always introduced when the people in the church no longer rely on the leading and empowering of the Holy Spirit for guidance. Idols and relics are poor substitutes for the indwelling power of the Holy Spirit. Today in the modern church with its emphasis on self and individual rights, the saints need to hear the message to Pergamos and take heed. The church leaders tolerate much today in order not to offend anyone.

The church of Pergamos allowed those who followed in the error of Balaam to remain in the church instead of excommunicating them. What was the error of Balaam? Allowing the women of the land to seduce the men of Israel into trespassing against the Lord. The story of Balaam is recorded in the Book of Numbers. Balak, the king of Moab, sought to hire Balaam to curse the children of Israel as they were passing through the land on their way to the Promised Land. Here we have a Gentile king plotting the extermination of the people of Israel. Balak believed that if he could hire Balaam to curse the people of Israel, they would indeed be cursed.

[1] And the children of Israel set forward, and pitched in the plains of Moab on this side Jordan by Jericho. [2] And Balak the son of Zippor saw all that Israel had done to the Amorites. [3] And Moab was sore afraid of the people, because they were

Revelation

many: and Moab was distressed because of the children of Israel. ⁴ And Moab said unto the elders of Midian, Now shall this company lick up all that are round about us, as the ox licketh up the grass of the field. And Balak the son of Zippor was king of the Moabites at that time. ⁵ He sent messengers therefore unto Balaam the son of Beor to Pethor, which is by the river of the land of the children of his people, to call him, saying, Behold, there is a people come out from Egypt: behold, they cover the face of the earth, and they abide over against me: ⁶ Come now therefore, I pray thee, curse me this people; for they are too mighty for me: peradventure I shall prevail, that we may smite them, and that I may drive them out of the land: for I wot that he whom thou blessest is blessed, and he whom thou cursest is cursed. ⁷ And the elders of Moab and the elders of Midian departed with the rewards of divination in their hand; and they came unto Balaam, and spake unto him the words of Balak. (Numbers 22:1-7)

However, Balaam blesses the people of Israel instead of cursing them because Balaam knows that the people of Israel are blessed:

¹ And when Balaam saw that it pleased the LORD to bless Israel, he went not, as at other times, to seek for enchantments, but he set his face toward the wilderness. ² And Balaam lifted up his eyes, and he saw Israel abiding in his tents according to their tribes; and the spirit of God came upon him. ³ And he took up his parable, and said, Balaam the son of Beor hath said, and the man whose eyes are open hath said: ⁴ He hath said, which heard the words of God, which saw the vision of the Almighty, falling into a trance, but having his eyes open: ⁵ How goodly are thy tents, O Jacob, and thy tabernacles, O Israel! ⁶ As the valleys are they spread forth, as gardens by the river's side, as the trees of lign aloes which the LORD hath planted, and as cedar trees beside the waters. ⁷ He shall pour the water out of his buckets, and his seed shall be in many waters, and his king shall be higher than Agag, and his kingdom shall be exalted. ⁸ God brought him forth out of Egypt; he hath as it were the strength of an unicorn: he shall eat up the nations his enemies, and shall break their bones, and pierce them through with his arrows. ⁹ He couched, he lay down as a lion, and as a great lion: who shall stir him up? Blessed is he that blesseth thee, and cursed is he that curseth thee. ¹⁰ And Balak's anger was kindled against Balaam, and he smote his hands together: and Balak said unto Balaam, I called thee to curse mine enemies, and, behold, thou hast altogether blessed them these three times. ¹¹ Therefore now flee thou to thy place: I thought to promote thee unto great honour; but, lo, the LORD hath kept thee back from honour. ¹² And Balaam said unto Balak, Spake I not also to thy messengers which thou sentest unto me, saying, ¹³ If Balak would give me his house full of silver and gold, I cannot go beyond the commandment of the LORD, to

do either good or bad of mine own mind; but what the LORD saith, that will I speak? (Numbers 24:1-13)

We can see that the error of Balaam was his ungodly council to Balak in order to receive money and fame from Balak (Revelation 2:14). It shows the heart of Balaam as riches and fame led to his downfall. Balaam knew the people of Israel were holy unto the Lord. He believed that if they sinned against the Lord, He would destroy them. Balaam's wicked counsel to Balak was to persuade the women of Balak's kingdom to seduce the men of Israel into sexual immorality and into the worship of their gods. It is amazing how evil entices men's hearts to obtain riches and fame.

¹ And Israel abode in Shittim, and the people began to commit whoredom with the daughters of Moab. ² And they called the people unto the sacrifices of their gods: and the people did eat, and bowed down to their gods. ³ And Israel joined himself unto Baalpeor: and the anger of the LORD was kindled against Israel. ⁴ And the LORD said unto Moses, Take all the heads of the people, and hang them up before the LORD against the sun, that the fierce anger of the LORD may be turned away from Israel. ⁵ And Moses said unto the judges of Israel, Slay ye everyone his men that were joined unto Baalpeor. (Numbers 25:1-5)

Balaam did not have much time to spend all that money because the Jews attacked the Midianites as directed by the Lord, and Balaam was killed not many days later:

¹ And the LORD spake unto Moses, saying, ² Avenge the children of Israel of the Midianites: afterward shalt thou be gathered unto thy people. ³ And Moses spake unto the people, saying, Arm some of yourselves unto the war, and let them go against the Midianites, and avenge the LORD of Midian. ⁴ Of every tribe a thousand, throughout all the tribes of Israel, shall ye send to the war. ⁵ So there were delivered out of the thousands of Israel, a thousand of every tribe, twelve thousand armed for war. ⁶ And Moses sent them to the war, a thousand of every tribe, them and Phinehas the son of Eleazar the priest, to the war, with the holy instruments, and the trumpets to blow in his hand. ⁷ And they warred against the Midianites, as the LORD commanded Moses; and they slew all the males. ⁸ And they slew the kings of Midian, beside the rest of them that were slain; namely, Evi, and Rekem, and Zur, and Hur, and Reba, five kings of Midian: Balaam also the son of Beor they slew with the sword. (Numbers 31:1-8)

The doctrine of Balaam walks softly on immorality, encouraging intermarriage with unbelievers and compromise with pagan worship. The goal of every person who attends church should be to make it to heaven.

Revelation

This means publicly confessing that Jesus of Nazareth is the Messiah, the Son of God, and to love one another. As a true child of God, we are commanded to love our brothers and sisters in Christ who have also committed their lives to the Lord Jesus Christ. It is important that the child of God walks in the truth and not after the doctrine of Balaam. Living an immoral lifestyle is contradictory to the commands of Jesus. Those who continue living in an immoral lifestyle jeopardize their entrance into heaven and the Kingdom of God. Balaam walked in error and not truth as he allowed greed, fame, and rewards to trip him up. He is presented in the Scriptures as what a child of God should not do.

Priests from Babylon

History tells us that when Babylon was conquered by the Medes and Persians, the 3,000 pagan priests from Babylon migrated westward to Pergama. By the first century, the pagan religions came via Pergama to the Pantheon in Rome; hence when Peter wrote his first epistle, he was writing from Rome, "She who is in Babylon greets you" (I Peter 5:13). Peter was not writing from the city of Babylon, but from Rome. This confirms the words of the Lord Jesus that the saints at Pergamos were dwelling where Satan's throne is. This was the place to where the priests of Babylon had migrated after the destruction of Babylon by the Medes and Persians. For more detail on this subject, I highly recommend the sermon "Roots of Babylon" by Jacob Prasch, the founder of Moriel Ministries. The late Alexander Hislop in his book, *The Two Babylons, or The Papal Worship Proven to be the Worship of Nimrod and His Wife*, also documents the migration of the priests from Babylon to Pergamos.

There is a prophecy in Zechariah 5:5-11, which has not been fulfilled yet as it has a future fulfillment:

⁵ Then the angel that talked with me went forth, and said unto me, Lift up now thine eyes, and see what is this that goeth forth. ⁶ And I said, what is it? And he said, this is an ephah that goeth forth. He said moreover, this is their resemblance through all the earth. ⁷ And, behold, there was lifted up a talent of lead: and this is a woman that sitteth in the midst of the ephah. ⁸ And he said, this is wickedness. And he cast it into the midst of the ephah; and he cast the weight of lead upon the mouth thereof. ⁹ Then lifted I up mine eyes, and looked, and, behold, there came out two women, and the wind was in their wings; for they had wings like the wings of a stork: and they lifted up the ephah between the earth and the heaven. ¹⁰ Then said I to the angel that talked with me, whither do these bear the ephah? ¹¹ And he said unto me, to

Letters to the Churches - Part One

build it an house in the land of Shinar: and it shall be established, and set there upon her own base. (Zechariah 5:5-11)

The prophecy clearly states that the mystery of the Babylonian Religion is going to return to the land of Shinar, where the Tower of Babel and the Babylonian Religion was first established. Hence the false religion will be returning to its original base in the land of Shinar. We will see when we get to Revelation chapters 17 and 18, that the wicked woman (false religion) will return to Babylon and that Zechariah 5 climaxes in Revelation 18, the destruction of Babylon the Great.

The third of the Kingdom parables that Jesus taught was concerning the mustard seed, which is an herb that grows into a tree and the birds of the air come to lodge in its branches. This parable that Jesus taught matches the description of the church of Pergamos. Pergamos is the third church addressed by our Lord in the Book of Revelation, and the parable of the mustard seed is the third Kingdom parable. It appears our Lord is saying that the church of Pergamos is to be compared to the mustard seed that grows into a tree. However, mustard seeds do not grow into trees, and the growth into a tree signifies cancerous growth, an abnormal growth. Thus Pergamos signifies a mixed marriage church, a church that is married to the world and yet holding to being called a Christian church. Paul warned the Corinthian church that they must not be married to the world in his epistle:

14And God hath both raised up the Lord, and will also raise up us by his own power. 15 Know ye not that your bodies are the members of Christ? shall I then take the members of Christ, and make them the members of an harlot? God forbid. 16 What? Know ye not that he which is joined to an harlot is one body? for two, saith he, shall be one flesh. (I Corinthians 6:14-16)

Constantine the Great

Emperor Constantine I is often credited with converting the Roman Empire to Christianity. He was credited with ending the persecution of Christians and was believed to have been converted to Christianity. It is believed his conversion began with a battle for control of the Western Roman Empire. Constantine battled the Western Roman Emperor Maxentius at the Tiber River's Mulvian Bridge in AD 312. Fourth-century historian Eusebius of Caesarea reported that before the great battle Constantine saw a flaming cross in the sky bearing the words "In this sign thou shalt conquer." Constantine did win the battle, routing and killing his enemy on a day that loomed large not only for the emperor but for the Christian faith.

The following year Constantine (now the Western Roman Emperor) and the Eastern Roman Emperor Licinius signed the Edict of Milan, which finally ensured religious tolerance for Christians. Christians were given specific rights such as the return of confiscated property and the right to worship. After his victory, history says that Constantine became a Christian, but that he made many compromises with the existing religions of the day. The compromises that were introduced by Constantine have convinced many scholars that Constantine's conversion was not a genuine conversion to Christianity.

The persecution of Christians was stopped. Now Caesar was a Christian and the priests of Mars and Venus hastened to their baptisms. There is a distinct connection between devil worship at Babylon and Pergamos, where Satan's throne was at one time declared to be. As time passed, the clergy became exalted and began lording over God's people. More and more confidence was placed in rituals.

Evil was growing in the church as Luke declared in his Gospel. Not everyone who attends church is truly born again.

18 Then said he, Unto what is the kingdom of God like? and whereunto shall I resemble it? 19 It is like a grain of mustard seed, which a man took, and cast into his garden; and it grew, and waxed a great tree; and the fowls of the air lodged in the branches of it. 20 And again he said, Whereunto shall I liken the kingdom of God? 21 It is like leaven, which a woman took and hid in three measures of meal, till the whole was leavened. (Luke 13:18-21)

23 Then said one unto him, Lord, are there few that be saved? And he said unto them, 24 Strive to enter in at the strait gate: for many, I say unto you, will seek to enter in, and shall not be able. 25 When once the master of the house is risen up, and hath shut to the door, and ye begin to stand without, and to knock at the door, saying, Lord, Lord, open unto us; and he shall answer and say unto you, I know you not whence ye are: 26 Then shall ye begin to say, We have eaten and drunk in thy presence, and thou hast taught in our streets. 27 But he shall say, I tell you, I know you not whence ye are; depart from me, all ye workers of iniquity. 28 There shall be weeping and gnashing of teeth, when ye shall see Abraham, and Isaac, and Jacob, and all the prophets, in the kingdom of God, and you yourselves thrust out. 29 And they shall come from the east, and from the west, and from the north, and from the south, and shall sit down in the kingdom of God. 30 And, behold, there are last which shall be first, and there are first which shall be last. 31 The same day there came certain of the

Pharisees, saying unto him, Get thee out, and depart hence: for Herod will kill thee. ³² And he said unto them, Go ye, and tell that fox, Behold, I cast out devils, and I do cures to day and tomorrow, and the third day I shall be perfected. ³³ Nevertheless I must walk to day, and tomorrow, and the day following: for it cannot be that a prophet perish out of Jerusalem. ³⁴ O Jerusalem, Jerusalem, which killest the prophets, and stonest them that are sent unto thee; how often would I have gathered thy children together, as a hen doth gather her brood under her wings, and ye would not! ³⁵ Behold, your house is left unto you desolate: and verily I say unto you, Ye shall not see me, until the time come when ye shall say, Blessed is he that cometh in the name of the Lord. (Luke 13:23-35)

The leaders of the church of Pergamos did not take a stand to cast out the leaven before it grew and impacted the church. We see the same concern today as many churches are not teaching the full counsel of God. During the Jesus movement in the 1970s the emphasis was on being filled, empowered and led by the Holy Spirit. Now, forty years later, many of those same churches are following church-growth programs, and seeking to gain members to join the church at the expense of training them to become disciples of the Lord. It is not possible for church programs to mentor and train disciples. The Lord Jesus will not allow this to happen. The Lord Jesus will not share His glory with men. The church growth that the Lord Jesus desires is growth that is under the anointing of the Holy Spirit. The Holy Spirit is not a machine that can be manipulated by a church program. The church leaders need to go back to basics and to train and mentor disciples under the leading and the anointing of the Holy Spirit.

The leaders of the church of Pergamos allowed error into the church. When the truth is compromised, the lies of the Devil can infiltrate the church like a cancer. If one does not believe the truth, one believes a lie. Believing and following a lie will not help anyone. The desired outcome is to make it to heaven and to take as many people as you can with you. The church leaders need to take heed to what Paul wrote to the Galatians and to make a stand against evil:

¹⁶ I say then: Walk in the Spirit, and you shall not fulfill the lust of the flesh. ¹⁷ For the flesh lusts against the Spirit, and the Spirit against the flesh; and these are contrary to one another, so that you do not do the things that you wish. ¹⁸ But if you are led by the Spirit, you are not under the law. ¹⁹ Now the works of the flesh are evident, which are: adultery,[1] fornication, uncleanness, lewdness, ²⁰ idolatry, sorcery, hatred, contentions, jealousies, outbursts of wrath, selfish ambitions, dissensions, heresies, ²¹ envy, murders,[1] drunkenness, revelries, and the like; of which I tell you

beforehand, just as I also told you in time past, that those who practice such things will not inherit the kingdom of God. (Galatians 5:16-21 NKJV)

    Paul is very blunt and to the point in his warning to the Galatian church. Those who are walking in the lusts of their own flesh are in danger of missing out on going to heaven and to be with the Lord Jesus for all eternity. John, in his first epistle in chapter 3, warns his readers that a Christian cannot be saved and continue to live in sin or practice sin. If a brother or a sister is living in sin and professes to be a Christian, the apostle John says that they are liars. These are very strong words from the apostle John. The point that he makes in his writings is for the believer not only to make it to heaven, but to experience the oneness, the communion, and the fellowship that the apostles experienced. Every believer should have that oneness with Jesus. Every believer needs to experience that Jesus is abiding in them and they are abiding in Him. Unfortunately, it is the practice of sin and the living in sin that robs a person of the precious promises that God the Father desires for all His creation.

Revelation 2:18-29
Letter to the church of Thyatira - Time Period: AD 590 – AD 1517
(In Greek meaning "Continuing Sacrifice")

And unto the angel of the church in Thyatira write; These things saith the Son of God, who hath his eyes like unto a flame of fire, and his feet are like fine brass; I know thy works, and charity, and service, and faith, and thy patience, and thy works; and the last to be more than the first. Notwithstanding I have a few things against thee, because thou sufferest that woman Jezebel, which calleth herself a prophetess, to teach and to seduce my servants to commit fornication, and to eat things sacrificed unto idols. And I gave her space to repent of her fornication; and she repented not. Behold, I will cast her into a bed, and them that commit adultery with her into great tribulation, except they repent of their deeds. And I will kill her children with death; and all the churches shall know that I am he which searcheth the reins and hearts: and I will give unto every one of you according to your works. But unto you I say, and unto the rest in Thyatira, as many as have not this doctrine, and which have not known the depths of Satan, as they speak; I will put upon you none other burden. But that which ye have already hold fast till I come. And he that overcometh, and keepeth my works unto the end, to him will I give power over the nations: and he shall rule them with a rod of iron; as the vessels of a potter shall they be broken to shivers: even as I received of my Father. And I will give him the morning star. He that hath an ear, let him hear what the Spirit saith unto the churches.

Letters to the Churches - Part One

The first fruits of an evil sowing are now being reaped. Jezebel is exalted from her throne and ministers unto Satan. Time for repentance is past; judgment now waits as Hebrews 4:13 states: God sees everything and nothing is hidden from Him. The church at Thyatira followed the deep things of Satan. Jezebel introduced Baal worship and persecuted those who worshiped the true and living God. She claimed to be a prophetess and seduced the Northern Kingdom of Israel into immorality, idolatry, and occult practices. She seduced the Lord's servants to eat food sacrificed to idols and to turn them away from the God of Israel. The Greek word for Thyatira means "continuing sacrifice," and this description is fitting for the church of Thyatira as the church leaders had replaced the power and leading of the Holy Spirit with sacrifices and rituals.

The church of Thyatira is believed to represent the churches during the "Dark Ages" from AD 500 to AD 1517. The Thyatira period of the church is thought to be during this Dark Age when the Roman Catholic Church reigned over much of Europe. According to many church historians and Bible scholars from the period of the Protestant Reformation, the Roman Catholic Church over the centuries fits the description of the church of Thyatira. There are scholars today who believe the same as those from the time of the Protestant Reformation.

The church of Thyatira was known for their works, faith, love, and perseverance. Their works are mentioned twice, which shows that the church has accomplished many good deeds. The Roman Catholic Church has missionaries doing good works all over the world. The Lord Jesus declares that there is a faithful remnant within the Roman Catholic Church. When we get to the church of Sardis, which is the church of the Protestant Reformation, we see that the Lord Jesus declares that there are only a few names in the church of Sardis that have remained true and faithful. The Roman Catholic Church has a faithful remnant that has remained true and faithful to the Lord. They have a promise to reign with the Lord Jesus when He returns to the earth.

God gave the Roman Catholic Church an opportunity to repent when Martin Luther nailed his 95 Theses to the Wittenberg Cathedral door on October 31, 1517. However, the pope and many of the leaders in the Vatican chose not to repent; instead they rejected the truth and persecuted the reformers. The church of Thyatira has a promise to go into the Great Tribulation for judgment and to experience the wrath of the Lamb (Revelation 2:22).

Revelation

Pope Gregory I (540 – 604) is often considered to have established the papacy. Known as Gregory the Great, he was the son of a Roman senator. The papacy developed continuously, but it was defined in its present form in 1870 when the popes, who had already ascribed to themselves the title of "Holy Father" in rejection of the plain teaching of Jesus in Matthew 23, had taken the title Jesus gave to the Father in John 17:11. They now ascribed to themselves divine infallibility when speaking "Ex-Cathedra" from the alleged throne of Saint Peter in Rome. There is only one Great High Priest who intercedes between man and God, and that is Jesus Christ as declared in the Book of Hebrews:

25 Wherefore he is able also to save them to the uttermost that come unto God by him, seeing he ever liveth to make intercession for them. 26 For such an high priest became us, who is holy, harmless, undefiled, separate from sinners, and made higher than the heavens; 27 Who needeth not daily, as those high priests, to offer up sacrifice, first for his own sins, and then for the people's: for this he did once, when he offered up himself. (Hebrews 7:25-27)

11But Christ being come an high priest of good things to come, by a greater and more perfect tabernacle, not made with hands, that is to say, not of this building; 12 Neither by the blood of goats and calves, but by his own blood he entered in once into the holy place, having obtained eternal redemption for us. (Hebrews 9:11-12)

12 But this man, after he had offered one sacrifice for sins for ever, sat down on the right hand of God; 13 From henceforth expecting till his enemies be made his footstool. 14 For by one offering he hath perfected for ever them that are sanctified. (Hebrews 10:12-14)

In the Book of Hebrews we see Jesus seated at the right hand of God. This is important as we move to Revelation 5 where the Lord Jesus will be seen no longer seated at the right hand of God. The doctrine of the Roman Catholic Mass constitutes a fundamental rejection of the sufficiency of the once-and-for-all death of Jesus, and reverts to the Old Testament practice of a separate priesthood and continuing sacrifices in direct abrogation of the unambiguous teaching of the epistle to the Hebrews. Under the blood of Jesus, the saint can come boldly with confidence unto the Father. All saints can come boldly unto the Father in prayer with the confidence that their prayer will be heard.

There is a faithful remnant within the church of Thyatira that has remained true and faithful to the Lord Jesus. The faithful remnant has a promise to reign with Jesus when He returns to establish His kingdom.

Chapter 3

Letters to the Churches, Part Two

Revelation 3:1-6
Letter to the Church of Sardis - Time Period: AD 1517 - AD 1730
(In Greek meaning "Incomplete")

And unto the angel of the church in Sardis write; these things saith he that hath the seven Spirits of God, and the seven stars; I know thy works, that thou hast a name that thou livest, and art dead. Be watchful, and strengthen the things which remain, that are ready to die: for I have not found thy works perfect before God. Remember therefore how thou hast received and heard, and hold fast, and repent. If therefore thou shalt not watch, I will come on thee as a thief, and thou shalt not know what hour I will come upon thee. Thou hast a few names even in Sardis which have not defiled their garments; and they shall walk with me in white: for they are worthy. He that overcometh, the same shall be clothed in white raiment; and I will not blot out his name out of the book of life, but I will confess his name before my Father, and before his angels. He that hath an ear, let him hear what the Spirit saith unto the churches.

THE MESSAGES TO the last three churches differ greatly from those to the first four churches, as the development of evil seems to have ceased. The church of Thyatira was following the depths of Satan and now evil cannot get any worse (Revelation 2:24). There is no word of commendation to the church of Sardis other than their works. Their heart gone, Christ is owned in word, but ignored in deed. His name read as they are reading from the Scriptures during the church services, His truth owned but not followed, and Himself forgotten. The church at Sardis believed that they were alive unto God because of their church attendance and works, but they were dead spiritually. The tragedy is that they were unaware that they were dead spiritually. The Lord desires to lead His church by the anointing and leading of the Holy Spirit. The church of Sardis has replaced the Holy Spirit with relics and traditions. Church historians and Bible scholars agree that the church of Sardis represents the Protestant churches that were established during and after the Protestant Reformation.

After 30 years the mighty reformation has stopped; orthodoxy is dead. The Greek word for Sardis is "incomplete," and indeed the church of Sardis started out well, but is now dying. The reformers failed to remove all the traditions and rituals that are present in the Roman Catholic Church. The mighty reformation was a time of great revival, but how far the church of Sardis has fallen—a church that once was led and controlled by the Holy Spirit. The church of Sardis is exhorted to become vigilant, to strengthen the remnant, to be faithful, to maintain good works, and to remember when they first came to Christ. They thought that their doctrine was right when they broke away from the Roman Catholic Church. They are exhorted to remember the early years of the Protestant Reformation. They are exhorted to remember the early days of their conversion to Christianity when they placed their faith in the Lord Jesus. They are in danger of missing the harpazo because they are not watching and not making themselves ready for His sudden appearing, as Matthew wrote in his Gospel:

42 Watch therefore: for ye know not what hour your Lord doth come. 43 But know this, that if the goodman of the house had known in what watch the thief would come, he would have watched, and would not have suffered his house to be broken up. 44 Therefore be ye also ready: for in such an hour as ye think not the Son of man cometh. (Matthew 24:42-44)

Many will not be ready for the Lord Jesus when He comes for His church. Many who attend the Protestant churches will be left behind. Jesus reveals that only a few will be saved and will be ready when He appears to call His church home to heaven to be with Him forever. The tragedy of the church of Sardis is that they did not recognize that they are dead spiritually.

The church at Sardis was dying through apathy and indifference. The struggle against pagan influence and worldly viewpoints has been lost. The Christians have given up the fight and are not reaching their world for Jesus Christ. Their zeal is gone, and they have compromised with the world around them; they have a terminal illness and they do not recognize the seriousness of their condition. Erasmus, who published his Greek New Testament from the Textus Receptus in 1516, predicted this would happen. Protestantism, in short, has become worse both morally and theologically than what it set out to correct and reform. The church at Sardis was unconcerned about their spiritual condition because they were not watching; they were asleep spiritually. They were unaware of the seriousness of their condition. They are in danger of having their names blotted out from the Book of Life. It is fair to say that God's standard for being part of the true church is to be born again as explained by Paul in Galatians:

[20]*I am crucified with Christ: nevertheless I live; yet not I, but Christ liveth in me: and the life which I now live in the flesh I live by the faith of the Son of God, who loved me, and gave himself for me.* (Galatians 2:20)

The history of the city of Sardis should be a warning to all the churches. It was said of King Cyrus that when he invaded Sardis it was like a thief in the night before anyone had time to put his shoes on. The city of Sardis believed that they could not be conquered and they were asleep and not watching. The saint is commanded to be alert and to be watching for the glorious appearing of Jesus, and not to be asleep. The church at Sardis eventually ceased to exist. The area surrounding Sardis became a center of Muslim influence and continues that way today.

Revelation 3:7-13
Letter to the Church of Philadelphia
Time Period – AD 1730 – AD 1900 (In Greek meaning "Brotherly love")

And to the angel of the church in Philadelphia write; These things saith he that is holy, he that is true, he that hath the key of David, he that openeth, and no man shutteth; and shutteth, and no man openeth; I know thy works: behold, I have set before thee an open door, and no man can shut it: for thou hast a little strength, and hast kept my word, and hast not denied my name. Behold, I will make them of the synagogue of Satan, which say they are Jews, and are not, but do lie; behold, I will make them to come and worship before thy feet, and to know that I have loved thee. Because thou hast kept the word of my patience, I also will keep thee from the hour of temptation, which shall come upon all the world, to try them that dwell upon the earth. Behold, I come quickly: hold that fast which thou hast, that no man take thy crown. Him that overcometh will I make a pillar in the temple of my God, and he shall go no more out: and I will write upon him the name of my God, and the name of the city of my God, which is new Jerusalem, which cometh down out of heaven

Revelation

from my God: and I will write upon him my new name. He that hath an ear, let him hear what the Spirit saith unto the churches.

Out of the church of Sardis comes the church of Philadelphia, which has no rebuke, and the church of Laodicea, which has no praise. God desires holiness and truth (Leviticus 11:44), and the church of Philadelphia has holiness and truth. The Greek work for Philadelphia means "brotherly love," and this is the love that the Lord Jesus is looking for; the love for one another. It pleases the Lord when the children of God are walking in truth and love.

[20]*And we know that the Son of God is come, and hath given us an understanding, that we may know him that is true, and we are in him that is true, even in his Son Jesus Christ. This is the true God, and eternal life.* (I John 5:20)

[3]*And this is life eternal, that they might know thee the only true God, and Jesus Christ, whom thou hast sent.* (John 17:3)

[15]*For thus saith the high and lofty One that inhabiteth eternity, whose name is Holy; I dwell in the high and holy place, with him also that is of a contrite and humble spirit, to revive the spirit of the humble, and to revive the heart of the contrite ones.* (Isaiah 57:15)

The character of God is holiness and truth. Without holiness and truth a man will not see the Lord. We are exhorted to love Jesus and to keep His Word. In order to keep the Word of God, the child of God must read and study the Word of God. The faithful church of Philadelphia was walking in holiness and truth. They were led by the anointing of the Holy Spirt as they ministered unto the Lord Jesus.

The key of David that is mentioned in Revelation 3:7 is the lordship of the Son of David over his house as hinted in Isaiah:

[15]*Thus saith the Lord GOD of hosts, Go, get thee unto this treasurer, even unto Shebna, which is over the house, and say,* [16] *What hast thou here? and whom hast thou here, that thou hast hewed thee out a sepulchre here, as he that heweth him out a sepulchre on high, and that graveth an habitation for himself in a rock?* [17] *Behold, the LORD will carry thee away with a mighty captivity, and will surely cover thee.* [18] *He will surely violently turn and toss thee like a ball into a large country: there shalt thou die, and there the chariots of thy glory shall be the shame of thy lord's house.* [19] *And I will drive thee from thy station, and from thy state shall he pull thee down.* [20] *And it shall come to pass in that day, that I will call my servant Eliakim the son of Hilkiah:* [21] *And I will clothe him with thy robe, and strengthen him with thy girdle,*

and I will commit thy government into his hand: and he shall be a father to the inhabitants of Jerusalem, and to the house of Judah. 22 And the key of the house of David will I lay upon his shoulder; so he shall open, and none shall shut; and he shall shut, and none shall open. 23 And I will fasten him as a nail in a sure place; and he shall be for a glorious throne to his father's house. 24 And they shall hang upon him all the glory of his father's house, the offspring and the issue, all vessels of small quantity, from the vessels of cups, even to all the vessels of flagons. (Isaiah 22:15-24)

The key mentioned in Revelation is similar to the key of David's day. The one who possessed the key had the authority to open or shut the doors without any opposition. This authority comes from the Lord Jesus, and even Satan and his forces have no authority to oppose this. This blessing is given to the church that is walking in truth and love.

The church of Philadelphia had works, and God has set an open door for them. The success of their ministry was the love for the Word of God and for study of the Word of God. An example of a church that adhered to the Word of God and taught the people the Scriptures are the Calvary Chapels in the United States during the 1970s and 1980s. The success of the Calvary Chapel movement during that time was their commitment to the Word of God.

The Lord Jesus commends the faithful church of Philadelphia for the little strength they have, their keeping of the Word of God, and for not denying Him before men. They have a promise of being raptured because they are watching for the Lord to return. Jesus did not say to them that He will come unto them quickly as He had said to the church at Ephesus and Pergamos!

The true and faithful church has a promise of being raptured. The Scripture verses in I Corinthians 15:51-52 prove that there is an event that will occur as the Lord Jesus will appear and remove the true and faithful saints to heaven. There is a harpazo that is to come. For those Bible scholars following the A-Tribulation view that declares that the Lord Jesus will not appear to take His church to heaven, the verses in I Corinthians 15 dispel that belief. For those Bible scholars who hold to the Partial Rapture view where only the true and faithful saints will ascend when the Lord Jesus appears, the message to the church of Philadelphia supports this view. Church membership is not enough to guarantee a church member to be taken up when the Lord Jesus appears. The message to the churches of Thyatira and Sardis is a proof text that there are members from these churches who will be left behind, and only a faithful remnant from Thyatira

Revelation

and a few members from the church of Sardis will be taken up when the Lord Jesus appears. The Lord Jesus in Luke 21:36 commanded His disciples to pray always that they may be worthy to escape all of these things that will be coming upon the earth.

The church of Philadelphia was a church that sent out missionaries to reach the lost. This was true of the churches during the time period from AD 1730 - AD 1900. It was during this period of church history that missionaries were sent out to preach the Gospel and to make disciples all over the world. This was a time of great revival as the Holy Spirit was moving in the hearts of men who were reaching out to take the Gospel message to the world. Those who never heard the Gospel were coming to faith in the Lord Jesus. There were signs and wonders that followed the missionaries in their service to the Lord. The Christians during this period in church history were actively hastening the coming of Jesus through personal faithfulness (II Peter 3:11-13), which according to related scriptural passages, is carrying out the Great Commission and acquiring the oil for our lamps before it is too late. This was a time where the church was actively engaged in reaching the lost and seeking to reach the entire world with the Gospel message.

Some Bible scholars believe that in the last days a time will come when the faithful church will be socially disenfranchised, hated, and surrounded like Lot and his family in Sodom. Opposition will even come from the unfaithful churches of Sardis and Laodicea. Like Lot, any positions God's people had in the community will become useless in negotiating away the pressure by the forces of evil. Irrespective of whatever temporal status they may have politically, financially, or in a professional business, media, or academic community before the harpazo, God's people will either sell out or be ostracized and then targeted.

Revelation 3:14-22
Letter to the Church of Laodicea - Time Period: AD 1900 - Present
(In Greek meaning "People's Opinions")

And unto the angel of the church of the Laodiceans write; These things saith the Amen, the faithful and true witness, the beginning of the creation of God; I know thy works, that thou art neither cold nor hot: I would thou wert cold or hot. So then because thou art lukewarm, and neither cold nor hot, I will spue thee out of my mouth. Because thou sayest, I am rich, and increased with goods, and have need of nothing; and knowest not that thou art wretched, and miserable, and poor, and blind, and naked: I counsel thee to buy of me gold tried in the fire, that thou mayest be rich; and

Letters to the Churches - Part Two

white raiment, that thou mayest be clothed, and that the shame of thy nakedness do not appear; and anoint thine eyes with eyesalve, that thou mayest see. As many as I love, I rebuke and chasten: be zealous therefore, and repent. Behold, I stand at the door, and knock: if any man hear my voice, and open the door, I will come in to him, and will sup with him, and he with me. To him that overcometh will I grant to sit with me in my throne, even as I also overcame, and am set down with my Father in his throne. He that hath an ear, let him hear what the Spirit saith unto the churches.

Paul wrote in his epistle to the Colossians a request that his epistle be read at Laodicea, and the Laodicean epistle be read at the Colossian church. There must have been an epistle that Paul wrote to Laodicea that was similar to what he wrote to the church of the Colossians. We see that the Lord's letter to the church of Laodicea reveals their ignorance of the Lord's sudden appearing, like foolish virgins as Matthew wrote in his Gospel:

¹ Then shall the kingdom of heaven be likened unto ten virgins, which took their lamps, and went forth to meet the bridegroom. ² And five of them were wise, and five were foolish. ³ They that were foolish took their lamps, and took no oil with them: ⁴ But the wise took oil in their vessels with their lamps. ⁵ While the bridegroom tarried, they all slumbered and slept. ⁶ And at midnight there was a cry made, Behold, the bridegroom cometh; go ye out to meet him. ⁷ Then all those virgins arose, and trimmed their lamps. ⁸ And the foolish said unto the wise, Give us of your oil; for our lamps are gone out. ⁹ But the wise answered, saying, Not so; lest there be not enough for us and you: but go ye rather to them that sell, and buy for yourselves. ¹⁰ And while they went to buy, the bridegroom came; and they that were ready went in with him to the marriage: and the door was shut. ¹¹ Afterward came also the other virgins, saying, Lord, Lord, open to us. ¹² But he answered and said, Verily I say unto you, I know you not. ¹³ Watch therefore, for ye know neither the day nor the hour wherein the Son of man cometh. (Matthew 25:1-13)

The church at Thyatira had a faithful remnant that followed after the Lord. The church at Sardis had only a few members that followed after the Lord. The Lord's message to the church of Laodicea was: if any man hears His voice and opens the door, He would come in and have supper (fellowship) with him. This shows that Jesus is outside, wanting to come in and have fellowship with the members of the church. This indicates that the church was in a sorry state, including the church leadership. The church at Laodicea had works, but the emphasis was on material possessions. They believed that material possessions were a sign of God's approval of their spiritual condition, much as we see today in some churches. The Lord Jesus considers this attitude to be nauseating. The Lord Jesus is looking for truth and love from the churches. The church of Laodicea had replaced truth and love with church attendance and works. Attendance and works are necessary, but they are not to replace truth and love.

Jesus is the faithful and true witness, and His church is to reflect His witness to the world. If the church is lukewarm, the passion to reach out to the lost disappears, the love grows cold, and the witness to the world is gone. Lukewarm hearts are disgusting to the Lord, and He will spew those who are lukewarm out of His mouth. For the one who leaves the lukewarm tradition of the Laodicean church, who recognizes the depths of his need, who turns away from self, who buys the full supply that the Lord gives without money and without price, the Lord Jesus shall raise that saint to the very throne of heaven. The church of Laodicea is exhorted to repent and to open the door of their hearts and minds to Jesus. The Lord calls them to confess their sins and to turn back to following Him so that they may be hot again in their love and service to Him.

The Greek word for Laodicea means "people's opinions." It is sad when the church has rejected Jesus as the head of the church and places people's opinions as the head of the church. By doing so the church becomes indifferent to the ways of the Lord. It is easy to profess, but more difficult to live out the life the Lord wants us to live. We can say the right words and make people think that we are Christians, but do we obey the Lord's Word as a habit of life? It was apparent that the church of Laodicea was spiritually weak as Jesus declared that they were blind and not able to see their true condition.

The Lord Jesus uses five highly descriptive words to speak of their real spiritual condition: wretched, miserable, poor, blind, and naked—all of which reveal that they were not true Christians at all. The church of Laodicea's first and foremost problem is that they were blind to their spiritual condition. They did not know that they were spiritually dead. They did not recognize the Lord Jesus knocking on the door of their hearts and desiring to come in. Jesus desires to have supper and fellowship with them. He desires the oneness and sharing that the apostle John refers to in his epistle:

³ That which we have seen and heard declare we unto you, that ye also may have fellowship with us: and truly our fellowship is with the Father, and with his Son Jesus Christ. ⁴ And these things write we unto you, that your joy may be full. (I John 1:3-4)

In his first epistle the apostle John emphasizes oneness and communion with the Father and the Son. It is the oneness and communion, which cannot be substituted with church attendance and works. The Lord Jesus desires to have a close communion and oneness with every saint. When we attend church we should see Jesus in our brothers and sisters in Christ because they also possess that oneness and communion with the Lord Jesus. If we attend church and do not see Jesus in our brothers and sisters in Christ, can we actually say that we attended church and worshipped the Lord? When we recognize that we have oneness and communion with the Father and the Son, the immediate result is fullness of joy that the apostle John declares. The apostle John had the fullness of joy because he knew that he was one with the Father and the Son.

Many church historians and Bible scholars refer to the period of church history that represents Laodicea as starting around the year AD 1900 and continuing to the present day. Tragically, we see the characteristics of the church of Laodicea in Purpose Driven or Emergent churches. In many of these churches the leading of the Holy Spirit has been replaced with church growth programs designed by men. Any element of truth in the Purpose Driven or Emergent churches is there merely to camouflage a trap—a trap which is not the snare of the pastors of these churches but of the Devil that uses them. There is always real cheese in a rat trap. Always! We may enjoy hot or iced tea, but no one likes lukewarm tea. Jesus Christ hates the mixture, and the good cannot be separated from the bad. One cannot drink the lukewarm tea and say that one will only swallow the hot or cold and spit out the lukewarm tea. In his second epistle, Peter warned of false teachers and false prophets who would mix truth and error side by side in their false doctrine. Elements of truth would be used to camouflage the false. There is always real cheese in the rat trap. The apostle John also warns of false teachers in his first epistle in chapter 2.

Even more tragic is the new eschatology that is being taught where the events prophesied by Jesus must be ignored with the aim of preventing them from ever transpiring. Those Christians who heed to the words of Jesus to be alert for the signs of His return are criminalized for not seeing an alternative Kingdom Now scenario. This scenario is sadly based on an interfaith Universalist view of salvation and the belief that the church of Jesus Christ can work together with Hindus, unbelieving Jews, Buddhists, or any people of any religion. Such a view is at fundamental odds with the divine peace plan of Jesus found in Daniel 2, Isaiah 52, and Ephesians 6. Daniel 2 clearly states God has already declared what the future of this world will be. But we have pastors of churches that teach contrary to the plain teaching in Daniel 2. Either God is lying or these men who teach contrary

Revelation

to the written Word of God are lying. They both cannot be declaring the truth. The author personally chooses to believe God, the Creator of all things.

Once a man begins to challenge the teachings of God, he moves to rewrite the Holy Scriptures. Today we see many new Bible translations being developed. We are seeing new Bible translations being written to remove the conviction of sin, to remove the personal responsibility that man needs to confess his sins and then to repent before the Holy God. But we see in the church of Laodicea that everyone is entitled to his own opinion. Indeed everyone is entitled to their own opinion in the church of Laodicea as the Greek word for Laodicea means "people's opinions."

History records that before the judgments recorded in Jeremiah came to pass, there was a period of real prosperity in Israel, and people did not believe in what Jeremiah prophesied was going to happen. Similarly, before the temple was destroyed in AD 70, there was an unprecedented period of prosperity under the Romans, and the people did not want to believe what the early Christians were telling them was going to happen according to prophecy. The people believed that material possessions were a sign of God's approval for the lifestyle they were living. The Lord revealed to the Christians that judgment was coming because the nation had rejected Jesus Christ as their Messiah. The wrath of God did come, and what happened in the past will happen in the future. The faithfulness of the church of Philadelphia is a warning to the churches of Ephesus, Pergamos, Thyatira, Sardis and Laodicea to repent. The true and faithful church is warning the other churches to repent because Jesus is returning soon. Just as the people did in Jeremiah's time, they will mock and choose not to believe, and then it will be too late for them.

Chapter 4

The Heavenly Scene

Revelation 4:1-6

After this I looked, and, behold, a door was opened in heaven: and the first voice which I heard was as it were of a trumpet talking with me; which said, Come up hither, and I will shew thee things which must be hereafter. And immediately I was in the spirit: and, behold, a throne was set in heaven, and one sat on the throne. And he that sat was to look upon like a jasper and a sardine stone: and there was a rainbow round about the throne, in sight like unto an emerald. And round about the throne were four and twenty seats: and upon the seats I saw four and twenty elders sitting, clothed in white raiment; and they had on their heads crowns of gold. And out of the throne proceeded lightnings and thunderings and voices: and there were seven lamps of fire burning before the throne, which are the seven Spirits of God. And before the throne there was a sea of glass like unto crystal: and in the midst of the throne, and round about the throne, were four beasts full of eyes before and behind.

THE INTRODUCTION TO Chapter 4 starts with the phrase, "After this," which in Greek is *meta tauta*, meaning "after these things." We need to ask, after what things? The answer is, after the church things of chapters 2 and 3. The Book of Revelation is written in three divisions (Revelation 1:19):

- The things that John saw in chapter 1;
- The things concerning the church, which John saw in chapters 2 and 3;
- The things of the future, which starts in chapter 4 and completes with chapter 22.

Revelation

Some Bible scholars see the harpazo of the church taking place at the introduction of chapter 4, using the Scriptures in Revelation 1:19 and Revelation 4:1 for their support. The fact that the Lord Jesus is seen no longer seated on the throne making intercession as a priest as portrayed in Revelation 5, indicates that He left the throne to gather His church in order to bring the saints to heaven to be with Him. In chapter 5, He is standing as a judge opening the book sealed with Seven Seals.

The Bible has two terms that need to be identified and defined to assist in understanding of end-time prophecy. They are the Day of Christ, and the Day of the Lord. The Day of Christ refers to the harpazo of the church, and the Day of the Lord immediately follows the Day of Christ. The Day of the Lord is a time of great judgment, a time where the wrath of the Lord will be poured out upon the earth. The Day of Christ is defined in Paul's epistle to the Thessalonians:

[1] Now we beseech you, brethren, by the coming of our Lord Jesus Christ, and by our gathering together unto him, [2] that ye be not soon shaken in mind, or be troubled, neither by spirit, nor by word, nor by letter as from us, as that the day of Christ is at hand. [3] Let no man deceive you by any means: for that day shall not come, except there come a falling away first, and that man of sin be revealed, the son of perdition; [4] Who opposeth and exalteth himself above all that is called God, or that is worshipped; so that he as God sitteth in the temple of God, shewing himself that he is God. (II Thessalonians 2:1-4)

The Bible is clear that there are two conditions that need to be fulfilled before the Day of Christ comes. One is the apostasy, and the second is the faithful church identifying the antichrist. The apostasy appears to have begun in the first century as the Lord Jesus rebukes the churches of Ephesus, Pergamos, Thyatira, Sardis, and Laodicea and exhorts them to repent. The second condition is the identification of the antichrist. There is much debate among Bible scholars concerning when this is to be fulfilled. Some Bible scholars believe this will be fulfilled when the antichrist signs a covenant with the nation of Israel for seven years. Other scholars believe that the antichrist will be revealed when he sets up his image in the rebuilt Jewish Temple. Others yet believe it is when the antichrist sets up his mark and orders that no man can buy or sell unless he has the mark of the beast (antichrist).

The Day of the Lord will immediately follow the Day of Christ, as once again Paul indicates in his writings to the Thessalonians:

The Heavenly Scene

13 But I would not have you to be ignorant, brethren, concerning them which are asleep, that ye sorrow not, even as others which have no hope. 14 For if we believe that Jesus died and rose again, even so them also which sleep in Jesus will God bring with him. 15 For this we say unto you by the word of the Lord, that we which are alive and remain unto the coming of the Lord shall not prevent them which are asleep. 16 For the Lord himself shall descend from heaven with a shout, with the voice of the archangel, and with the trump of God: and the dead in Christ shall rise first: 17 Then we which are alive and remain shall be caught up together with them in the clouds, to meet the Lord in the air: and so shall we ever be with the Lord. 18 Wherefore comfort one another with these words. 5 But of the times and the seasons, brethren, ye have no need that I write unto you. 2 For yourselves know perfectly that the day of the Lord so cometh as a thief in the night. 3 For when they shall say, Peace and safety; then sudden destruction cometh upon them, as travail upon a woman with child; and they shall not escape. 4 But ye, brethren, are not in darkness, that that day should overtake you as a thief. 5 Ye are all the children of light, and the children of the day: we are not of the night, nor of darkness. 6 Therefore let us not sleep, as do others; but let us watch and be sober. (I Thessalonians 4:13-5:6)

The Day of the Lord will be a time of judgment and wrath that will come upon the entire world immediately following the Day of Christ.

There are Bible scholars who believe that the harpazo takes place in chapter 4, and the church is complete in heaven in chapter 4. There are two views of the harpazo that we will review here:

- Pre-Tribulation view
- Before the First Seal is opened view

From the Scriptures in Daniel 9:24-27, we know that there is a seven year period that will start when the antichrist signs a covenant with the nation of Israel. Those who follow the Pre-Tribulation view believe that the harpazo commences before the antichrist signs his covenant with the nation of Israel. They believe that the faithful church will be able to identify the antichrist before he signs a covenant with the nation of Israel.

Scholars who hold to the view that the harpazo will be Before the First Seal is opened believe that the church will have to be on the earth for the start of the seventieth week of Daniel to identify the antichrist as he signs the covenant with the nation of Israel. The one who signs the covenant with the nation of Israel will be identified by the faithful church as the antichrist. Sometime after the identification of the antichrist, Jesus will return for His church and the church will be complete in heaven Before the First Seal is opened. Both hold

Revelation

to the view that the church is complete in heaven in chapter 4, but they have a different view on when the harpazo will take place.

The scholars from both the Pre-Tribulation view and Before the First Seal is opened view use the verses below from Genesis as their proof text that God will not destroy the righteous with the wicked:

> ²²*And the men turned their faces from thence, and went toward Sodom: but Abraham stood yet before the LORD. ²³ And Abraham drew near, and said, Wilt thou also destroy the righteous with the wicked? ²⁴ Peradventure there be fifty righteous within the city: wilt thou also destroy and not spare the place for the fifty righteous that are therein? ²⁵ That be far from thee to do after this manner, to slay the righteous with the wicked: and that the righteous should be as the wicked, that be far from thee: Shall not the Judge of all the earth do right? ²⁶ And the LORD said, If I find in Sodom fifty righteous within the city, then I will spare all the place for their sakes. ²⁷ And Abraham answered and said, Behold now, I have taken upon me to speak unto the LORD, which am but dust and ashes: ²⁸ Peradventure there shall lack five of the fifty righteous: wilt thou destroy all the city for lack of five? And he said, If I find there forty and five, I will not destroy it. ²⁹ And he spake unto him yet again, and said, Peradventure there shall be forty found there. And he said, I will not do it for forty's sake. ³⁰ And he said unto him, Oh let not the LORD be angry, and I will speak: Peradventure there shall thirty be found there. And he said, I will not do it, if I find thirty there. ³¹ And he said, Behold now, I have taken upon me to speak unto the LORD: Peradventure there shall be twenty found there. And he said, I will not destroy it for twenty's sake. ³² And he said, Oh let not the LORD be angry, and I will speak yet but this once: Peradventure ten shall be found there. And he said, I will not destroy it for ten's sake.* (Genesis 18:22-32)

> ¹⁵ *And when the morning arose, then the angels hastened Lot, saying, Arise, take thy wife, and thy two daughters, which are here; lest thou be consumed in the iniquity of the city. ¹⁶ And while he lingered, the men laid hold upon his hand, and upon the hand of his wife, and upon the hand of his two daughters; the LORD being merciful unto him: and they brought him forth, and set him without the city. ¹⁷ And it came to pass, when they had brought them forth abroad, that he said, Escape for thy life; look not behind thee, neither stay thou in all the plain; escape to the mountain, lest thou be consumed. ¹⁸ And Lot said unto them, Oh, not so, my LORD: ¹⁹ Behold now, thy servant hath found grace in thy sight, and thou hast magnified thy mercy, which thou hast shewed unto me in saving my life; and I cannot escape to the mountain, lest some evil take me, and I die: ²⁰ Behold now, this city is near to flee unto, and it is a little one: Oh, let me escape thither, (is it not a little one?) and my soul shall live. ²¹ And he said unto him, See, I have accepted thee concerning this*

thing also, that I will not overthrow this city, for the which thou hast spoken. [22] *Haste thee, escape thither; for I cannot do anything till thou be come thither. Therefore the name of the city was called Zoar.* (Genesis 19:15-22)

Both views of the harpazo of the church follow these verses in Genesis that the God of the earth will not destroy the righteous with the wicked. In the example where there are only ten righteous men surrounded by a multitude of wicked men, the God of earth will not destroy the righteous with the wicked.

One key difference between the Pre-Tribulation view and Before the First Seal is opened view is the identification of the antichrist as noted by Paul in his epistle to the Thessalonians:

[1]*Now we beseech you, brethren, by the coming of our Lord Jesus Christ, and by our gathering together unto him,* [2] *That ye be not soon shaken in mind, or be troubled, neither by spirit, nor by word, nor by letter as from us, as that the day of Christ is at hand.* [3] *Let no man deceive you by any means: for that day shall not come, except there come a falling away first, and that man of sin be revealed, the son of perdition;* [4] *Who opposeth and exalteth himself above all that is called God, or that is worshipped; so that he as God sitteth in the temple of God, shewing himself that he is God.* (II Thessalonians 2:1-4)

Scholars who follow the Pre-Tribulation view believe the antichrist will be identified before the seventieth week of Daniel begins. The problem with that view is that there are no Scriptures that can be used to show that the antichrist will be identified before he signs the covenant with the nation of Israel. The Pre-Tribulation view is based on assumption and has no scriptural support. The Scriptures in Genesis 18:22-32 and Genesis 19:15-22 cannot be used to prove that the antichrist will be revealed to the true and faithful church before the covenant is signed.

Those scholars that believe that Jesus will come for His church Before the First Seal is opened do have scriptural support for this view. They quote Daniel 9:24-27 as their proof text. The true and faithful church must identify the antichrist before the harpazo. These scholars believe that the church is complete in heaven before the Lord Jesus opens the book with the Seven Seals that He received from His Father in Revelation 5.

Many Bible scholars do not believe the antichrist will be clearly identified when he signs a covenant with the nation of Israel. Some of these scholars interpret II Thessalonians 2:1-4 being fulfilled when the antichrist sets up his image in the rebuilt Jewish Temple and demands to be worshipped as God. Other scholars see these verses being fulfilled when the mark of the beast is set up and the number 666 is introduced. Those scholars that hold to the harpazo occurring after the mark of the beast is established will quote the uniform body of evidence from the early church fathers of the 1st, 2nd, and 3rd centuries that held to the belief that the apostles taught that the antichrist would have to be clearly identified to the faithful church prior to the coming of Jesus for His church. They believe the man who signs the covenant with the nation of Israel would not be conclusive to identify the coming antichrist. Irenaeus, the disciple of Polycarp, who was a disciple of John, believed that the church would see the abomination of desolation spoken of by Daniel the prophet, which would signify that the church would be on the earth for the first three-and-a-half years and Christ will come for His church at the start of the Great Tribulation period. These views will be covered in greater detail later in the book.

There is a passage in the Gospel of Luke that suggests that the harpazo will occur Before the First Seal is opened. The Lord commands us to pray always that we may escape all these judgments that will begin to come to pass when the seals of the book are being opened in Revelation 6:

> *34And take heed to yourselves, lest at any time your hearts be overcharged with surfeiting, and drunkenness, and cares of this life, and so that day come upon you unawares. 35 For as a snare shall it come on all them that dwell on the face of the whole earth. 36 Watch ye therefore, and pray always, that ye may be accounted worthy to escape all these things that shall come to pass, and to stand before the Son of man.* (Luke 21:34-36)

Jesus declares in Luke to pray always to escape all of these things that are coming upon the earth. Jesus did not say some of these things or most of these things, but He exhorted His disciples to pray always to escape all of these things that are coming upon the earth.

The church does not know the day or the hour of the coming of Jesus for His church, but the church is to recognize that the day of His coming is near. There are signs that indicate that these are the last days. Apostasy is growing in the churches and the characteristics of the church of Laodicea are becoming more prevalent today. These are signs that these are indeed the last days.

The concept of the harpazo is not something new that was introduced in the New Testament. There are Scriptures in the Old and New Testaments which describe the harpazo that is to come. In the Book of Exodus there is the suggestion of the harpazo:

The Heavenly Scene

¹⁶ *And it came to pass on the third day in the morning, that there were thunders and lightnings, and a thick cloud upon the mount, and the voice of the trumpet exceeding loud; so that all the people that was in the camp trembled.* ¹⁷ *And Moses brought forth the people out of the camp to meet with God; and they stood at the nether part of the mount.* ¹⁸ *And Mount Sinai was altogether on a smoke, because the LORD descended upon it in fire: and the smoke thereof ascended as the smoke of a furnace, and the whole mount quaked greatly.* ¹⁹ *And when the voice of the trumpet sounded long, and waxed louder and louder, Moses spake, and God answered him by a voice.* ²⁰ *And the LORD came down upon Mount Sinai, on the top of the mount: and the LORD called Moses up to the top of the mount; and Moses went up.* (Exodus 19:16-20)

In the Book of Exodus, we see the Lord descending when the trumpet is sounding. The Lord called Moses to come up and Moses ascended to meet the Lord. The prophet Isaiah also reveals the harpazo in his writings:

¹*The righteous perisheth, and no man layeth it to heart: and merciful men are taken away, none considering that the righteous is taken away from the evil to come.* (Isaiah 57:1)

In addition to I Thessalonians 4:13-17, there are other Scriptures in the New Testament that support the harpazo:

¹*Let not your heart be troubled: ye believe in God, believe also in me.* ² *In my Father's house are many mansions: if it were not so, I would have told you. I go to prepare a place for you.* ³ *And if I go and prepare a place for you, I will come again, and receive you unto myself; that where I am, there ye may be also.* (John 14:1-3)

⁵¹*Behold, I shew you a mystery; We shall not all sleep, but we shall all be changed,* ⁵² *in a moment, in the twinkling of an eye, at the last trump: for the trumpet shall sound, and the dead shall be raised incorruptible, and we shall be changed.* (I Corinthians 15:51-52)

Following are two graphs. The first graph shows the Pre-Tribulation view. The second shows the Before the First Seal is opened view. It is interesting to note that there is no indication in the Scriptures as to the period of time once the antichrist signs a covenant with the nation of Israel until the opening of the First Seal. There may be a period of many days between these events.

PRE-TRIBULATION RAPTURE VIEW
70th Week of Daniel
Pre-Tribulation Rapture
Second Coming
Antichrist signs covenant
Abomination of Desolation
Tribulation
The Great Tribulation
MIDPOINT
3 1/2 years
3 1/2 years

BEFORE FIRST SEAL RAPTURE VIEW
70th Week of Daniel
SEALS
Before the First Seal Rapture
Second
Coming
Antichrist signs covenant
Abomination of Desolation
1
2
3
4
5
6
7
Tribulation
The Great Tribulation
MIDPOINT
3 1/2 years
3 1/2 years

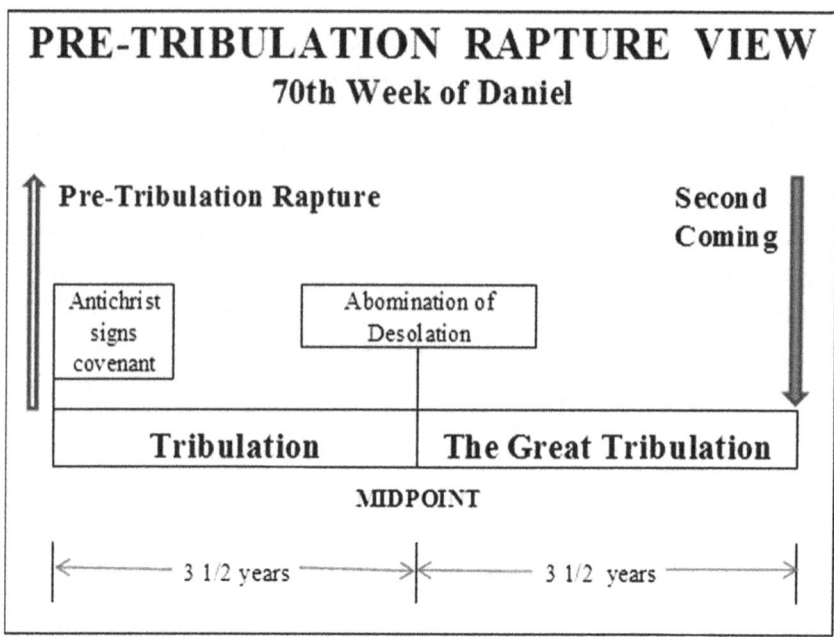

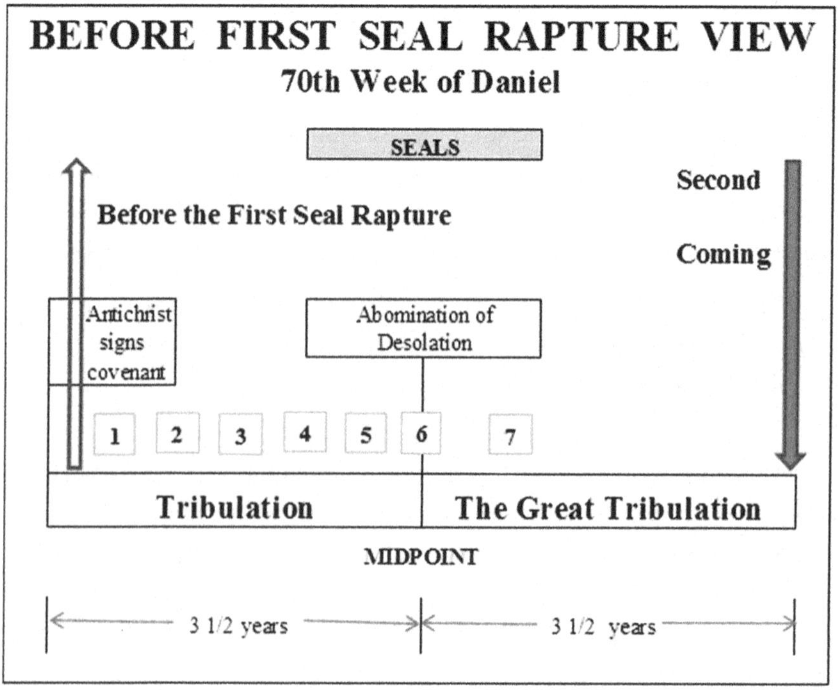

The Heavenly Scene

As we continue in Revelation 4:2-6, when he gets to heaven John sees many glorious events in the following order:

- A Throne in heaven, the seat of government, final authority;
- God is seated on the Throne;
- A rainbow around the Throne indicating that God remembers Noah and the flood;
- The twenty four lesser thrones around the Throne;
- The twenty four elders seated on the lesser thrones wearing crowns of gold on their heads;
- Visual and audio events;
- The seven lamps;
- The sea of glass;
- The four living creatures.

The Throne of God is also described in Daniel 7, and the rainbow around the Throne, which is the sign of the covenant with Noah, is recorded in the Book of Genesis:

9 I beheld till the thrones were cast down, and the Ancient of days did sit, whose garment was white as snow, and the hair of his head like the pure wool: his throne was like the fiery flame, and his wheels as burning fire. 10 A fiery stream issued and came forth from before him: thousand thousands ministered unto him, and ten thousand times ten thousand stood before him: the judgment was set, and the books were opened. (Daniel 7:9-10)

8 And God spake unto Noah, and to his sons with him, saying, 9 And I, behold, I establish my covenant with you, and with your seed after you; 10 And with every living creature that is with you, of the fowl, of the cattle, and of every beast of the earth with you; from all that go out of the ark, to every beast of the earth. 11 And I will establish my covenant with you, neither shall all flesh be cut off any more by the waters of a flood; neither shall there any more be a flood to destroy the earth. 12 And God said, This is the token of the covenant which I make between me and you and every living creature that is with you, for perpetual generations: 13 I do set my bow in the cloud, and it shall be for a token of a covenant between me and the earth. 14 And it shall come to pass, when I bring a cloud over the earth, that the bow shall be seen in the cloud: 15 And I will remember my covenant, which is between me and you and every living creature of all flesh; and the waters shall no more become a flood to destroy all flesh. 16 And the bow shall be in the cloud; and I will look upon it, that I may remember the everlasting covenant between God and every living creature of all flesh that is upon the earth.

Revelation

¹⁷ And God said unto Noah, This is the token of the covenant, which I have established between me and all flesh that is upon the earth. (Genesis 9:8-17)

John also sees around the Throne twenty four elders clothed in white robes, indicating that their resurrection has already taken place. Some scholars see these elders as the twelve apostles and twelve patriarchs, but there are no Scriptures to support this theory. John also sees seven lamps burning before the Throne and the glassy sea. These objects take us back to the Jewish Tabernacle and Temple. The seven lamps are symbolic of the seven golden lampstands in the Tabernacle. The glassy sea is symbolic of the molten sea that King Solomon created. The calm glassy sea in Revelation 4 is not quite so calm in Revelation 15:2 once the wrath of God has commenced.

Revelation 4:7-11
The Four Living Creatures

And the first beast was like a lion, and the second beast like a calf, and the third beast had a face as a man, and the fourth beast was like a flying eagle. And the four beasts had each of them six wings about him; and they were full of eyes within: and they rest not day and night, saying, Holy, holy, holy, LORD God Almighty, which was, and is, and is to come. And when those beasts give glory and honour and thanks to him that sat on the throne, who liveth for ever and ever, The four and twenty elders fall down before him that sat on the throne, and worship him that liveth for ever and ever, and cast their crowns before the throne, saying, Thou art worthy, O Lord, to receive glory and honour and power: for thou hast created all things, and for thy pleasure they are and were created.

The prophet Ezekiel also saw the four living creatures as described in Ezekiel 1:4-28 and 10:1-22. They are mentioned in the Book of Ezekiel twelve times in the first ten chapters. Ezekiel 10:20 clearly indicates that they are Cherubim. This must have been an overwhelming experience for John when he saw the four living creatures and the twenty four elders seated before the Throne of the Lord God Almighty.

It is here in chapter 4 that we see the reason why man was created. This is an age old question that man has been pondering for centuries, which is the reason for the existence of mankind on planet earth. Now we have the answer to that question in chapter 4. Man was created to give God pleasure. If we come into harmony with God's plan for all mankind, then man will live and experience life to its fullest. But when man seeks the pleasures of this world instead of pleasing God, then man will die spiritually, for the wages of sin is death as declared in Romans 6:23. God desires to have fellowship with man as recorded by the apostle John in his first epistle:

> *³That which we have seen and heard declare we unto you, that ye also may have fellowship with us: and truly our fellowship is with the Father, and with his Son Jesus Christ. ⁴ And these things write we unto you, that your joy may be full.* (I John 1:3-4)

John taught that we can be one with God; that we can experience a communion, a sharing, and an oneness with God. When we come into harmony with God's ideal for our life, we can experience fullness of joy as we fellowship with the Creator of all things. However, there is an obstacle for man that hinders fellowship with God. Sin—unconfessed sin—separates the saint from oneness and fellowship with God. The solution to the sin problem is to confess the sin, and to turn from that sin as John writes in his epistle:

> *⁹If we confess our sins, he is faithful and just to forgive us our sins, and to cleanse us from all unrighteousness.* (I John 1:9)

It does not matter what the sin is or for how long one may be in bondage to that sin. All God wants us to do is confess that sin before Him and turn from it. If man does his part which is to confess, Jesus will do His part and forgive us. And not only does He forgive us, but He also cleanses us from that sin. Living in sin will separate the saint from a life of oneness, the common sharing with the Father and the Son as John declares:

> *⁴ Whosoever committeth sin transgresseth also the law: for sin is the transgression of the law. ⁵ And ye know that he was manifested to take away our sins; and in him is no sin. ⁶ Whosoever abideth in him sinneth not: whosoever sinneth hath not seen him, neither known him. ⁷ Little children, let no man deceive you: he that doeth righteousness is righteous, even as he is righteous. ⁸ He that committeth sin is of the devil; for the devil sinneth from the beginning. For this purpose the Son of God was manifested, that he might destroy the works of the devil. ⁹ Whosoever is born of God doth not commit sin; for his seed remaineth in him: and he cannot sin, because he is born of God.* (I John 3:4-9)

All men have fallen into sin, but what John is declaring here is that if a man is living a lifestyle that is contrary to the commandments of God, then that man does not have fellowship with God. For the man that is walking in fellowship with God, it is not possible to live in sin; to practice sin. The indwelling Holy Spirit will convict that man to confess his sins and to repent, to change, to turn from sin and to continue in fellowship with God. The Word of God declares that all have sinned and fallen short of the Glory of God (Romans 3:23). No one is perfect. The man that is truly walking in fellowship with the Lord Jesus will confess his sin and then repent, and turn away from that sin. Paul in his epistle to the Galatians reveals that the man who is living a lifestyle contrary to the commandments of the Lord will not inherit the Kingdom of God:

[19]Now the works of the flesh are manifest, which are these; Adultery, fornication, uncleanness, lasciviousness, [20] Idolatry, witchcraft, hatred, variance, emulations, wrath, strife, seditions, heresies, [21] Envyings, murders, drunkenness, revellings, and such like: of the which I tell you before, as I have also told you in time past, that they which do such things shall not inherit the kingdom of God. (Galatians 5:19-21)

We must not be deceived, for those who live a lifestyle as described in Galatians 5 do not live in fellowship and oneness with God. Today in some churches there are church members that live in sin as Paul declared in Galatians. The leaders of those churches have not effectively warned the church members to turn away from their sin. Therefore, the church members will believe that what they are doing is acceptable to God and that continuing to be a church member is all God desires from them. The Scriptures clearly teach that living in sin and attending church will not guarantee anyone entrance into heaven. It is better to heed the exhortation of the apostle John and the apostle Paul to confess and turn from sin than to continue in sin and trust in church attendance to be saved from the lake of fire which was prepared for the Devil and his angels. The goal of every church member should be to make it to heaven. Any sin or lifestyle that threatens to keep a church member out of heaven should be confessed and turned from.

Chapter 5

The Lion and the Book

Revelation 5:1-7
The Book Sealed with Seven Seals

And I saw in the right hand of him that sat on the throne a book written within and on the backside, sealed with seven seals. And I saw a strong angel proclaiming with a loud voice, Who is worthy to open the book, and to loose the seals thereof? And no man in heaven, nor in earth, neither under the earth, was able to open the book, neither to look thereon. And I wept much, because no man was found worthy to open and to read the book, neither to look thereon. And one of the elders saith unto me, Weep not: behold, the Lion of the tribe of Judah, the Root of David, hath prevailed to open the book, and to loose the seven seals thereof. And I beheld, and, lo, in the midst of the throne and of the four beasts, and in the midst of the elders, stood a Lamb as it had been slain, having seven horns and seven eyes, which are the seven Spirits of God sent forth into all the earth. And he came and took the book out of the right hand of him that sat upon the throne.

THE SCENE IN heaven now shifts to the book that is sealed with Seven Seals, that is in the right hand of God the Father. A strong angel bars the way to the book. Is the book the title deed to the earth as many Bible scholars suggest? The book does reveal the judgment that is due to come before Jesus returns to the earth.

We see that no one is worthy to open the book or read it. No one in heaven, or on the earth, or under the earth was found worthy. The scene shifts to the Lord Jesus Christ, and we see that the Lord Jesus Christ is no longer seated on His Throne next to His Father. This is significant as it is showing that the age of intercession has come to its close according to the Book of Hebrews as some Bible scholars have indicated:

¹ *God, who at sundry times and in divers manners spake in time past unto the fathers by the prophets,* ² *Hath in these last days spoken unto us by his Son, whom he hath appointed heir of all things, by whom also he made the worlds;* ³ *Who being the brightness of his glory, and the express image of his person, and upholding all things by the word of his power, when he had by himself purged our sins, sat down on the right hand of the Majesty on high:* ⁴ *Being made so much better than the angels, as he hath by inheritance obtained a more excellent name than they.* (Hebrews 1:1-4)

²² *By so much was Jesus made a surety of a better testament.* ²³ *And they truly were many priests, because they were not suffered to continue by reason of death:* ²⁴ *But this man, because he continueth ever, hath an unchangeable priesthood.* ²⁵ *Wherefore he is able also to save them to the uttermost that come unto God by him, seeing he ever liveth to make intercession for them.* ²⁶ *For such an high priest became us, who is holy, harmless, undefiled, separate from sinners, and made higher than the heavens;* ²⁷ *Who needeth not daily, as those high priests, to offer up sacrifice, first for his own sins, and then for the people's: for this he did once, when he offered up himself.* (Hebrews 7:22-27)

¹ *Now of the things which we have spoken this is the sum: We have such an high priest, who is set on the right hand of the throne of the Majesty in the heavens;* ² *A minister of the sanctuary, and of the true tabernacle, which the Lord pitched, and not man.* ³ *For every high priest is ordained to offer gifts and sacrifices: wherefore it is of necessity that this man have somewhat also to offer.* (Hebrews 8:1-3)

We see from these verses in Hebrews that the Lord Jesus Christ sat down next to His Father, because the sacrifice for the sins of the world was now complete. When our Lord was seated in heaven, He was making intercession for those that believed in Him. In Revelation 5, we no longer see Him sitting next to His Father. He has left the Throne next to His Father which provides a strong indication that the church age is over. The Lord Jesus is now operating as the Lion of the tribe of Judah and not as the Lamb.

The Bible scholars who believe in the Pre-Tribulation view of the harpazo, and those scholars who believe that the harpazo will take place Before the First Seal is opened, believe that the sign of the Lord Jesus not seated on His Throne is proof that the harpazo has already occurred. They

The Lion and the Book

both point to the fact that the Lord Jesus is now acting as judge before He returns the second time to the earth.

As the Day of the Lord immediately follows the harpazo, those scholars who hold to the view that the harpazo takes place Before the First Seal is opened also believe that the Day of the Lord begins when the Lord Jesus takes the book from the Father. Those scholars who believe in a Pre-Tribulation rapture are compelled to declare that the Day of the Lord had already commenced before the seventieth week of Daniel. There are no Scriptures to support the view that the Day of the Lord has started before the seventieth week of Daniel. This is another weakness in the Pre-Tribulation view. The prophet Elijah will need to appear before the seventieth week of Daniel as he must come before the Day of the Lord (Malachi 4:5). This is yet another weakness in the Pre-Tribulation view as the ministry of the two witnesses covers only 1,260 days, and the two witnesses are killed during the Great Tribulation period. Marvin Rosenthal in his book, *The Pre-Wrath Rapture of the Church*, provides detailed analysis to show that the Pre-Tribulation view is based on assumption and lacks scriptural support.

The wrath of the Lamb does not occur until the Sixth Seal is opened, and the fiery wrath of God does not take place until the Vial or Bowl judgments begin. However, it is in taking possession of the book which contains the Seal, Trumpet, and Bowl judgments, that indicates the beginning of the Day of the Lord as some scholars believe. This is the view that is held by those who hold that the harpazo occurs Before the First Seal is opened and before the Lord Jesus takes the book from God the Father.

There are some suggestions from some Bible scholars that the Lord Jesus still shows the marks of His crucifixion. As the Lamb of God, He paid the price to open the book. Does He still bear the marks of the beating that He endured before He went to the cross as this passage in chapter 5 may suggest?

Revelation 5:8-14
The Lamb Becomes a Lion

And when he had taken the book, the four beasts and four and twenty elders fell down before the Lamb, having every one of them harps, and golden vials full of odours, which are the prayers of saints. And they sung a new song, saying, Thou art worthy to take the book, and to open the seals thereof: for thou wast slain, and hast redeemed us to God by thy blood out of every kindred, and tongue, and people, and

Revelation

nation; And hast made us unto our God kings and priests: and we shall reign on the earth. And I beheld, and I heard the voice of many angels round about the throne and the beasts and the elders: and the number of them was ten thousand times ten thousand, and thousands of thousands; Saying with a loud voice, Worthy is the Lamb that was slain to receive power, and riches, and wisdom, and strength, and honour, and glory, and blessing. And every creature which is in heaven, and on the earth, and under the earth, and such as are in the sea, and all that are in them, heard I saying, Blessing, and honour, and glory, and power, be unto him that sitteth upon the throne, and unto the Lamb for ever and ever. And the four beasts said, Amen. And the four and twenty elders fell down and worshipped him that liveth for ever and ever.

Chapter 4 begins with the words, "the things which must be after [the church age]." Chapter 5 of the Book of Revelation provides scriptural support that the church is in heaven and in their glorified bodies Before the First Seal of the book is opened. The elders have received their crowns of reward, and are now singing the song of the redeemed church:

^{9} And they sung a new song, saying, Thou art worthy to take the book, and to open the seals thereof: for thou wast slain, and hast redeemed **us** to God by thy blood out of every kindred, and tongue, and people, and nation; ^{10} And hast made **us** unto our God kings and priests: and **we** shall reign on the earth. (Revelation 5:9-10)

This is not a song of Israel. The church (which includes Jews and Gentiles) are the only ones that can sing this song. Even angels cannot sing this song. Verses 9 and 10 provide strong evidence that the church is in heaven before the Lord Jesus is presented with the book as some scholars have concluded. Depending on which manuscript is followed for translation of the Bible, the interpretation of verses 9 and 10 is different. The manuscript evidence falls into basically two camps: the Received Text and the Alexandrian manuscripts.

The Received Text and the majority of the manuscript evidence support the pronouns "us" in verse 9 and "us" and "we" in verse 10. The manuscripts that make up the Received Text are roughly 90 percent of the manuscript evidence today.

The Codex Vaticanus (found on a forgotten bookshelf in the Vatican) and the Codex Sinaiticus (discovered in a wastepaper basket at Mount Sinai) support "them" and "they" in verses 9 and 10. The Codex Vaticanus and Codex Sinaiticus are two of the most well-known manuscripts that make up the Alexandrian manuscripts.

With evidence from the majority of the manuscripts, support is given to show that the church of Jesus Christ is in heaven before the Lord Jesus receives the book from the Father. If credence is given to the Codex Vaticanus and Codex Sinaiticus, then there is no Scripture support for the church being in heaven in chapter 5. Below is a comparison of the King James Version which was translated from the Received Text and the English Standard Version which was translated from the Codex Sinaiticus and the Codex Vaticanus:

⁹ And they sung a new song, saying, Thou art worthy to take the book, and to open the seals thereof: for thou wast slain, and hast redeemed **us** to God by thy blood out of every kindred, and tongue, and people, and nation; ¹⁰ And hast made **us** unto our God kings and priests: and **we** shall reign on the earth.

⁹ And they sang a new song, saying, "Worthy are you to take the scroll and to open its seals, for you were slain, and by your blood you ransomed **people** for God from every tribe and language and people and nation, ¹⁰ and you have made **them** a kingdom and priests to our God, and **they** shall reign on the earth." (ESV)

There is a difference in these two verses depending on the manuscript evidence that is held to. Those who follow the Received Text and the majority of the manuscript evidence, hold to the reading as noted in the King James Version. The Bible scholars who follow that the harpazo occurs much later in the Book of Revelation, such as the Sixth Seal, Pre-Wrath or Mid-Tribulation view will say that the New Testament saints have not yet received their glorified bodies and that the church is not yet complete in heaven before the Throne of God. They will also note that the saints under the altar in the Fifth Seal that were martyred for their faith have not received their gloried bodies (Revelation 6:9-11). There are some scholars who use the Received Text and believe that the church is not yet complete in heaven, and the harpazo will occur later. They use the example of the saints under the altar in the Fifth Seal that their number is not yet complete.

Those who follow that the harpazo has already occurred and that the church is in heaven in chapter 5 indicate that Jesus is not sitting upon the Throne. He is acting as a Lion now, getting ready to return to the earth as He will begin to open the sealed book. The Day of the Lord has started as some scholars conclude.

There are Bible scholars who hold to the language in the Codex Sinaiticus and Codex Vaticanus and to the interpretation as noted in the English Standard Version and many of the modern English translations that are based on the Codex Sinaiticus and Codex Vaticanus. As a rule, most of them believe that the harpazo will occur much later.

There are thousands of differences between the Textus Receptus and the Alexandrian manuscripts. We have about 5,255 manuscripts today. Ninety percent of these are in perfect agreement and they are referred to as the "Received Text" or "Textus Receptus." These are dated as early as the fifth century. The other 10 percent can be traced to Alexandria, Egypt, and these are commonly called the "Alexandrian manuscripts." These 10 percent are NOT in perfect agreement with the Received Text and are not in agreement with each other.

The Codex Vaticanus is the oldest complete manuscript that we have today. It is dated at AD 300 and was discovered on a forgotten bookshelf in the Vatican library. The Codex Vaticanus differs from the Received Text also.

The Codex Sinaiticus is the second oldest manuscript and it is dated at AD 400. This manuscript was discovered in 1859 in a wastepaper basket in Mt. Sinai. It differs not only from the Received Text, but from all other manuscripts.

One valid reason for the differences between the Received Text and the Alexandrian manuscripts is Gnosticism that developed in Alexandria, Egypt, and had its headquarters there. Today all of our English translations are based on the Codex Vaticanus or the Codex Sinaiticus or the other Alexandrian manuscripts. Only the King James Version and the first edition of the New King James Version are based on the Received Text. It is for this reason that the author has deferred to use the King James Version as the main text since it is based on the Received Text.

Below are some of the thousands of differences in the translations that are derived from these Greek New Testaments. The author has selected only a few differences between the different types of manuscripts. The words that are found in the Received Text and are missing from the Alexandrian manuscripts are bolded:

Matthew 9:13 English Standard Version (ESV)

[13] *Go and learn what this means, 'I desire mercy, and not sacrifice.' For I came not to call the righteous, but sinners."*

Matthew 9:13 King James Version

[13] *But go ye and learn what that meaneth, I will have mercy, and not sacrifice: for I am not come to call the righteous, but sinners* **to repentance***.*

The Lion and the Book

The Codex Vaticanus and Codex Sinaiticus omit the words "to repentance." Only two words are deleted, but the context of the verse is changed by that omission.

Acts 8:36-38 English Standard Version (ESV)

36 And as they were going along the road they came to some water, and the eunuch said, "See, here is water! What prevents me from being baptized?"[a] 38 And he commanded the chariot to stop, and they both went down into the water, Philip and the eunuch, and he baptized him.

Acts 8:36-38 King James Version

36 And as they went on their way, they came unto a certain water: and the eunuch said, See, here is water; what doth hinder me to be baptized? 37 **And Philip said, If thou believest with all thine heart, thou mayest. And he answered and said, I believe that Jesus Christ is the Son of God.** *38 And he commanded the chariot to stand still: and they went down both into the water, both Philip and the eunuch; and he baptized him.*

The Codex Vaticanus and Codex Sinaiticus omit verse 37 which contains the man's profession that Jesus Christ is the Son of God in order to be born again. This is a very important deletion and such deletions and omissions were a common practice of the Gnostics that were centered in Alexandria, Egypt

Mark 16:9-20 English Standard Version (ESV)

[Some of the earliest manuscripts do not include 16:9-20.][a]

Mark 16:9-20 King James Version

9 Now when Jesus was risen early the first day of the week, he appeared first to Mary Magdalene, out of whom he had cast seven devils. 10 And she went and told them that had been with him as they mourned and wept. 11 And they, when they had heard that he was alive, and had been seen of her, believed not. 12 After that he appeared in another form unto two of them as they walked, and went into the country. 13 And they went and told it unto the residue: neither believed they them. 14 Afterward he appeared unto the eleven as they sat at meat, and upbraided them with their unbelief and hardness of heart, because they believed not them which had seen him after he was risen. 15 And he said unto them, Go ye into all the world, and preach the gospel to every creature. 16 He that believeth and is baptized shall be saved; but he that believeth not shall be damned. 17 And these signs shall follow them that believe; In my name shall they cast out devils; they shall speak with new tongues; 18 They

Revelation

shall take up serpents; and if they drink any deadly thing, it shall not hurt them; they shall lay hands on the sick, and they shall recover. [19] So then after the Lord had spoken unto them, he was received up into heaven, and sat on the right hand of God. [20] And they went forth, and preached every where, the Lord working with them, and confirming the word with signs following. Amen.

In the examples above, there may be one or two words that are deleted from the Alexandrian manuscripts but found in the Received Text. In Matthew 9:13, the words "to repentance" have been deleted. These are important words to delete as the meaning of the text is altered. In Acts 8, the confession that Jesus Christ is the Son of God has been deleted in the Alexandrian manuscripts. That is a very important omission. In the Gospel of Mark, the resurrection, the appearance of Jesus to the disciples, and the great commission have all been deleted. The Alexandrian manuscripts have the tomb found empty and everyone afraid, and thus ends Mark's Gospel. The Alexandrian manuscripts also alter the message of Revelation 5, but in the Received Text the message clearly states that the church is in heaven.

There are those Bible scholars who believe the Alexandrian manuscripts are correct in Revelation 5, with the use of "them" and "they," but they are not correct in Mark 16 with the deletion of verses 9 through 20. However, this is just picking and choosing Scriptures out of the Alexandrian manuscripts and not allowing the manuscripts to stand by themselves. Just like in the message to the church of Laodicea, one cannot just swallow the good mixture and spit out the lukewarm mixture. It is interesting to note that the church age, which represents Laodicea, is the church age in which many new Bible translations are being printed. The word Laodicea means "people's opinions" and how fitting that during this church age there are many new Bible translations coming out to suit man's opinion. Indeed everyone in Laodicea is entitled to his own opinion—which Bible translation to use.

The historical time period of the church of Laodicea is believed to be from AD 1900 to the present day. It was just before the year of AD 1900 that the first English translations of the Codex Sinaiticus and the Codex Vaticanus appeared. The erosion of the Word of God has become apparent during the time period of the Laodicean church.

The King James Version is not a perfect translation of the Greek manuscripts. Some words have changed their meaning over the centuries. For example, the Greek word "agape" is translated "love" in I Corinthians 13 in many of our English translations today. In the KJV, the word agape is translated as "charity." In the seventeenth century the word charity was used for love. Over the centuries the English word charity has changed in meaning. Today the word charity refers to "generous actions or donations to aid the poor, ill, or helpless." The changes in the meanings of some of the words over the centuries show a weakness of the KJV. The strength of the KJV is that it was translated from the Received Text.

The strength of the English translations from the Alexandrian manuscripts is in the modern English words. These translations do provide clarification on many of the old English words that are in the King James Version.

It is beyond the scope of this book to go into detail on the manuscript evidence. Therefore, the author recommends the books below by David Fuller:

- *True or False?*
- *Which Bible?*
- *Counterfeit or Genuine Mark 16? John 8?*

The author has had the pleasure of personally corresponding with David Fuller. He is a very devoted Christian. Mr. Fuller's research is well documented as he brings to light how we have obtained the English translations that we have today.

To show a brief summary of the erosion that is taking place in the English translations today, the author will use two phrases: "Lord Jesus" and "Lord Jesus Christ" and then will show the count of the number of occurrences that each phrase occurs in the English translations below:

Passage in the text	KJV	NIV	The Message
Lord Jesus	115	102	0
Lord Jesus Christ	82	60	0

The Message is an English translation that was created by Eugene Peterson in 2002. The Message does not contain the two phrases. It reveals the erosion that has taken place in the Word of God over the years.

Chapter 6

Opening of the Seals

Revelation 6:1-2
The First Seal is Opened

And I saw when the Lamb opened one of the seals, and I heard, as it were the noise of thunder, one of the four beasts saying, Come and see. And I saw, and behold a white horse: and he that sat on him had a bow; and a crown was given unto him: and he went forth conquering, and to conquer.

THE MOMENT THE Lamb opened the First Seal John saw a rider on a white horse. Most Bible scholars agree that he is not Jesus Christ since He is pictured as returning to the earth in Revelation 19 to make war with the nations. They believe this rider to be the antichrist. The rider wears a crown while Jesus wears many crowns. The Greek word for a crown in Revelation 6:2 is *stephanos*, meaning a crown worn by a victor. The Greek word for crowns in Revelation 19:12 is *diadema*, meaning crowns of royalty. The rider in chapter 6 is given a great sword which emphasizes unusual powers and declares his authority and influence over the affairs of planet earth.

There is a seven-year period marked by a treaty between the antichrist and Israel. At some point after the treaty is signed the Lamb of God will open the First Seal. The Scriptures are silent as to the timeframe from the start of the seventieth week of Daniel to the opening of the First Seal. It is possible that during that time the antichrist may be consolidating his power before he reveals his true nature. Even dictators such as Adolf Hitler appeared as a man of peace in the beginning as he was secretly building up his military. At the midpoint of the seventieth week of Daniel, the antichrist will show his true character when he breaks his covenant with the nation of Israel by setting up his image in the Holy of Holies in the rebuilt Temple, declaring himself to be God.

The Seals, Trumpets, and Vial or Bowl judgments in the Book of Revelation are events, not timelines. John records the events and sometimes the duration of the events in the Book of Revelation, but the timeline of the Book of Revelation is provided in the Book of Daniel. The timeline is a seven-year period that starts when the antichrist signs a treaty or covenant with the nation of Israel. The starting point of the seven-year period does not correspond with the opening of the First Seal as there is no scriptural evidence to support this.

The antichrist is also called the son of perdition in II Thessalonians. This same title or description is given to Judas Iscariot as he is called the son of perdition (John 17:12). Judas and the antichrist are the only men in the Bible declared to be possessed by Satan. The antichrist is also referred to as the little horn in the Book of Daniel:

> [19] *Then I would know the truth of the fourth beast, which was diverse from all the others, exceeding dreadful, whose teeth were of iron, and his nails of brass; which devoured, brake in pieces, and stamped the residue with his feet;* [20] *And of the ten horns that were in his head, and of the other which came up, and before whom three fell; even of that horn that had eyes, and a mouth that spake very great things, whose look was more stout than his fellows.* [21] *I beheld, and the same horn made war with the saints, and prevailed against them;* [22] *Until the Ancient of days came, and judgment was given to the saints of the most High; and the time came that the saints possessed the kingdom.* [23] *Thus he said, The fourth beast shall be the fourth kingdom upon earth, which shall be diverse from all kingdoms, and shall devour the whole earth, and shall tread it down, and break it in pieces.* [24] *And the ten horns out of this kingdom are ten kings that shall arise: and another shall rise after them; and he shall be diverse from the first, and he shall subdue three kings.* [25] *And he shall speak great words against the most High, and shall wear out the saints of the most High, and think to change times and laws: and they shall be given into his hand until a time and times and the dividing of time.* [26] *But the judgment shall sit, and they shall take away his dominion, to consume and to destroy it unto the end.* (Daniel 7:19-26)

The passage in Daniel clearly indicates that the antichrist will not come to power until the ten kingdom confederacy has been established. Once the ten nation or kingdom confederacy is set up, this man referred to as the beast, or the antichrist, will begin to rise to power. He will most likely be a great orator, similar to Antiochus Epiphanes, who was able to seduce multitudes with his persuasive words. The antichrist will lead everyone to believe that he is a man of peace.

The wars of the antichrist are revealed in Daniel 11 as he conquers Egypt and Ethiopia during his time in power:

> ³⁶ *And the king shall do according to his will; and he shall exalt himself, and magnify himself above every god, and shall speak marvellous things against the God of gods, and shall prosper till the indignation be accomplished: for that that is determined shall be done.* ³⁷ *Neither shall he regard the God of his fathers, nor the desire of women, nor regard any god: for he shall magnify himself above all.* ³⁸ *But in his estate shall he honour the God of forces: and a god whom his fathers knew not shall he honour with gold, and silver, and with precious stones, and pleasant things.* ³⁹ *Thus shall he do in the most strong holds with a strange god, whom he shall acknowledge and increase with glory: and he shall cause them to rule over many, and shall divide the land for gain.* ⁴⁰ *And at the time of the end shall the king of the south push at him: and the king of the north shall come against him like a whirlwind, with chariots, and with horsemen, and with many ships; and he shall enter into the countries, and shall overflow and pass over.* ⁴¹ *He shall enter also into the glorious land, and many countries shall be overthrown: but these shall escape out of his hand, even Edom, and Moab, and the chief of the children of Ammon.* ⁴² *He shall stretch forth his hand also upon the countries: and the land of Egypt shall not escape.* ⁴³ *But he shall have power over the treasures of gold and of silver, and over all the precious things of Egypt: and the Libyans and the Ethiopians shall be at his steps.* ⁴⁴ *But tidings out of the east and out of the north shall trouble him: therefore he shall go forth with great fury to destroy, and utterly to make away many.* ⁴⁵ *And he shall plant the tabernacles of his palace between the seas in the glorious holy mountain; yet he shall come to his end, and none shall help him.* (Daniel 11:36-45)

As revealed in the Book of Daniel, the antichrist will be a man of war and will conquer many nations.

The Lord Jesus warned His disciples concerning the events that will occur in the last days. The events of the Book of Revelation are described in the Gospels. The First Seal is described in the Gospels as false Christs arising and deceiving many:

> ³*And as he sat upon the Mount of Olives, the disciples came unto him privately, saying, Tell us, when shall these things be? And what shall be the sign of thy coming, and of the end of the world?* ⁴ *And Jesus answered and said unto them, Take heed that no man deceive you.* ⁵ *For many shall come in my name, saying, I am Christ; and shall deceive many.* (Matthew 24:3-5)

Revelation

³*And as he sat upon the Mount of Olives over against the temple, Peter and James and John and Andrew asked him privately,* ⁴ *tell us, when shall these things be? And what shall be the sign when all these things shall be fulfilled?* ⁵ *And Jesus answering them began to say, Take heed lest any man deceive you:* ⁶ *for many shall come in my name, saying, I am Christ; and shall deceive many.* (Mark 13:3-6)

⁷*And they asked him, saying, Master, but when shall these things be? And what sign will there be when these things shall come to pass?* ⁸ *And he said, Take heed that ye be not deceived: for many shall come in my name, saying, I am Christ; and the time draweth near: go ye not therefore after them.* (Luke 21:7-8)

Along with the nations of the world being deceived, the nation of Israel will also follow after the deception of the antichrist as revealed in John 5:43. The eyes of the nation of Israel will not be opened to recognize this false Christ until after he betrays them and when the abomination of desolation is set up as revealed in the Gospel of Matthew:

¹⁵*When ye therefore shall see the abomination of desolation, spoken of by Daniel the prophet, stand in the holy place, (whoso readeth, let him understand:)* ¹⁶ *Then let them which be in Judaea flee into the mountains:* ¹⁷ *Let him which is on the housetop not come down to take any thing out of his house:* ¹⁸ *Neither let him which is in the field return back to take his clothes.* ¹⁹ *And woe unto them that are with child, and to them that give suck in those days!* ²⁰ *But pray ye that your flight be not in the winter, neither on the sabbath day:* ²¹ *For then shall be great tribulation, such as was not since the beginning of the world to this time, no, nor ever shall be.* ²² *And except those days should be shortened, there should no flesh be saved: but for the elect's sake those days shall be shortened.* (Matthew 24:15-22)

Once the true nature of the antichrist is revealed and the Jews realize that they have been deceived, it will be a time of great tribulation for the Jews. The antichrist will move speedily against them at this time as the Scriptures indicate that the Jews will be fleeing their country quickly to escape the wrath of the antichrist.

Revelation 6:3-4
The Second Seal is Opened

And when he had opened the second seal, I heard the second beast say, Come and see. And there went out another horse that was red: and power was given to him that sat thereon to take peace from the earth, and that they should kill one another: and there was given unto him a great sword.

Opening of the Seals

As the First Seal was revealed in the Gospels, so also are Seals Two through Six revealed. Wars and rumors of wars were foretold by our Lord. These wars may be the result of nations resisting the antichrist and his policies as he is looking to expand his influence and power throughout the world. Jesus revealed this warning to His disciples:

⁶ *And ye shall hear of wars and rumours of wars: see that ye be not troubled: for all these things must come to pass, but the end is not yet.* ⁷ *For nation shall rise against nation, and kingdom against kingdom: and there shall be famines, and pestilences, and earthquakes, in divers places.* ⁸ *All these are the beginning of sorrows.* (Matthew 24:6-8)

⁷ *And when ye shall hear of wars and rumours of wars, be ye not troubled: for such things must needs be; but the end shall not be yet.* ⁸ *For nation shall rise against nation, and kingdom against kingdom: and there shall be earthquakes in divers places, and there shall be famines and troubles: these are the beginnings of sorrows.* (Mark 13:7-8)

⁹ *But when ye shall hear of wars and commotions, be not terrified: for these things must first come to pass; but the end is not by and by.* ¹⁰ *Then said he unto them, Nation shall rise against nation, and kingdom against kingdom.* (Luke 21:9-10)

Revelation 6:5-6
The Third Seal is Opened

And when he had opened the third seal, I heard the third beast say, Come and see. And I beheld, and lo a black horse; and he that sat on him had a pair of balances in his hand. And I heard a voice in the midst of the four beasts say, A measure of wheat for a penny, and three measures of barley for a penny; and see thou hurt not the oil and the wine.

Famine usually takes place during and immediately following a war. The Greek word for penny is *denarius*. A Roman denarius was equal to a day's wages, which indicates that the food supply will be scarce and people will be spending most of their money on food just to survive. From history we see that when man develops weapons of great firepower, not only do the towns and cities suffer, but the food supply becomes endangered. During World War II there was a tremendous food shortage across all of Europe as farmlands were destroyed and captured. Here in the Gospels, Jesus again foretells of this great plague:

Revelation

⁷For nation shall rise against nation, and kingdom against kingdom: and there shall be famines, and pestilences, and earthquakes, in divers places. ⁸ All these are the beginning of sorrows. (Matthew 24:7-8)

¹¹And great earthquakes shall be in divers places, and famines, and pestilences; and fearful sights and great signs shall there be from heaven. (Luke 21:11)

In the Gospel of Matthew these plagues are mentioned as just the beginning of sorrows. Wars and famine are horrible and it is hard to imagine that events upon the world can get worse. But these are the beginning of sorrows, and the worst is yet to come.

Revelation 6:7-8
The Fourth Seal is Opened

And when he had opened the fourth seal, I heard the voice of the fourth beast say, Come and see. And I looked, and behold a pale horse: and his name that sat on him was Death, and Hell followed with him. And power was given unto them over the fourth part of the earth, to kill with sword, and with hunger, and with death, and with the beasts of the earth.

One fourth of the world's population will be dead as the result of wars, famine and pestilences. In Matthew 24 this is noted as the beginning of sorrows. The beginning of sorrows is often referred to as a woman in the beginning stages of labor. The labor pains will increase as the time for the birth of the baby is to come. So too, in the Book of Revelation the sorrows that have been experienced so far are just the beginning of sorrows. During the second half of the seventieth week of Daniel, as the coming of the Lord Jesus is soon to be expected, the labor pains that the world will experience will intensify. During the Sixth Trumpet judgment in chapter 9 one-third of the remaining population will be killed. This would be equal, at minimum, to one-half of the world's population that would be killed starting from the opening of the First Seal until the end of the Sixth Trumpet judgment. The Fourth Seal judgment is likened to a sword that is approved to commit murder or government action against its citizens. The number of people killed during this time will far exceed the total of the first two world wars.

- In WW I some sources estimate 16.5 million perished (military and civilian).
- In WW II some sources estimate 72.4 million perished (military and civilian).

Opening of the Seals

Revelation 6:9-11
The Fifth Seal is Opened

And when he had opened the fifth seal, I saw under the altar the souls of them that were slain for the word of God, and for the testimony which they held: And they cried with a loud voice, saying, How long, O Lord, holy and true, dost thou not judge and avenge our blood on them that dwell on the earth? And white robes were given unto every one of them; and it was said unto them, that they should rest yet for a little season, until their fellowservants also and their brethren, that should be killed as they were, should be fulfilled.

A scapegoat needs to be found for the wars, famines, and pestilences that have taken place. The scapegoat will be those who believe the antichrist is evil and must be stopped. Those who believe that the antichrist is evil and is responsible for what has happened upon the earth will be persecuted and put to death. Many will most likely be passive and observe with displeasure what is transpiring, but they will remain silent.

The persecution described from the Fifth Seal was foretold by Jesus in the Gospels:

⁹ Then shall they deliver you up to be afflicted, and shall kill you: and ye shall be hated of all nations for my name's sake. ¹⁰ And then shall many be offended, and shall betray one another, and shall hate one another. ¹¹ And many false prophets shall rise, and shall deceive many. ¹² And because iniquity shall abound, the love of many shall wax cold. ¹³ But he that shall endure unto the end, the same shall be saved. (Matthew 24:9-13)

⁹But take heed to yourselves: for they shall deliver you up to councils; and in the synagogues ye shall be beaten: and ye shall be brought before rulers and kings for my sake, for a testimony against them. ¹⁰ And the gospel must first be published among all nations. ¹¹ But when they shall lead you, and deliver you up, take no thought beforehand what ye shall speak, neither do ye premeditate: but whatsoever shall be given you in that hour, that speak ye: for it is not ye that speak, but the Holy Ghost. ¹² Now the brother shall betray the brother to death, and the father the son; and children shall rise up against their parents, and shall cause them to be put to death. ¹³ And ye shall be hated of all men for my name's sake: but he that shall endure unto the end, the same shall be saved. (Mark 13:9-13)

¹²But before all these, they shall lay their hands on you, and persecute you, delivering you up to the synagogues, and into prisons, being brought before kings and rulers for my name's sake. ¹³ And it shall turn to you for a testimony. ¹⁴ Settle it therefore in your hearts, not to meditate before what ye shall answer: ¹⁵ For I will give

Revelation

you a mouth and wisdom, which all your adversaries shall not be able to gainsay nor resist. 16 And ye shall be betrayed both by parents, and brethren, and kinsfolks, and friends; and some of you shall they cause to be put to death. 17 And ye shall be hated of all men for my name's sake. 18 But there shall not an hair of your head perish. 19 In your patience possess ye your souls. (Luke 21:12-19).

This will be a time of great persecution and many will be betrayed and sentenced to death for opposing the kingdom of antichrist. It will be a time when family members will betray one another.

There are two schools of thought regarding the identity of the multitude of souls seen under the altar when the Fifth Seal is opened. Some scholars believe that these souls represent the church and others believe that the souls under the altar represent those who came to faith in the Lord Jesus after the harpazo.

The souls under the altar represent the church

Those scholars who hold to the view that the souls under the altar represent the church believe that the harpazo has not yet occurred. They hold to the belief that the church is not yet complete in heaven. The Codex Vaticanus and the Codex Sinaiticus do support that the church is not yet complete in heaven, as we discussed earlier in chapter 5. They believe the souls under the altar represent the great multitude that came out of the Great Tribulation from Revelation 7:9-17:

9After this I beheld, and, lo, a great multitude, which no man could number, of all nations, and kindreds, and people, and tongues, stood before the throne, and before the Lamb, clothed with white robes, and palms in their hands; 10 And cried with a loud voice, saying, Salvation to our God which sitteth upon the throne, and unto the Lamb. 11 And all the angels stood round about the throne, and about the elders and the four beasts, and fell before the throne on their faces, and worshipped God, 12 Saying, Amen: Blessing, and glory, and wisdom, and thanksgiving, and honour, and power, and might, be unto our God for ever and ever. Amen. 13 And one of the elders answered, saying unto me, what are these which are arrayed in white robes? And whence came they? 14 And I said unto him, Sir, thou knowest. And he said to me, These are they which came out of great tribulation, and have washed their robes, and made them white in the blood of the Lamb. 15 Therefore are they before the throne of God, and serve him day and night in his temple: and he that sitteth on the throne shall dwell among them. 16 They shall hunger no more, neither thirst any more; neither shall the sun light on them, nor any heat. 17 For the Lamb which is in the midst of the throne shall feed them, and shall lead them unto living fountains of waters: and God shall wipe away all tears from their eyes. (Revelation 7:9-17)

Opening of the Seals

The Lord speaks to those under the altar, urging them to remain patient until their number is complete. The persecution will need to run its course as the antichrist continues to expand his power and authority over the world.

The scholars who support the view that the harpazo will occur after the Fifth Seal use the great multitude as their example. Their argument is, how can such a multitude of people come to faith in Christ from the churches of Pergamos, Thyatira, Sardis and Laodicea if the harpazo occurred earlier? The members and leadership of these churches have no discernment to recognize truth from error. In Christ's letter to the seven churches we saw that there was only a remnant within the church of Thyatira that was faithful, and only a few who were faithful to the Lord from the church of Sardis. Only the members from the churches of Philadelphia and Smyrna have the discernment to recognize truth from error.

There are Bible scholars who believe that the true and faithful believers will be spared the horrors of the Great Tribulation and will take part in the harpazo. The Lord will provide a hedge of protection around them. The members of the backslidden churches of Pergamos, Thyatira, Sardis and Laodicea will experience the horrors of the Great Tribulation.

The souls under the altar do not represent the church

Those scholars who hold to the view that the harpazo occurred earlier believe that the church is complete in heaven. (The Received Text does support the fact that the church is complete in heaven as we discussed earlier in chapter 5.) They believe that the souls under the altar represent the great multitude that came to faith in the Lord Jesus Christ after the harpazo, meaning they represent the saints that came out of the Great Tribulation from Revelation 7:9-17.

This view is difficult to accept when the churches of Pergamos, Thyatira, Sardis and Laodicea have no discernment and cannot recognize truth from error. It is difficult to comprehend that these churches would be carrying the truth to the unsaved world, a world being ruled by the antichrist.

In defense of those who do believe that the church is in heaven in Revelation 5 and that this multitude represents a vast multitude of people that came to faith in Jesus Christ after the harpazo occurs, there is the possibility that the Lord will send a great revival across the entire world. The author has had the privilege to listen to Dr. J. Edwin Orr in 1982. Pastor Chuck Smith came to Franklin, Pennsylvania, as part of a pastors' seminar for the local pastors on the east coast of the United States. Pastor Chuck

Revelation

brought Dr. J. Edwin Orr to Franklin with him to speak to the pastors and church leaders.

Dr. Orr was one of the leading experts on revivals across the world. Billy Graham stated that Dr. Orr was the leading authority on revivals in the Protestant world. The author had the privilege to listen to Dr. Orr speak about the great revivals in Europe and the United States over the centuries, and it was very enlightening. Dr. Orr revealed that when the Lord sent a revival it was always His sovereign work. Dr. Orr spoke of multitudes of sinners falling on their hands and knees in repentance as they went about their day-to-day activities. Churches were packed all day and all night as multitudes came to faith in Jesus Christ. Dr. Orr observed that all revivals throughout history had three essential ingredients: prayer, confession of sin, and repentance. All three must be present for a true revival to take place. It is possible that the Lord will send one last revival after the church is gone as He has done in the past—one last call to mankind as the antichrist is growing in power and seeking to stomp out all that resist him.

Dr. Orr taught that in the past the Lord would often send a revival before a great war occurred. He showed that before the Civil War, World War I, and World War II, the Lord sent a great awaking that filled the churches with many who came to hear the Gospel.

According the Scriptures, when the antichrist comes to power he will be a man of war. There is always the possibility that the Lord may send one last revival before the wars of the antichrist commence. No one can say for certain that such a revival can or will take place, but this is one explanation for the multitude that is seen under the altar as part of the Fifth Seal judgment.

Another point that indicates that this multitude may be the saints that came to believe in Christ after the church was raptured is found in Acts 7:60. Contrast the Fifth Seal to the cry of Stephen for mercy on those who were stoning him. It appears that the age of grace is over as those under the altar were crying out for justice because their blood was shed. The saints were under the altar of sacrifice and not the altar of incense that is described in Revelation 6. Since the text says that they "had been slain," it implies that their deaths occurred prior to the Fifth Seal.

For those under the altar, the Lord speaks to them to remain patient until their number is complete. The persecution will need to run its course as the antichrist continues to expand his power and authority over the world.

The wrath of God and of the Lamb will now be revealed when the Sixth Seal is opened.

Opening of the Seals

Revelation 6:12-17
The Sixth Seal is Opened

And I beheld when he had opened the sixth seal, and, lo, there was a great earthquake; and the sun became black as sackcloth of hair, and the moon became as blood; And the stars of heaven fell unto the earth, even as a fig tree casteth her untimely figs, when she is shaken of a mighty wind. And the heaven departed as a scroll when it is rolled together; and every mountain and island were moved out of their places. And the kings of the earth, and the great men, and the rich men, and the chief captains, and the mighty men, and every bondman, and every free man, hid themselves in the dens and in the rocks of the mountains; And said to the mountains and rocks, Fall on us, and hide us from the face of him that sitteth on the throne, and from the wrath of the Lamb: For the great day of his wrath is come; and who shall be able to stand?

The Sixth Seal announces the wrath of the Lamb with the following events that will occur:
- A great earthquake;
- The sun turns black;
- The moon turns red as blood;
- The stars of heaven appear to be falling to the earth;
- The heaven departed as a scroll when it is rolled up;
- Every mountain and island is moved out of its place;
- Great fear falls upon all mankind from great to the small as they recognize from where these judgments are originating.

This is the first time that the wrath of God has been introduced in the Book of Revelation. The Greek word for wrath introduced in the Sixth Seal is *orge*. Orge means "punishment," "anger." There is another Greek word for wrath that is used in the Book of Revelation and that word is *thumos* which means "fierce anger," "fiery indignation." Here in the Sixth Seal, the word *orge* is used.

There are two views of the harpazo of the church that relate to the Sixth Seal. We will cover them in more detail in this chapter. They are:

The Sixth Seal View - the belief that the coming of Christ for His church coincides with the announcement of the Sixth Seal and the church will not experience any of the plagues of the Sixth Seal.

The Intra-Seal View - the belief that the coming of Christ for His church will be after the announcement of the Sixth Seal but before the Seventh Seal is opened. There is a pause after the announcement of the Sixth

Revelation

Seal before the plagues of the Sixth Seal are unleashed upon the earth. Before the pause is over, Christ comes for His church and the awful plagues of the Sixth Seal are unleashed.

The earthquake described in the Sixth Seal is a "great earthquake." It coincides with changes in the heavens as well as remarkable alterations on the surface of the earth. The entire population is in a panic and world leaders have no answers for what is now occurring on the earth. The stars are often referred to as angels in the Scripture, especially in the Book of Revelation. Bible scholars believe that the stars here in the Sixth Seal refer to Satan and his angels being thrown out of heaven as described in Revelation 12:

> [7] *And there was war in heaven: Michael and his angels fought against the dragon; and the dragon fought and his angels,* [8] *and prevailed not; neither was their place found any more in heaven.* [9] *And the great dragon was cast out, that old serpent, called the Devil, and Satan, which deceiveth the whole world: he was cast out into the earth, and his angels were cast out with him.* [10] *And I heard a loud voice saying in heaven, Now is come salvation, and strength, and the kingdom of our God, and the power of his Christ: for the accuser of our brethren is cast down, which accused them before our God day and night.* [11] *And they overcame him by the blood of the Lamb, and by the word of their testimony; and they loved not their lives unto the death.* [12] *Therefore rejoice, ye heavens, and ye that dwell in them. Woe to the inhabiters of the earth and of the sea! For the devil is come down unto you, having great wrath, because he knoweth that he hath but a short time.* [13] *And when the dragon saw that he was cast unto the earth, he persecuted the woman which brought forth the man child.* [14] *And to the woman were given two wings of a great eagle, that she might fly into the wilderness, into her place, where she is nourished for a time, and times, and half a time, from the face of the serpent.* [15] *And the serpent cast out of his mouth water as a flood after the woman, that he might cause her to be carried away of the flood.* [16] *And the earth helped the woman, and the earth opened her mouth, and swallowed up the flood which the dragon cast out of his mouth.* [17] *And the dragon was wroth with the woman, and went to make war with the remnant of her seed, which keep the commandments of God, and have the testimony of Jesus Christ.* (Revelation 12:7-17)

It is apparent from Revelation 12 that Satan and his angels are cast out of heaven at the midpoint of the seventieth week of Daniel. The last three-and-a-half years of the seventieth week of Daniel are referred to as the Great Tribulation and also as the time of Jacob's Trouble. It appears as if the Sixth Seal occurs at the halfway point of the seven-year period. The dragon will begin to persecute the Jews and those who have the testimony

Opening of the Seals

of Jesus Christ. At this point the antichrist begins to show his true character as he turns against the Jews. Those saints who were identified as under the altar in the Fifth Seal will have their number complete towards the end of the seventieth week of Daniel. Those who have the testimony of Jesus Christ will experience much hardship as the plagues of God are being poured out upon the earth against the kingdom of antichrist.

As with the previous Seals, the Sixth Seal is described in the Gospels:

²⁹ Immediately after the tribulation of those days shall the sun be darkened, and the moon shall not give her light, and the stars shall fall from heaven, and the powers of the heavens shall be shaken: ³⁰ And then shall appear the sign of the Son of man in heaven: and then shall all the tribes of the earth mourn, and they shall see the Son of man coming in the clouds of heaven with power and great glory. ³¹ And he shall send his angels with a great sound of a trumpet, and they shall gather together his elect from the four winds, from one end of heaven to the other (Matthew 24:29-31).

Many Bible scholars believe that the harpazo will occur at the Sixth Seal, and they will point to the verses here in Matthew 24:29-31 and compare them to the Sixth Seal in Revelation 6:12-17 as the wording appears identical. The people on the earth will see Jesus appearing in the sky and coming for His church, and then as the world is watching this event on the Internet or cable television, the wrath of the Lamb will begin. This event cannot be confused with the angels that some say are commissioned to bring back the Jews into the Promised Land at the end of the seventieth week of Daniel. The angels have not been commissioned to bring back the Jews into the land of Israel when Jesus returns to the earth to reign as King of Kings and Lord of Lords. It is men who are commissioned by the Lord to search out, find and bring back the Jews to the Promised Land after Jesus returns to the earth. This is clearly revealed in Isaiah 14:2, Isaiah 66:19-20, Jeremiah 16:14-16, and Jeremiah 23:5-8. Again, those who follow the Sixth Seal harpazo will point to the sign of the Son of Man (Jesus) appearing in the sky and gathering His church into the heavens to be with Him forever. This would be a visible event of the harpazo of the church, and the world is now witnessing this great event as the saints are rising up to meet Jesus. The verses in Matthew and Revelation offer strong support that the harpazo occurs at the Sixth Seal. After the harpazo the Day of the Lord will commence.

Those scholars who believe that the harpazo will take place Before the First Seal is opened see two appearances of the Lord Jesus in Matthew 24:29-31—the appearing when He comes for His church and the Second Coming as thus:

Revelation

²⁹ *Immediately after the tribulation of those days shall the sun be darkened, and the moon shall not give her light, and the stars shall fall from heaven, and the powers of the heavens shall be shaken:* ³⁰ *And then shall appear the sign of the Son of man in heaven: and then shall all the tribes of the earth mourn.* (Matthew 24:29-30a)

They believe that the rest of verse 30 refers to the second coming and that verse 31 describes the harpazo that took place Before the First Seal is opened.

³⁰ᵇ*And they shall see the Son of man coming in the clouds of heaven with power and great glory.* ³¹ *And he shall send his angels with a great sound of a trumpet, and they shall gather together his elect from the four winds, from one end of heaven to the other.* (Matthew 24:30b-31)

The Sixth Seal is also described in the Gospel of Mark and Luke:

²⁴ *But in those days, after that tribulation, the sun shall be darkened, and the moon shall not give her light,* ²⁵ *and the stars of heaven shall fall, and the powers that are in heaven shall be shaken.* ²⁶ *And then shall they see the Son of man coming in the clouds with great power and glory.* ²⁷ *And then shall he send his angels, and shall gather together his elect from the four winds, from the uttermost part of the earth to the uttermost part of heaven.* (Mark 13:24-27)

The description here in Mark presents the harpazo as occurring at the Sixth Seal, and supports the view that the Lord Jesus is coming for His church at this time.

²⁵ *And there shall be signs in the sun, and in the moon, and in the stars; and upon the earth distress of nations, with perplexity; the sea and the waves roaring;* ²⁶ *Men's hearts failing them for fear, and for looking after those things which are coming on the earth: for the powers of heaven shall be shaken.* ²⁷ *And then shall they see the Son of man coming in a cloud with power and great glory.* ²⁸ *And when these things begin to come to pass, then look up, and lift up your heads; for your redemption draweth nigh.* (Luke 21:25-28)

The verses in the Gospel of Luke are a little different, as there is no mention of the harpazo. Luke is writing to Gentiles, unlike Matthew and Mark who are writing to the Jews. Luke 21:28 can easily be interpreted to prepare the Gentile church to be ready for the harpazo when the events of the beginning of the chapter are starting to come to pass. Scholars who hold to a Sixth Seal view and Before the First Seal view of the harpazo will quote these verses as their proof texts. The only difference being the interpretation of the passage in Luke. Those who follow the Sixth Seal view will see the

Opening of the Seals

events of the Sixth Seal as a fulfillment of Luke 21:28. Those scholars who hold to the view that Jesus will come for His church Before the First Seal is opened see the events that are introduced at the beginning of the chapter (Luke 21:8-9), which warn about the coming antichrist, as the fulfillment of Luke 21:28.

The Sixth Seal is also described in Luke 17 and is compared to the days of Noah and Lot:

24 For as the lightning, that lighteneth out of the one part under heaven, shineth unto the other part under heaven; so shall also the Son of man be in his day. 25 But first must he suffer many things, and be rejected of this generation. 26 And as it was in the days of Noe, so shall it be also in the days of the Son of man. 27 They did eat, they drank, they married wives, they were given in marriage, until the day that Noah entered into the ark, and the flood came, and destroyed them all. (Luke 17:24-27)

The harpazo will be a visible event which will be seen by who dwell upon the earth. The Lord Jesus will be visible in the sky when He returns to gather His church and take them home to heaven. The Greek word for "caught up" is *harpazo* and it is fully described in I Thessalonians 4:16-17:

16 For the Lord himself shall descend from heaven with a shout, with the voice of the archangel, and with the trump of God: and the dead in Christ shall rise first: 17 Then we which are alive and remain shall be caught up together with them in the clouds, to meet the Lord in the air: and so shall we ever be with the Lord. (I Thessalonians 4:16-17)

The events of the Sixth Seal are also prophesied in the Old Testament:

30 And I will shew wonders in the heavens and in the earth, blood, and fire, and pillars of smoke. 31 The sun shall be turned into darkness, and the moon into blood, before the great and terrible day of the LORD come. (Joel 2:30-31)

9 And it shall come to pass in that day, saith the Lord GOD, that I will cause the sun to go down at noon, and I will darken the earth in the clear day: 10 And I will turn your feasts into mourning, and all your songs into lamentation; and I will bring up sackcloth upon all loins, and baldness upon every head; and I will make it as the mourning of an only son, and the end thereof as a bitter day. (Amos 8:9-10)

10 Enter into the rock, and hide thee in the dust, for fear of the LORD, and for the glory of his majesty. 11 The lofty looks of man shall be humbled, and the haughtiness of men shall be bowed down, and the LORD alone shall be exalted in that day. 12 For the day of the LORD of hosts shall be upon every one that is proud and lofty, and upon every one that is lifted up; and he shall be brought low: 13 And upon all the cedars of Lebanon, that are high and lifted up, and upon all the oaks of Bashan,

Revelation

¹⁴ And upon all the high mountains, and upon all the hills that are lifted up, ¹⁵ And upon every high tower, and upon every fenced wall, ¹⁶ And upon all the ships of Tarshish, and upon all pleasant pictures. ¹⁷ And the loftiness of man shall be bowed down, and the haughtiness of men shall be made low: and the LORD alone shall be exalted in that day. ¹⁸ And the idols he shall utterly abolish. ¹⁹ And they shall go into the holes of the rocks, and into the caves of the earth, for fear of the LORD, and for the glory of his majesty, when he ariseth to shake terribly the earth. (Isaiah 2:10-19)

The Scriptures in Joel and Isaiah provide strong support for the harpazo of the church to occur at the Sixth Seal. The Day of Christ is the harpazo, where the Lord Jesus comes for His church. The Day of the Lord immediately follows the harpazo of the church.

⁶ Howl ye; for the day of the LORD is at hand; it shall come as a destruction from the Almighty. ⁷ Therefore shall all hands be faint, and every man's heart shall melt: ⁸ And they shall be afraid: pangs and sorrows shall take hold of them; they shall be in pain as a woman that travaileth: they shall be amazed one at another; their faces shall be as flames. ⁹ Behold, the day of the LORD cometh, cruel both with wrath and fierce anger, to lay the land desolate: and he shall destroy the sinners thereof out of it. ¹⁰ For the stars of heaven and the constellations thereof shall not give their light: the sun shall be darkened in his going forth, and the moon shall not cause her light to shine. ¹¹ And I will punish the world for their evil, and the wicked for their iniquity; and I will cause the arrogancy of the proud to cease, and will lay low the haughtiness of the terrible. ¹² I will make a man more precious than fine gold; even a man than the golden wedge of Ophir. ¹³ Therefore I will shake the heavens, and the earth shall remove out of her place, in the wrath of the LORD of hosts, and in the day of his fierce anger. (Isaiah 13:6-13)

¹ Behold, the LORD maketh the earth empty, and maketh it waste, and turneth it upside down, and scattereth abroad the inhabitants thereof. ² And it shall be, as with the people, so with the priest; as with the servant, so with his master; as with the maid, so with her mistress; as with the buyer, so with the seller; as with the lender, so with the borrower; as with the taker of usury, so with the giver of usury to him. ³ The land shall be utterly emptied, and utterly spoiled: for the LORD hath spoken this word. ⁴ The earth mourneth and fadeth away, the world languisheth and fadeth away, the haughty people of the earth do languish. ⁵ The earth also is defiled under the inhabitants thereof; because they have transgressed the laws, changed the ordinance, broken the everlasting covenant. ⁶ Therefore hath the curse devoured the earth, and they that dwell therein are desolate: therefore the inhabitants of the earth are burned, and few men left. ⁷ The new wine mourneth, the vine languisheth, all the

merryhearted do sigh. ⁸ The mirth of tabrets ceaseth, the noise of them that rejoice endeth, the joy of the harp ceaseth. ⁹ They shall not drink wine with a song; strong drink shall be bitter to them that drink it. ¹⁰ The city of confusion is broken down: every house is shut up, that no man may come in. ¹¹ There is a crying for wine in the streets; all joy is darkened, the mirth of the land is gone. ¹² In the city is left desolation, and the gate is smitten with destruction. ¹³ When thus it shall be in the midst of the land among the people, there shall be as the shaking of an olive tree, and as the gleaning grapes when the vintage is done. ¹⁴ They shall lift up their voice, they shall sing for the majesty of the LORD, *they shall cry aloud from the sea. ¹⁵ Wherefore glorify ye the* LORD *in the fires, even the name of the* LORD *God of Israel in the isles of the sea. ¹⁶ From the uttermost part of the earth have we heard songs, even glory to the righteous. But I said, My leanness, my leanness, woe unto me! the treacherous dealers have dealt treacherously; yea, the treacherous dealers have dealt very treacherously. ¹⁷ Fear, and the pit, and the snare, are upon thee, O inhabitant of the earth. ¹⁸ And it shall come to pass, that he who fleeth from the noise of the fear shall fall into the pit; and he that cometh up out of the midst of the pit shall be taken in the snare: for the windows from on high are open, and the foundations of the earth do shake. ¹⁹ The earth is utterly broken down, the earth is clean dissolved, the earth is moved exceedingly. ²⁰ The earth shall reel to and fro like a drunkard, and shall be removed like a cottage; and the transgression thereof shall be heavy upon it; and it shall fall, and not rise again.* (Isaiah 24:1-20)

The Hebrew word for wrath in Isaiah 13:9 is *qatsaph*, and it is similar to *orge*. Therefore, the wrath of God described in the Book of Isaiah is similar to the wrath of the Lamb described in the Book of Revelation. *Orge* in the Greek means "punishment," "anger." The first time *orge* is used in the Book of Revelation is the Sixth Seal. The other occurrences of *orge* in the Book of Revelation are in Revelation 11:18; 16:19; and 19:15. *Orge* commences with the Sixth Seal and ends when Jesus returns to the earth and makes war with the antichrist and his armies. The verses in Isaiah do support the harpazo occurring at the Sixth Seal.

The other Greek word for "wrath" in the Book of Revelation is *thumos*. *Thumos* in English means "fierceness," "fiery indignation." This is more intense than *orge*. The first occurrence of *thumos* in the Scriptures is when Satan is cast out of heaven and he is very, very angry, and will take out his anger upon mankind. The first time that God the Father uses *thumos* is in Revelation 14:8 as He judges Babylon. The next occurrences are in reference to those who worship the antichrist and take his mark in Revelation 14:10, the battle of Armageddon in 14:19, the Vial judgments in 15:1; 15:7; and 16:1, and finally in the destruction of Babylon in 18:3.

Revelation

There are some very important Scriptures in the Book of Thessalonians that tie directly to the wrath of God described in the Book of Revelation. The apostle Paul uses the Greek word *orge* when he writes about the wrath of God in his epistle to the Thessalonians.

^{10}And to wait for his Son from heaven, whom he raised from the dead, even Jesus, which delivered us from the wrath to come. (I Thessalonians 1:10)

^{9} For God hath not appointed us to wrath, but to obtain salvation by our Lord Jesus Christ. (I Thessalonians 5:9)

From Paul's writing to the Thessalonians, it is clear that the church is not appointed to *orge*, which is the wrath of the Lamb. Indeed, one can substitute the words (Sixth Seal) for wrath in Paul's epistle and it can be correctly interpreted that God has not appointed us (His church) to the Sixth Seal. Therefore, the church is not appointed to the Sixth Seal and the harpazo of the church cannot occur after the Sixth Seal as this would contradict the Scriptures! This is a very important truth as the church will not experience the wrath of the Lamb when it begins.

In summary, the harpazo of the church is an event that will occur in the future. The Lord Jesus will appear in the sky for all to see, and will call His church home to heaven. There are Scriptures that support the view that Jesus will come for His church Before the First Seal is opened (as discussed earlier) and there are Scriptures to support the view that the Lord Jesus will come for His church at the start of the Sixth Seal when it is opened. There is no direct scriptural evidence to support the Pre-Tribulation view that Jesus will come for His church before the start of the seventieth week of Daniel. The Pre-Tribulation view is a pure assumption that the antichrist will be revealed to the true and faithful church before he signs a seven-year treaty with the nation of Israel.

What the apostle Paul declared in his epistle to the Thessalonians, that the church is not appointed to the wrath (*orge*) of God, is significant. The harpazo cannot occur after the Sixth Seal as this would contradict the Scriptures. Any view of the harpazo that is declared after the wrath (*orge*) of God has commenced is not scripturally correct. Therefore, the following views of the harpazo of the church cannot be correct as they would contradict the Scriptures:

- Post-Tribulational view
- Post-Tribulational view but earlier – (the view that the harpazo occurs before the Vial or Bowl judgments).

There may be those who believe the church will be raptured late in the tribulation period, past the event of the Sixth Seal. However, a true believer in Christ will eventually understand that the church will not see the *orge* of God. For those who teach that the church will be raptured after the wrath of the Lamb, those teachers are not correct, and preach from the pulpit that which is contrary to the Scriptures. It is best to stay away from such men and to find a church where the Word of God is proclaimed in truth and in love.

There are those who believe that men can redeem society so that the events described in the Book of Revelation need not occur. They believe that by working together, men can prevent these awful events from happening. Stay away from those who teach such nonsense, as their view is in direct contraction to the Book of Daniel, especially Daniel 2. Those who teach that the events in Revelation can be prevented are also teaching falsely and need to be avoided.

There are Bible scholars who hold to a Mid-Tribulation view on the harpazo of the church. If the Sixth Seal occurs before the Mid-Point of the final seven year period, then the Mid-Tribulation view cannot be correct. If the Sixth Seal occurs at the Mid-Point of the seventieth week of Daniel, then those who hold to a Sixth Seal view and a Mid-Tribulation view could be correct in their view, if indeed the Lord Jesus returns for His church at the start of the Sixth Seal. Below is a graph of the Sixth Seal view.

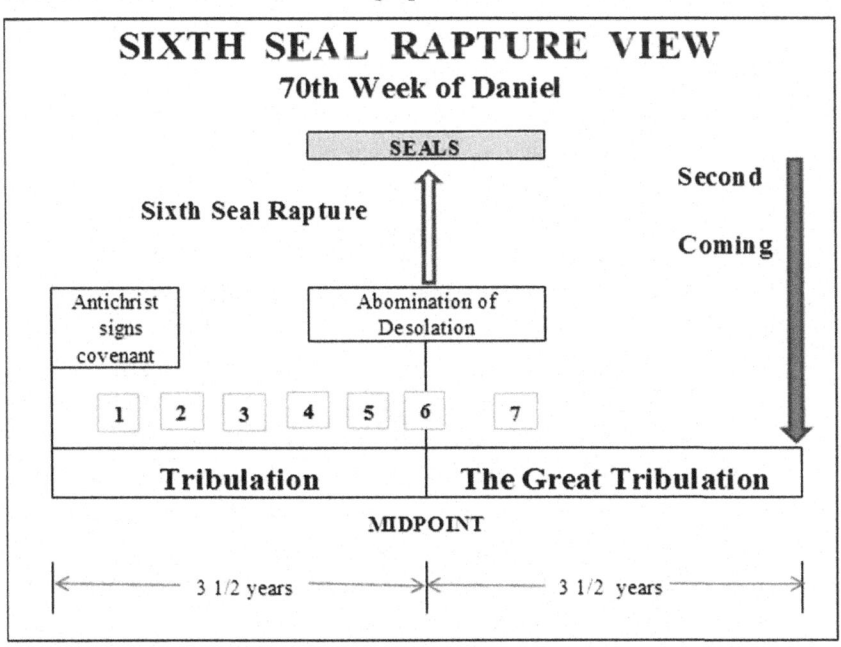

Revelation

Intra-Seal View

The Intra-Seal view also follows the view that the church is not appointed to the Sixth Seal. This view believes that the church will be raptured after the start of the Sixth Seal but before the Seventh Seal is opened. Those who hold to this view also believe that the true and faithful church will not experience any of the plagues of the Sixth Seal but will be raptured before the plagues occur. Therefore, this view holds to the truth that the church will not experience the wrath of God. The Bible scholars who favor the Intra-Seal view believe that after the opening of the Sixth Seal in Revelation 6:12, there will be a pause before the final plagues of the Sixth Seal commence. During the pause there would be one final call to the world to repent and turn to Jesus as their Savior and Lord. Some of the key points of the Intra-Seal view are:

- Once the faithful church has been removed, God will turn His purpose and prophetic focus back on the salvation of Israel and the restoration of the kingdom to the Jews as we will see in Revelation 7 when the 144,000 Israelites are sealed. Ezekiel 9:1-11 reveals the Glory of the Lord departing. This is symbolic of the harpazo. Then occurs the marking of His people (which is symbolic of the 144,000 Israelites being sealed) before judgment commences and then the wrath of God is poured out. This would coincide with the Mid-Tribulation view providing these events occur at the middle of the seventieth week of Daniel.

- The Intra-Seal view maintains that the antichrist will be revealed to the faithful church when his image is set up in the Temple (II Thessalonians 2:1-4) and establishes the mark that all men must have in order to buy and sell (Revelation 13:11-18). The faithful church will have the wisdom to identify the antichrist once the mark of the beast has been established. The church will experience the beginning of the Great Tribulation, except for the true and faithful believers as they will be protected from its horrors. The plagues of the Sixth Seal will begin after the harpazo which signifies the start of the wrath (*orge*) of God (Matthew 24:29-31; Revelation 6:12-17; I Thessalonians 1:10; I Thessalonians 5:9). At this time the church will be complete in heaven and in their glorified bodies. The Day of the Lord commences immediately after the harpazo (Isaiah 13:6-13; Isaiah 24:1-20; Joel 2:31), as the sun shall be turned to darkness and the moon into blood before the great and terrible day of the Lord comes.

Opening of the Seals

- An example of the Intra-Seal view would be in the time of Noah. As Noah was building the ark and witnessing to the world concerning the coming deluge, he was ridiculed. When the ark was completed, Noah and his family entered the ark with the animals and the Lord closed the door. Once the door was closed, Noah and his family were protected from the coming judgment. However, the rest of the world was now locked out. The closing of the door represents in type the close of the church age. At this point the restrainer is no longer restraining evil in the world. This allows for the wrath of God to begin. The rain and water are typologically analogous to the first six Seals. After the animals entered the ark there was a pause before the deluge occurred (Genesis 7:9-10). After Noah and his family were safe inside, the rain came. The water reaching the flood level, causing the ark to ascend above the deluge, corresponds to the harpazo taking place before the judgments commence, at which point the lost will understand. But it will be too late for them.
- Another example of the Intra-Seal view is in Daniel 3, where Shadrach, Meshach and Abed-Nego refused to bow down to the golden image that King Nebuchadnezzar had set up. Everyone in the king's province was ordered to bow and to worship the golden image. Shadrach, Meshach and Abed-Nego gave testimony before the king that the God of Israel was able to rescue them before being cast into the furnace of affliction, but that He may not do so (Daniel 3:16-18). The king commanded these three men to be cast alive into the fiery furnace. After they were cast into the furnace they were seen walking in the furnace along with a fourth person who appeared to be a Son of God. The God of Israel allowed the three Hebrew men to be cast into the furnace of affliction, but He was right there beside them and protecting them. The scholars that follow the Intra-Seal view hold to the fact that the children of Israel being cast into the fiery furnace is a type of the Great Tribulation period when the antichrist sets up his image and his mark, and demands everyone in the world to worship the image and to take the mark of the beast. This is a shadow of the rescue of God's people that will not take place until the image of the beast has been set up. Again, this is fully consistent with what Jesus stated in the Olivet Discourse in Matthew 24:15 and by Paul in II Thessalonians 2.
- And then finally, the ancient Jewish historian Flavius Josephus describes the events leading up to the destruction of the Temple in AD 70. He writes that the events were indeed astounding and included signs in the sky where visions of invading armies were seen in the

Revelation

clouds. Josephus also reports the instance of a red heifer giving birth to a lamb with obvious Messianic connotations comparing Christ to the red heifer ordinance in Numbers 19. He gives further account of a comet in the form of a sword staying in place over Jerusalem for a whole year before the Temple was destroyed, and people described as "madmen" running around Jerusalem proclaiming doom. Interesting, only two years prior there had been an economic boom that brought a prosperity that was unprecedented under Roman domination.

The writing of Josephus is very interesting. It shows that what happened in the past may indeed happen once again in the future. After the sign in the heavens occurs at the start of the Sixth Seal, there is a pause before the final plagues begin and the wrath of the Lamb is introduced. During the pause there will be one final call to the lost not to receive the mark of the beast. Right before the terrible judgments of the Sixth Seal, the harpazo occurs. The world quickly sees the events that are occurring once the church is taken up as the people of the world try to hide themselves from the wrath of the Lamb that has begun. Jacob Prasch's book, *Harpazo: The Intra-Seal Rapture of the Church*, is a very good read as Mr. Prasch explains in great detail the Intra-Seal view of the harpazo of the church. Below is the graph of the Intra-Seal Rapture view.

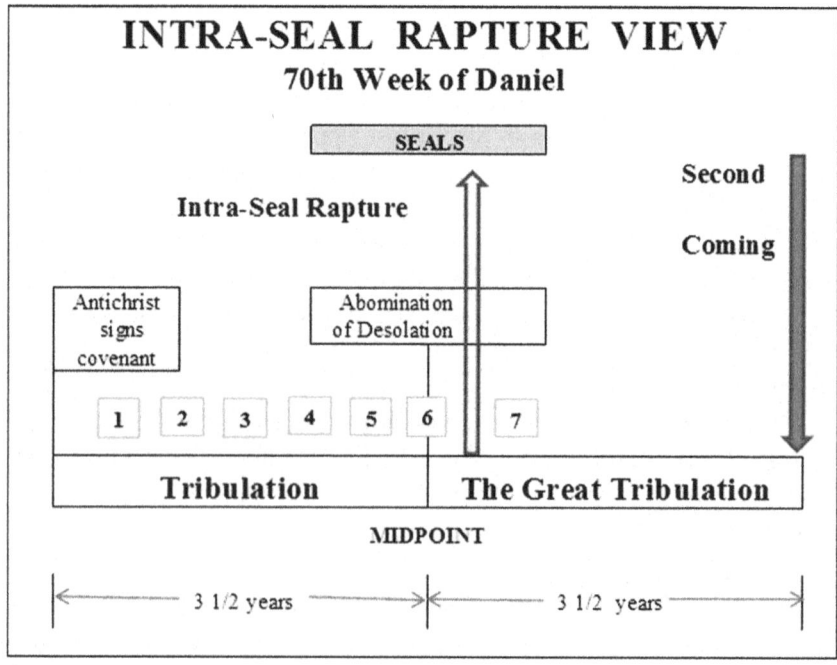

Opening of the Seals

Pre-Wrath View

There is another view of the harpazo recognizing that the church will not experience God's wrath. However, according to this view the wrath (*orge*) of God does not start until the opening of the Seventh Seal. This is called the Pre-Wrath view. Once the Seventh Seal is opened, the harpazo occurs, and immediately the Day of the Lord begins. Those who follow the Pre-Wrath view believe that the Sixth Seal represents only cosmic disturbances and not the commencement of the wrath of God. This view also holds to the fact that the events of the Fifth Seal commence once the antichrist sets up his image in the rebuilt Jewish Temple declaring that he is God and demanding to be worshipped as God. Those scholars who follow this view adhere to the fact that the church will experience the Great Tribulation, except for the true and faithful church as the true and faithful believers will be protected from the horrors of the Great Tribulation. The scholars believe the Great Tribulation does not last three-and-a-half years as the Lord will shorten the days (Matthew 24:22). At the end of the Great Tribulation, Jesus returns for His church, and then begins the Day of the Lord with the plagues of the Seventh Seal which consists of the Seven Trumpets and Seven Bowls. Marvin Rosenthal's book, *The Pre-Wrath Rapture of the Church*, is a good read as Mr. Rosenthal explains in great detail the Pre-Wrath view of the harpazo of the church. Below is the graph of the Pre-Wrath view.

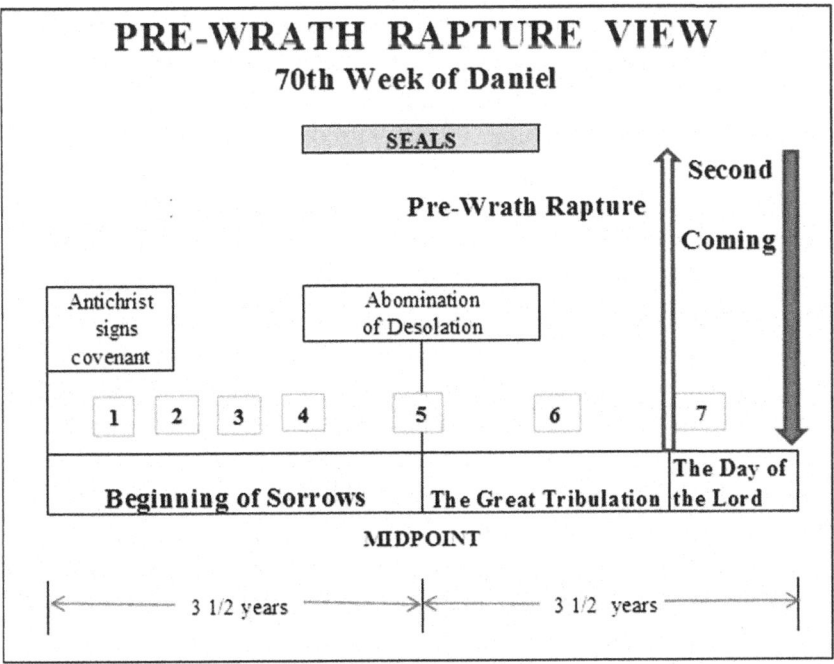

Revelation

In summary, the views of the Sixth Seal rapture, the Intra-Seal rapture, and Pre-Wrath rapture of the church hold to the following: They all hold to the teaching that the church is not destined to see the wrath (*orge*) of God. However, they do differ on when the *orge* of God begins.

- **Sixth Seal view** - Those scholars who follow the Sixth Seal view believe the sign in heaven is Jesus Christ and that He is visible to the entire world. At this point the church is called home, and then come the terrible plagues of the Sixth Seal.
- **Intra-Seal view** - Those scholars who follow the Intra-Seal view believe that there is a sign in heaven that is visible to the world, but there is a pause before the harpazo as there was a pause in AD 70 before Jerusalem fell. Before the pause is over, the harpazo occurs and then come the terrible plagues of the Sixth Seal.
- **Pre-Wrath view** - Those scholars who follow the Pre-Wrath view believe that the Sixth Seal represents only cosmic disturbances and that the wrath of God is unleashed with the Seventh Seal. When the Seventh Seal is opened the harpazo takes place and then terrible Trumpet judgments are unleashed upon the world.

Mid-Tribulation View

The Mid-Tribulation view is recent in origin and is believed to have started in 1940. A major advocate of the Mid-Tribulation theory was Norman B. Harrison. He published a book in 1941 titled, *The End: Rethinking the Revelation*. The Mid-Tribulation view was introduced at the same time when Nazi Germany was conquering Western and Eastern Europe.

When Adolf Hitler came to power some Bible scholars believed he was the rider on the white horse when the First Seal was opened. Adolf Hitler was a great orator and had tremendous power of persuasion. When World War II was underway and when Nazi Germany seemed unstoppable, some scholars related the war in Europe to Seals Two, Three, and Four being opened. Then when the concentration camps were set up, they believed that Seal Five was opened. The scholars are now waiting for the events of the Sixth Seal to begin. As you can see, the Mid-Tribulation view was gaining popularity at that time. However, after the fall of Nazi Germany and Adolf Hitler, it was quickly realized that World War II was not related to the opening of the book in heaven.

Adolf Hitler was not the antichrist, but he was most assuredly a type and shadow of the beast that is to come. He was a great orator and possessed power to persuade men with his words. The antichrist will possess the same qualities. He will be a man of great persuasion. He will command armies that will seem to be unstoppable as Nazi Germany appeared to be unstoppable under the leadership of Adolf Hitler. As Germany followed Adolf Hitler to the bitter end hoping for a victory, even so will the followers of the antichrist follow after the beast to the bitter end. The end will take place when the Lord Jesus returns again to the earth in Revelation 19 and defeats the armies of antichrist and sentences the antichrist and the false prophet to the lake of fire that is reserved for Satan and his angels. Below is the graph of the Mid-Tribulation view.

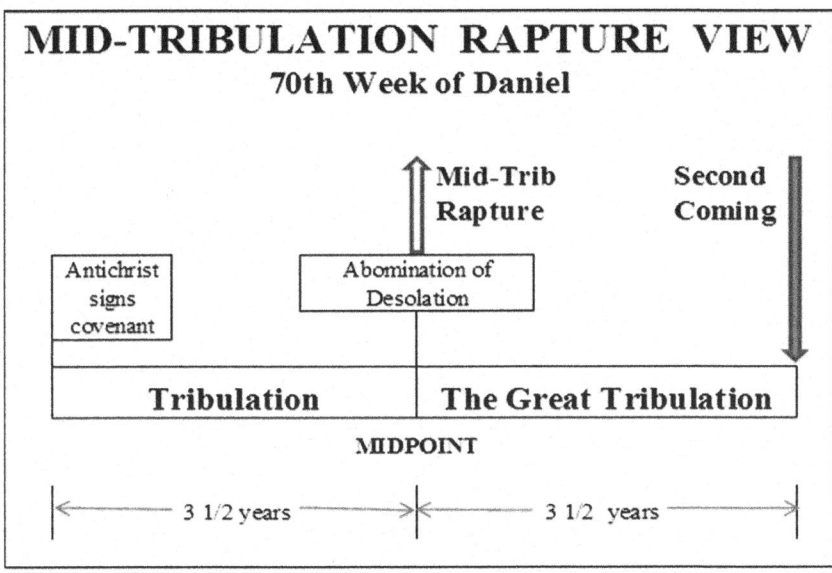

Chapter 7

Multitude of Witnesses

Revelation 7:1-8
Sealing of the 144,000

And after these things I saw four angels standing on the four corners of the earth, holding the four winds of the earth, that the wind should not blow on the earth, nor on the sea, nor on any tree. And I saw another angel ascending from the east, having the seal of the living God: and he cried with a loud voice to the four angels, to whom it was given to hurt the earth and the sea, Saying, Hurt not the earth, neither the sea, nor the trees, till we have sealed the servants of our God in their foreheads. And I heard the number of them which were sealed: and there were sealed an hundred and forty and four thousand of all the tribes of the children of Israel. Of the tribe of Juda were sealed twelve thousand. Of the tribe of Reuben were sealed twelve thousand. Of the tribe of Gad were sealed twelve thousand. Of the tribe of Asher were sealed twelve thousand. Of the tribe of Naphtali were sealed twelve thousand. Of the tribe of Manasseh were sealed twelve thousand. Of the tribe of Simeon were sealed twelve thousand. Of the tribe of Levi were sealed twelve thousand. Of the tribe of Issachar were sealed twelve thousand. Of the tribe of Zebulun were sealed twelve thousand. Of the tribe of Joseph were sealed twelve thousand. Of the tribe of Benjamin were sealed twelve thousand.

ALL JUDGMENT IS suspended until the twelve tribes of Israel are sealed and protected. The judgment resumes in Revelation 8 during the Trumpet judgments. The Lord is very detailed to reveal that those who are sealed and protected are indeed Jews. The sealing of the 144,000

Revelation

takes place after the first Six Seals have been opened. The Greek word *meta* is again used to signify that the sealing of the 144,000 Israelites takes place after the first Six Seals have been opened.

The tribes of Dan and Ephraim are not mentioned. This could be because Dan and Ephraim led the nation into Calf-Worship. Calf-Worship was set up in two cities, Bethel and Dan, during the reign of King Jeroboam when the northern tribes of Israel rebelled against King Rehoboam of Judah. Dan was the first tribe to go into idolatry as recorded in Judges 17 and 18. Ephraim followed later into Calf-Worship when the tribes from the north separated to establish their own kingdom. In Ezekiel 48:30-34 the gates of the Messianic city in the kingdom age will have the names of the original sons of Jacob as indicated in Genesis 35:22-26. The tribes of Dan and Ephraim will be restored during the reign of Jesus Christ upon the earth.

There are different opinions among the scholars as to what is being targeted in Revelation 7:1-3. One interpretation is symbolic: The earth represents Israel, the sea represents the Gentiles, and the trees represent those in authority as these symbols are defined in Judges 9. The four corners of the earth would seem to indicate that the world is being targeted, including the kingdom of the antichrist.

A second interpretation is literal: the land, the seas and trees are targeted. With targeting the land, the seas, and the trees, indeed the whole earth is impacted. It is believed that the antichrist has defiled the Temple by placing his image in the most Holy Place within the Temple at this time.

There is a third interpretation that suggests that both views are correct. Both the governments of the earth and the earth itself are targeted. This interpretation is similar to the letters to the seven churches as those were literal churches that existed and symbolic of the types of churches that exist today and throughout church history. This type of pattern is consistent with the style of the Book of Revelation as more than one view is correct. Winds are a symbol for judgment that is to begin. The four winds indicate that the judgment is widespread. The world and the leaders of the world are being targeted because of their rebellion against Almighty God, the Creator of all things, and for worshipping the antichrist and confessing that he is God.

Before judgment commences, the Lord will mark and protect those Jews who have not followed the antichrist when he revealed his true nature by declaring that he is God and demanding to be worshipped as God. The event of marking and sealing the righteous before judgment begins did occur elsewhere in the Scriptures. A marking of the people is mentioned in the Book of Ezekiel before the Lord brought judgment against Judah:

⁹ He cried also in mine ears with a loud voice, saying, Cause them that have charge over the city to draw near, even every man with his destroying weapon in his hand. ² And, behold, six men came from the way of the higher gate, which lieth toward the north, and every man a slaughter weapon in his hand; and one man among them was clothed with linen, with a writer's inkhorn by his side: and they went in, and stood beside the brasen altar. ³ And the glory of the God of Israel was gone up from the cherub, whereupon he was, to the threshold of the house. And he called to the man clothed with linen, which had the writer's inkhorn by his side; ⁴ And the LORD said unto him, Go through the midst of the city, through the midst of Jerusalem, and set a mark upon the foreheads of the men that sigh and that cry for all the abominations that be done in the midst thereof. ⁵ And to the others he said in mine hearing, Go ye after him through the city, and smite: let not your eye spare, neither have ye pity: ⁶ Slay utterly old and young, both maids, and little children, and women: but come not near any man upon whom is the mark; and begin at my sanctuary. Then they began at the ancient men which were before the house. ⁷ And he said unto them, Defile the house, and fill the courts with the slain: go ye forth. And they went forth, and slew in the city. ⁸ And it came to pass, while they were slaying them, and I was left, that I fell upon my face, and cried, and said, Ah Lord GOD! wilt thou destroy all the residue of Israel in thy pouring out of thy fury upon Jerusalem? ⁹ Then said he unto me, The iniquity of the house of Israel and Judah is exceeding great, and the land is full of blood, and the city full of perverseness: for they say, The LORD hath forsaken the earth, and the LORD seeth not. ¹⁰ And as for me also, mine eye shall not spare, neither will I have pity, but I will recompense their way upon their head. ¹¹ And, behold, the man clothed with linen, which had the inkhorn by his side, reported the matter, saying, I have done as thou hast commanded me. (Ezekiel 9:1-11)

Notice in Ezekiel that the Glory of the Lord is departing. This is symbolic of the harpazo and then the marking of His people (which is symbolic of the 144,000 Israelites being sealed) before judgment commences, and the wrath of God is poured out in chapter 8. This passage in Ezekiel does support the following views of the harpazo of the church:

- The Sixth Seal View
- The Intra-Seal View

The sealing and protecting of the 144,000 is significant. In the Old Testament, the saints were marked and protected in Exodus 12:22-23. They were also marked and protected in Ezekiel 9:1-4. The Lord marked His people for protection before His judgment was to come. In the New Testament a different approach was used. The Christian was identified

Revelation

because of the Holy Spirit who indwelt the believer. The New Testament saint was one with the Father and with the Son because of the indwelling Holy Spirit. Now in Revelation 7 the saints are once again being marked for protection. The marking of the 144,000 signifies two things:

- The harpazo has occurred and the church age is over;
- The Holy Spirit's function as the restrainer of evil will be removed from the earth. However, He will continue to be with the saints.

In the Old Testament the Spirit of God was upon the earth and in the lives of men such as Moses, Samuel and David. The Holy Spirit will be with the saints on the earth after the harpazo but He will no longer be restraining evil once the antichrist comes to power. The saints in the Great Tribulation will be indwelt by the Holy Spirit because of the testimony that will be presented before the evil rulers of the world as Mark writes:

9 But take heed to yourselves: for they shall deliver you up to councils; and in the synagogues ye shall be beaten: and ye shall be brought before rulers and kings for my sake, for a testimony against them. 10 And the gospel must first be published among all nations. 11 But when they shall lead you, and deliver you up, take no thought beforehand what ye shall speak, neither do ye premeditate: but whatsoever shall be given you in that hour, that speak ye: for it is not ye that speak, but the Holy Ghost. 12 Now the brother shall betray the brother to death, and the father the son; and children shall rise up against their parents, and shall cause them to be put to death. 13 And ye shall be hated of all men for my name's sake: but he that shall endure unto the end, the same shall be saved. (Mark 13:9-13)

Revelation 7:9-17
Those Who Came Out of Great Tribulation

After this I beheld, and, lo, a great multitude, which no man could number, of all nations, and kindreds, and people, and tongues, stood before the throne, and before the Lamb, clothed with white robes, and palms in their hands; And cried with a loud voice, saying, Salvation to our God which sitteth upon the throne, and unto the Lamb. And all the angels stood round about the throne, and about the elders and the four beasts, and fell before the throne on their faces, and worshipped God, Saying, Amen: Blessing, and glory, and wisdom, and thanksgiving, and honour, and power, and might, be unto our God for ever and ever. Amen. And one of the elders answered, saying unto me, What are these which are arrayed in white robes? And whence came they? And I said unto him, Sir, thou knowest. And he said to me, These are they which came out of great tribulation, and have washed their robes, and made them white in the blood of the Lamb. Therefore are they before the throne of God, and serve him day and night in his temple: and he that sitteth on the throne shall dwell among them. They shall hunger no more, neither thirst any more; neither shall the sun light on them, nor any heat. For the Lamb which is in the midst of the throne shall feed them, and shall lead them unto living fountains of waters: and God shall wipe away all tears from their eyes.

A great multitude from many nations will be saved during the seventieth week of Daniel. There are two views concerning the identity of this great multitude. Some Bible scholars believe that this is the church of Jesus Christ and the harpazo has not yet occurred. Others believe that this is not the church of Jesus Christ because the church was raptured earlier.

Those scholars who hold the view that this multitude is not the church believe that they represent the saints who were seen under the altar when the Fifth Seal was opened. The saints under the altar were killed for their faith. Their number becomes complete during the Great Tribulation period which starts when the antichrist sets his image up in the most Holy Place in the Temple. This multitude endured the plagues that were upon the earth during the Great Tribulation period. The plagues that are described here appear to be part of the Seven Bowl or Vial judgments which take place during the wrath (*thumos*) of God, unto which the church is not appointed to (Revelation 7:16). The wrath (*thumos*) of God takes place after the wrath (*orge*) of God has started. The church is not appointed to experience the wrath (*orge*) of God either. The apostle John does not recognize this great multitude, which gives evidence that this is not the church (Revelation 7:13-14). The church was seen in heaven in Revelation 5 according to the Received Text. This multitude is the same group that appears in heaven in Revelation 20:4. The only explanation for this great multitude to be the body of believers who came to believe in the Lord Jesus once the church is gone is that the Lord must have sent one last revival upon the earth during the darkest days of the planet. As Dr. Orr indicated in his books on revival, revival is always the work of the Lord and not man, where God in His mercy pours out His Spirit upon the earth.

The Bible scholars who believe that this multitude represents the church are those who hold to one of the following views of the harpazo:

- The Mid-Tribulation view;
- The Sixth Seal view;
- The Intra-Seal view;
- The Pre-Wrath view;

Revelation

- The Post-Tribulation view but earlier;
- The Post-Tribulation view.

All six views recognize that the antichrist has already set up his image in the Jewish Temple and demands to be worshipped as God. They all hold the view that this multitude represents the church that was seen under the altar when the Fifth Seal was opened. The scholars who support these views believe that this multitude must be the church, as how could a great multitude of people from the backslidden churches of Pergamos, Thyatira, Sardis and Laodicea come to faith in Jesus Christ when they have no discernment and cannot recognize truth from error? If the members from these churches cannot recognize truth from error before the antichrist appears, how will they recognize the deception of the antichrist and his false prophet? The scholars who support these views tend to agree that the Lord will not send a revival during this time as the Holy Spirit is no longer restraining the evil that has come upon the earth. They use II Thessalonians 2 as their proof text. Most of the scholars who support one of these views will lean to the Alexandrian manuscript evidence that the church is not yet complete in heaven in Revelation 5.

The great multitude of believers in chapter 7 will serve God day and night in His Temple. This appears to be a different role than the Lamb's Bride, which also gives credence that this multitude is not the church. They endured the plagues of famine and of the sun that occurred during the Vial or Bowl judgments when the wrath (*thumos*) of God was poured out upon the kingdom of antichrist. The Lamb of God shall feed them and lead them and they will follow Him. This multitude may not include the 144,000 Israelites who were sealed from the tribes of Israel. They are redeemed from the earth and follow the Lamb wherever He goes as noted in Revelation 14:

¹And I looked, and, lo, a Lamb stood on the mount Sion, and with him an hundred forty and four thousand, having his Father's name written in their foreheads. ² And I heard a voice from heaven, as the voice of many waters, and as the voice of a great thunder: and I heard the voice of harpers harping with their harps: ³ And they sung as it were a new song before the throne, and before the four beasts, and the elders: and no man could learn that song but the hundred and forty and four thousand, which were redeemed from the earth. ⁴ These are they which were not defiled with women; for they are virgins. These are they which follow the Lamb whithersoever he goeth. These were redeemed from among men, being the firstfruits unto God and to the Lamb. ⁵ And in their mouth was found no guile: for they are without fault before the throne of God. (Revelation 14:1-5)

Chapter 8

Trumpet Judgments - Part One

Revelation 8:1-7
The Seventh Seal and the First Trumpet Judgment

And when he had opened the seventh seal, there was silence in heaven about the space of half an hour. And I saw the seven angels which stood before God; and to them were given seven trumpets. And another angel came and stood at the altar, having a golden censer; and there was given unto him much incense, that he should offer it with the prayers of all saints upon the golden altar which was before the throne. And the smoke of the incense, which came with the prayers of the saints, ascended up before God out of the angel's hand. And the angel took the censer, and filled it with fire of the altar, and cast it into the earth: and there were voices, and thunderings, and lightnings, and an earthquake. And the seven angels which had the seven trumpets prepared themselves to sound. The first angel sounded, and there followed hail and fire mingled with blood, and they were cast upon the earth: and the third part of trees was burnt up, and all green grass was burnt up.

THE SEVENTH SEAL is not a judgment; it is a new beginning. The book is now opened and the seals have been removed. Now seven messengers come forth, each with a trumpet to sound further judgments. It was the Lord Jesus who opened the book. Now it is the Holy Spirit who appears in the form of the seven messengers to blow the Seven Trumpets.

There is silence in heaven for the space of half an hour once the Seventh Seal is opened. Imagine going to a sporting event where it is very loud and then silence.

Revelation

It is in Revelation 8:1 that those who follow the Pre-Wrath view of the harpazo hold to the belief that this is when the Lord Jesus appears to remove the true and faithful church to heaven. They believe that the Trumpet judgments that signify the wrath (*orge*) of God are to commence and that the Sixth Seal was just a cosmic disturbance. The key point is that the Pre-Wrath view also agrees that the church will not experience the wrath (*orge*) of God as Paul revealed in his epistle to the Thessalonians.

Therefore, any view of the harpazo that believes the true and faithful church is upon the earth once the wrath of God has started is a direct contradiction of Scripture. Paul wrote that the church will not experience the wrath (*orge*) of God. This is very plain and to the point. The view that the harpazo occurs at the end of the seventieth week of Daniel, which is a view defined as Post-Tribulation, has a problem. This view has no strong and convincing scriptural support to show that the harpazo occurs at the end of the seventieth week of Daniel. It is possible to take a few verses from Matthew 24 out of context and ignore the rest of the Scriptures that speak of the End Times in order to come up with the view that Jesus returns at the end of the seventieth week of Daniel. However, taking verses out of context and ignoring the rest of the Scriptures is never a good idea. Below is the graph of the Post-Tribulation view.

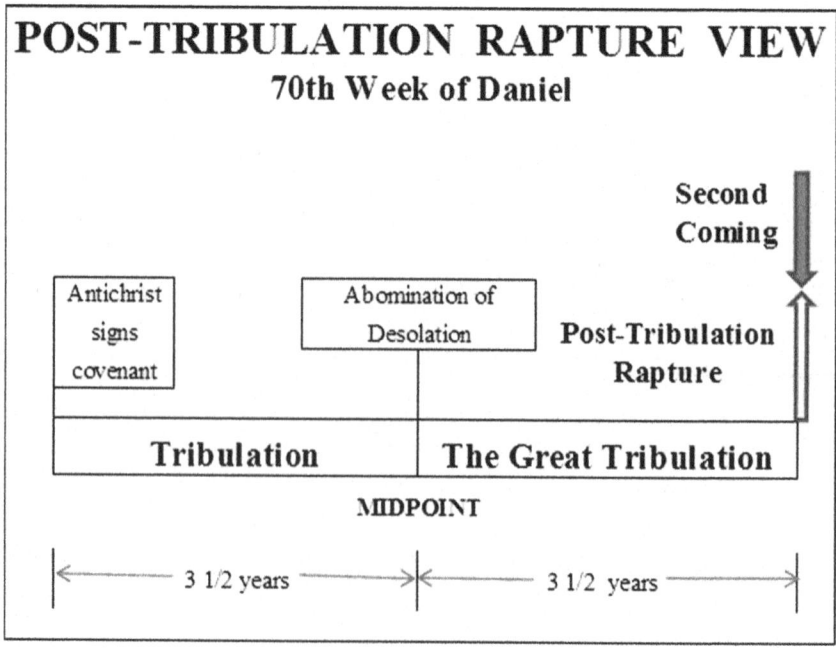

There is another view of the Post-Tribulation which places the harpazo before the Bowl or Vial judgments in Revelation 15. This is known as the Post-Tribulation view, but earlier. It is true that the wrath of God concludes with the Bowl or Vial judgments, but the Greek wording is different. The Bowl or Vial judgments unleash the wrath (*thumos*) of God. *Thumos* is defined as the fiery indignation of the Lord. However, the apostle Paul used the Greek word *orge* and not the Greek word *thumos* when he wrote about the wrath of God. Paul wrote that the church will not experience *orge*. If the apostle Paul had used the Greek word *thumos*, then one could conclude that the church would experience the terrible Trumpet judgments that begin in Revelation 8. Paul used the Greek word *orge*, and therefore we can conclude that the church will not experience the events of the Sixth Seal recorded in chapter 6 and any of the events recorded starting in chapter 8 as some scholars believe.

In Revelation 8:3, there is another messenger standing at the altar and he has in his hand a golden censor which is used for intercession and then judgment. The golden altar is the altar of incense. The prayers that are offered are from all the saints. Before the Temple was destroyed in AD 70, every morning and evening the priests on the earth would use a golden censor to put incense on the altar of incense in front of the second veil of the Tabernacle or Temple. Once a year the High Priest would enter the Most Holy Place with the incense and the golden censor. The incense would fill the Most Holy Place so that the High Priest would not be stricken down before the Lord when he entered the Most Holy Place (Leviticus 16:13). The censor in heaven which has held the incense for the worship of God is now filled with fire from the altar, and this fire is cast upon the earth. The judgment fire comes from the altar where the lamb was slain and body consumed. Now the wrath of God is poured out upon the earth based upon the suffering of the Lord Jesus on Calvary. The crime of condemning and putting to death the Messiah needs to be punished. It is true that Jesus suffered and died for the sins of the world, but the actual crime of rejecting and putting to death the Messiah and now choosing a false Messiah, a man who declares to everyone that he is God, these acts need to be punished. It is only the Lord Jesus who deserves to be worshipped as God as He paid the price to redeem man back to God, but now another steps in to receive that praise and worship. Now the wrath of God is to be poured out.

Men thought that the Sixth Seal, which had them hiding in fear, was terrifying, but the worst is yet to come. These judgments in chapter 8 impact a third of the earth. There is some mercy as two-thirds of the earth's population has not experienced this pain directly.

It is believed that the Trumpet and Vial judgments take place in the last three-and-a-half years of the seventieth week of Daniel. They will appear as birth pangs, which occur more frequently and in greater intensity when the baby is to be delivered. These plagues will grow in intensity in a shorter time frame as the Lord Jesus is about to be revealed when He comes in glory. The prophet Zephaniah declares the great day of the Lord that is to come:

> *14 The great day of the LORD is near, it is near, and hasteth greatly, even the voice of the day of the LORD: the mighty man shall cry there bitterly. 15 That day is a day of wrath, a day of trouble and distress, a day of wasteness and desolation, a day of darkness and gloominess, a day of clouds and thick darkness, 16 A day of the trumpet and alarm against the fenced cities, and against the high towers. 17 And I will bring distress upon men, that they shall walk like blind men, because they have sinned against the LORD: and their blood shall be poured out as dust, and their flesh as the dung. 18 Neither their silver nor their gold shall be able to deliver them in the day of the LORD's wrath; but the whole land shall be devoured by the fire of his jealousy: for he shall make even a speedy riddance of all them that dwell in the land.* (Zephaniah 1:14-18)

This will truly be a time of trouble and distress as men are now choosing the antichrist over Jesus Christ. The wealth of the world cannot deliver anyone from the wrath of God.

As the First Trumpet sounds, hail and fire impact one third of the earth. God has used hail as a means of judgment in the past:

> *23 And Moses stretched forth his rod toward heaven: and the LORD sent thunder and hail, and the fire ran along upon the ground; and the LORD rained hail upon the land of Egypt. 24 So there was hail, and fire mingled with the hail, very grievous, such as there was none like it in all the land of Egypt since it became a nation. 25 And the hail smote throughout all the land of Egypt all that was in the field, both man and beast; and the hail smote every herb of the field, and brake every tree of the field.* (Exodus 9:23-25)

> *2 Behold, the Lord hath a mighty and strong one, which as a tempest of hail and a destroying storm, as a flood of mighty waters overflowing, shall cast down to the earth with the hand.* (Isaiah 28:2)

> *22 Hast thou entered into the treasures of the snow? or hast thou seen the treasures of the hail, 23 Which I have reserved against the time of trouble, against the day of battle and war?* (Job 38:22-23)

The world has experienced hurricanes that have resulted in much destruction, but now a fiery hailstorm does so much damage that a third of the planet is directly impacted.

The Day of the Lord

Because of Paul's epistle to the Thessalonians, we know that the Day of the Lord immediately follows the harpazo of the church. We know that the sun will become dark and the moon will turn to blood before the Day of the Lord comes as prophesied in Joel 2. We know that the prophet Elijah will be one of the two witnesses. He will come before the Day of the Lord and may appear before the harpazo of the church according to Malachi 4. We know that the Day of the Lord will be complete when Jesus returns to the earth to set up His kingdom and to sit on the throne of King David. We know from Paul's letter to the Thessalonians that the great apostasy and the revealing of the antichrist must occur before the Day of the Lord comes. We know that the Day of the Lord precedes the wrath (*orge*) of God, but we do not know the length of time between the Day of the Lord and *orge*.

Orge and *Thumos*

There are two different Greek words for wrath used in the Book of Revelation. It is important to understand the differences between the two. *Orge* is defined as "punishment," "anger," "indignation," and "vengeance." The Greek word *thumos* is more intense than *orge*, and is defined as "fierceness," "indignation" and "wrath."

Orge begins at the Sixth Seal (the Pre-Wrath view is that it commences after the Seventh Seal is opened) and concludes when the Lord Jesus returns to the earth (Second Coming). Paul revealed in his letter to the Thessalonians that the church is not appointed to wrath, and he used the Greek word *orge*. Therefore Paul is writing, under the inspiration of the Holy Spirit, that the church will not experience the wrath of God when it commences with the opening of the Sixth Seal or with the events that come forth after the opening of the Sixth Seal.

Thumos is used to describe the wrath of the Lord in the Bowl or Vial judgments, for the destruction of Babylon and the kingdom of antichrist. Just as for a woman who is about to give birth, the labor pains are the most intense, even so are the Bowl or Vial judgments more intense than the Trumpet judgments as Jesus is about to return to the earth. *Thumos* is shorter in duration than *orge* and concludes at the Battle of Armageddon.

Revelation 8:8-9
The Second Trumpet Judgment

And the second angel sounded, and as it were a great mountain burning with fire was cast into the sea: and the third part of the sea became blood; And the third part of the creatures which were in the sea, and had life, died; and the third part of the ships were destroyed.

The first plague of Egypt in Exodus 7:14-21 turned the water of the Nile into blood. Here we see a great mountain that is cast into the sea causing a third of it to become blood. Bible scholars agree that a mountain is symbolic of a nation in the Scriptures. This judgment could refer to a Gentile nation being destroyed which results in great distress among the nations:

^{25} And there shall be signs in the sun, and in the moon, and in the stars; and upon the earth distress of nations, with perplexity; the sea and the waves roaring; ^{26} Men's hearts failing them for fear, and for looking after those things which are coming on the earth: for the powers of heaven shall be shaken. (Luke 21:25-26)

What John could have seen is a large asteroid striking the earth, resulting in much damage. This may refer to Rome and the Vatican being destroyed as there is an unfulfilled prophecy in the Book of Jeremiah concerning Babylon:

^{25} Behold, I am against thee, O destroying mountain, saith the LORD, which destroyest all the earth: and I will stretch out mine hand upon thee, and roll thee down from the rocks, and will make thee a burnt mountain. ^{26} And they shall not take of thee a stone for a corner, nor a stone for foundations; but thou shalt be desolate for ever, saith the LORD. (Jeremiah 51:25-26)

Jeremiah 51:25-26 refers to Babylon as a burnt mountain. Could this refer to Religious Babylon? Could this judgment include the religious institutions that assisted the beast to get into power? Could this prophecy also include the fulfillment of the judgment against the church of Thyatira and those churches that fit the description of the church of Thyatira? The Lord Jesus did pronounce a judgment against the church of Thyatira that will most likely be fulfilled after the mid-point of the seventieth week of Daniel:

^{18} And unto the angel of the church in Thyatira write; These things saith the Son of God, who hath his eyes like unto a flame of fire, and his feet are like fine brass; ^{19} I know thy works, and charity, and service, and faith, and thy patience, and thy works; and the last to be more than the first. ^{20} Notwithstanding I have a few

things against thee, because thou sufferest that woman Jezebel, which calleth herself a prophetess, to teach and to seduce my servants to commit fornication, and to eat things sacrificed unto idols. ²¹ And I gave her space to repent of her fornication; and she repented not. ²² Behold, I will cast her into a bed, and them that commit adultery with her into great tribulation, except they repent of their deeds. ²³ And I will kill her children with death; and all the churches shall know that I am he which searcheth the reins and hearts: and I will give unto every one of you according to your works. (Revelation 2:18-23)

However, this judgment appears to be larger than the destruction of Rome as even the marine life in the sea is impacted. This plague would greatly reduce the food supply that has already been depleted due to the wars of the antichrist.

It is thought by some scholars that the pope will assist the antichrist in his rise to power. This is covered in more detail in chapter 17. Once the antichrist has established his power and has apparently recovered from a deadly wound, he no longer needs the pope. The antichrist will also have no need for any church organization that may be on the earth at this time. The pope and the church organization are now standing in the way of the antichrist and his ambition to be worshiped as God. This is something that even the Roman Catholic Church will quickly oppose. The antichrist will move quickly against the Roman Catholic Church once he sets himself up as God and demands to be worshipped as God.

Revelation 8:10-11
The Third Trumpet Judgment

And the third angel sounded, and there fell a great star from heaven, burning as it were a lamp, and it fell upon the third part of the rivers, and upon the fountains of waters; And the name of the star is called Wormwood: and the third part of the waters became wormwood; and many men died of the waters, because they were made bitter.

A star is seen falling from heaven, a big star, burning as a lamp. Could this be a comet? This star is called wormwood and it pollutes the rivers and fountains of water. The drinking water is polluted with this plague. There is a prophecy in Jeremiah 9:15 and Jeremiah 23:15 that the Lord will give to the profane, wormwood to drink in judgment. Just as Babylon has polluted the world by its wickedness and rebellion, the Lord in judgment provides bitter water for those following the antichrist as the antichrist follows after the wicked practices of Babylon. First the marine life, and now the drinking water, is impacted. The plagues will soon get worse as the sun will now be impacted with the Fourth Trumpet judgment.

Revelation 8:12-13
The Fourth Trumpet Judgment

And the fourth angel sounded, and the third part of the sun was smitten, and the third part of the moon, and the third part of the stars; so as the third part of them was darkened, and the day shone not for a third part of it, and the night likewise. And I beheld, and heard an angel flying through the midst of heaven, saying with a loud voice, Woe, woe, woe, to the inhabiters of the earth by reason of the other voices of the trumpet of the three angels, which are yet to sound.

The Fourth Trumpet impacts the earth as the sun, moon, and stars are targeted. The sun, moon, and stars are also symbols of human government. There will be utter chaos upon the earth with this plague as the world leaders have no answers, but the worst is yet to come as the birth pangs become stronger.

The Fourth Trumpet most likely refers literally to the sun, moon, and stars, because a third part of the day will be dark as twilight before and after the sun rises and sets. This plague will affect plant life, as the plants need the sun to live and grow. As with the First Trumpet judgment, this judgment is similar to one of the plagues in Egypt when God sent a thick darkness upon the land.

[21] And the LORD said unto Moses, Stretch out thine hand toward heaven, that there may be darkness over the land of Egypt, even darkness which may be felt. [22] And Moses stretched forth his hand toward heaven; and there was a thick darkness in all the land of Egypt three days: [23] They saw not one another, neither rose any from his place for three days: but all the children of Israel had light in their dwellings. (Exodus 10:21-23)

The judgments recorded in the books of Exodus and Isaiah describe the effects upon the earth when the Lord stretches out His hand upon the sun, moon, and stars. There are many more prophecies that reveal that the heavens and earth will experience great signs as the hand of Lord is stretched out in judgment against the earth because men worship the antichrist and reject Jesus Christ.

[25] And there shall be signs in the sun, and in the moon, and in the stars; and upon the earth distress of nations, with perplexity; the sea and the waves roaring. (Luke 21:25)

Trumpet Judgments - Part One

¹⁰ *For the stars of heaven and the constellations thereof shall not give their light: the sun shall be darkened in his going forth, and the moon shall not cause her light to shine.* ¹¹ *And I will punish the world for their evil, and the wicked for their iniquity; and I will cause the arrogancy of the proud to cease, and will lay low the haughtiness of the terrible.* ¹² *I will make a man more precious than fine gold; even a man than the golden wedge of Ophir.* ¹³ *Therefore I will shake the heavens, and the earth shall remove out of her place, in the wrath of the LORD of hosts, and in the day of his fierce anger.* (Isaiah 13:10-13)

Both the Gospel of Luke and the Book of Isaiah prophesy what the future will be like as Almighty God pours out His wrath upon the world because of the wickedness of man.

Today the earth rotates on its axis every 24 hours. At the time of the Fourth Trumpet judgment the earth's tilt of its axis will be altered. This will result in a 16-hour day. The clocks of the world may need to be changed to accommodate a 16-hour day. This judgment will have a great impact on the entire world as the Lord is changing the orbit and the tilt of its axis as described in Isaiah 13:13.

There are other Scriptures that indicate how awful this time will be for men upon the earth. The Day of the Lord starts immediately after Jesus comes for His church as revealed in I Thessalonians 5:2. This period will be a time of great trouble:

¹⁸ *Woe unto you that desire the day of the LORD! To what end is it for you? The day of the LORD is darkness, and not light.* ¹⁹ *As if a man did flee from a lion, and a bear met him; or went into the house, and leaned his hand on the wall, and a serpent bit him.* ²⁰ *Shall not the day of the LORD be darkness, and not light? Even very dark, and no brightness in it?* (Amos 5:18-20)

² *God is jealous, and the LORD revengeth; the LORD revengeth, and is furious; the LORD will take vengeance on his adversaries, and he reserveth wrath for his enemies.* ³ *The LORD is slow to anger, and great in power, and will not at all acquit the wicked: the LORD hath his way in the whirlwind and in the storm, and the clouds are the dust of his feet.* ⁴ *He rebuketh the sea, and maketh it dry, and drieth up all the rivers: Bashan languisheth, and Carmel, and the flower of Lebanon languisheth.* ⁵ *The mountains quake at him, and the hills melt, and the earth is burned at his presence, yea, the world, and all that dwell therein.* ⁶ *Who can stand before his indignation? And who can abide in the fierceness of his anger? His fury is poured out like fire, and the rocks are thrown down by him.* ⁷ *The LORD is good, a strong hold in the day of trouble; and he knoweth them that trust in him.* ⁸ *But with an*

overrunning flood he will make an utter end of the place thereof, and darkness shall pursue his enemies. ⁹ What do ye imagine against the LORD? *He will make an utter end: affliction shall not rise up the second time.* ¹⁰ *For while they be folden together as thorns, and while they are drunken as drunkards, they shall be devoured as stubble fully dry.* ¹¹ *There is one come out of thee, that imagineth evil against the* LORD, *a wicked counsellor.* ¹² *Thus saith the* LORD; *though they be quiet, and likewise many, yet thus shall they be cut down, when he shall pass through. Though I have afflicted thee, I will afflict thee no more.* ¹³ *For now will I break his yoke from off thee, and will burst thy bonds in sunder.* ¹⁴ *And the* LORD *hath given a commandment concerning thee, that no more of thy name be sown: out of the house of thy gods will I cut off the graven image and the molten image: I will make thy grave; for thou art vile.* (Nahum 1:2-14)

The Lord will take vengeance on the antichrist and on those who worship him, as Nahum writes in his prophecy. It will be a time of great trouble as the Almighty God pours out his judgments against the kingdom of antichrist. There is a prophecy in Ezekiel which will have its complete fulfillment during the Day of the Lord, when the kingdom of antichrist is targeted by Almighty God for judgment:

¹*And it came to pass in the twelfth year, in the twelfth month, in the first day of the month, that the word of the* LORD *came unto me, saying,* ² *Son of man, take up a lamentation for Pharaoh king of Egypt, and say unto him, Thou art like a young lion of the nations, and thou art as a whale in the seas: and thou camest forth with thy rivers, and troubledst the waters with thy feet, and fouledst their rivers.* ³ *Thus saith the Lord* GOD; *I will therefore spread out my net over thee with a company of many people; and they shall bring thee up in my net.* ⁴ *Then will I leave thee upon the land, I will cast thee forth upon the open field, and will cause all the fowls of the heaven to remain upon thee, and I will fill the beasts of the whole earth with thee.* ⁵ *And I will lay thy flesh upon the mountains, and fill the valleys with thy height.* ⁶ *I will also water with thy blood the land wherein thou swimmest, even to the mountains; and the rivers shall be full of thee.* ⁷ *And when I shall put thee out, I will cover the heaven, and make the stars thereof dark; I will cover the sun with a cloud, and the moon shall not give her light.* ⁸ *All the bright lights of heaven will I make dark over thee, and set darkness upon thy land, saith the Lord* GOD. (Ezekiel 32:1-8)

What was prophesied against Pharaoh and Egypt will have its complete fulfillment against the kingdom of antichrist. Finally, in Zephaniah we see that the Day of the Lord will be cruel to those on the earth who choose to follow the antichrist:

Trumpet Judgments - Part One

¹*The word of the Lord which came unto Zephaniah the son of Cushi, the son of Gedaliah, the son of Amariah, the son of Hizkiah, in the days of Josiah the son of Amon, king of Judah.* ²*I will utterly consume all things from off the land, saith the Lord.* ³*I will consume man and beast; I will consume the fowls of the heaven, and the fishes of the sea, and the stumbling blocks with the wicked: and I will cut off man from off the land, saith the Lord.* (Zephaniah 1:1-3)

Some Bible scholars believe that the first Four Trumpet judgments may follow one another very closely.

- The First Trumpet judgment could refer to a fiery meteor shower resulting in a third of the trees and all the green grass being burned up.
- The Second Trumpet judgment could refer to a large asteroid striking the earth. When it hits the earth, a third of all the living creatures in the sea die, and a third of the ships are destroyed.
- The Third Trumpet judgment could refer to a comet that strikes the earth, resulting in the fresh water supply being bitter. This could be where a comet collides with an asteroid in space and sends both the asteroid and the comet on a collision course with the earth.
- The Fourth Trumpet judgment is the side effect of the great meteor or asteroid striking the earth, impacting its rotation and orbit around the sun and resulting in the day being shortened from 24 hours to 16 hours.

Whatever these deadly Four Trumpets judgments are, the people of the earth have not seen anything yet, as there are three more woes or Trumpets to sound.

If there is a large asteroid that will strike the earth as noted in the Second Trumpet judgment, the question arises as to the location of the impact. It is difficult, if not impossible, to determine the location of the impact, but we can easily determine the location where the asteroid will not impact the earth. For example, the Middle East will not be impacted as the people of the Middle East are mentioned after the first Four Trumpet judgments. The same can be said of Asia as the people of the Far East will invade the West as part of the battle of Armageddon. Africa will not be impacted as Africa is also mentioned as part of the conquests by the antichrist. The area of Russia west of the Ural Mountains will not be impacted as the people of Western Russia are from the north countries that will attack the antichrist along with the people of the east during the battle of Armageddon. Europe does not seem possible, as Europe will most likely be a part of the kingdom of the antichrist that will be destroyed later by Almighty God as part of the Bowl or Vial judgments. We know from the Scriptures that a third of the ships will be destroyed, so it must be a country with a well-developed shipping industry. When the geography of the earth is altered because of the Sixth Seal judgment, it would be difficult to predict where an asteroid would strike the earth (Revelation 6:12-17).

As part of this great judgment, could Religious Babylon also be targeted? When the beast demands to be worshipped as God, and those religious institutions that assisted the beast in coming to power are now betrayed by the beast, will those religious institutions become targeted by the beast as part of this great plague? In order to consolidate his power, the beast must eliminate any institution that will challenge his claim to be God and to be worshipped as God.

Chapter 9
Trumpet Judgments - Part Two

Revelation 9:1-12
The Fifth Trumpet Judgment

And the fifth angel sounded, and I saw a star fall from heaven unto the earth: and to him was given the key of the bottomless pit. And he opened the bottomless pit; and there arose a smoke out of the pit, as the smoke of a great furnace; and the sun and the air were darkened by reason of the smoke of the pit. And there came out of the smoke locusts upon the earth: and unto them was given power, as the scorpions of the earth have power. And it was commanded them that they should not hurt the grass of the earth, neither any green thing, neither any tree; but only those men which have not the seal of God in their foreheads. And to them it was given that they should not kill them, but that they should be tormented five months: and their torment was as the torment of a scorpion, when he striketh a man. And in those days shall men seek death, and shall not find it; and shall desire to die, and death shall flee from them. And the shapes of the locusts were like unto horses prepared unto battle; and on their heads were as it were crowns like gold, and their faces were as the faces of men. And they had hair as the hair of women, and their teeth were as the teeth of lions. And they had breastplates, as it were breastplates of iron; and the sound of their wings was as the sound of chariots of many horses running to battle. And they had tails like unto scorpions, and there were stings in their tails: and their power was to hurt men five months. And they had a king over them, which is the angel of the bottomless pit, whose name in the Hebrew tongue is Abaddon, but in the Greek tongue hath his name Apollyon. One woe is past; and, behold, there come two woes more hereafter.

Revelation

BIBLE SCHOLARS BELIEVE that Satan and his angels have been cast out of heaven during the Sixth Seal (Revelation 6:12-13), and this event is detailed Revelation 6:12-13 and 12:7-9:

12 And I beheld when he had opened the sixth seal, and, lo, there was a great earthquake; and the sun became black as sackcloth of hair, and the moon became as blood; 13 And the stars of heaven fell unto the earth, even as a fig tree casteth her untimely figs, when she is shaken of a mighty wind. (Revelation 6:12-13)

7 And there was war in heaven: Michael and his angels fought against the dragon; and the dragon fought and his angels, 8 and prevailed not; neither was their place found any more in heaven. 9 And the great dragon was cast out, that old serpent, called the Devil, and Satan, which deceiveth the whole world: he was cast out into the earth, and his angels were cast out with him. (Revelation 12:7-9)

In Isaiah, Satan has been described as falling from heaven when he desired to exalt his throne above the Throne of God. Satan is also described as falling from heaven in the Gospels when Jesus empowered His disciples to be witnesses upon the earth. Satan will be cast out of heaven again, this time on a permanent basis. What happened in the past will be replayed again in the future. This will be the time of Satan's greatest wrath as he knows his time is short after he is cast out of heaven for good.

12 How art thou fallen from heaven, O Lucifer, son of the morning! How art thou cut down to the ground, which didst weaken the nations! 13 For thou hast said in thine heart, I will ascend into heaven, I will exalt my throne above the stars of God: I will sit also upon the mount of the congregation, in the sides of the north: 14 I will ascend above the heights of the clouds; I will be like the most High. 15 Yet thou shalt be brought down to hell, to the sides of the pit. (Isaiah 14:12-15)

17 And the seventy returned again with joy, saying, Lord, even the devils are subject unto us through thy name. 18 And he said unto them, I beheld Satan as lightning fall from heaven. (Luke 10:17-18)

The Greek word for fall in Revelation 9:1 is *pipto*, which means "to fall," "fall down." This is not the same Greek word used to describe Satan being cast out of heaven as in Revelation 12. The Greek word in Revelation 12:9 is *ballo*, which means that Satan had been thrown or tossed out of heaven during the Sixth Seal judgment. With Satan being cast out of heaven earlier, could this be one of the fallen angels returning to heaven to receive the key to the bottomless pit and then returning back to the earth with the key to open the bottomless pit? The star in Revelation 9:1 is identified by the personal pronoun "him," indicating a real personality. It is very likely that one of Satan's angels is granted permission to return to heaven, obtain the key, and then fall back to the earth. The bottomless pit is also referred to as "the pit of the abyss." The abyss is a place where certain beings that have come under the judgment of God are being restrained as noted in Peter's epistle:

⁴ For if God spared not the angels that sinned, but cast them down to hell, and delivered them into chains of darkness, to be reserved unto judgment. (II Peter 2:4)

There is a place more terrible than Hades, where the demons are currently being held as noted in Luke and Isaiah:

²⁶ And they arrived at the country of the Gadarenes, which is over against Galilee. ²⁷ And when he went forth to land, there met him out of the city a certain man, which had devils long time, and ware no clothes, neither abode in any house, but in the tombs. ²⁸ When he saw Jesus, he cried out, and fell down before him, and with a loud voice said, What have I to do with thee, Jesus, thou Son of God most high? I beseech thee, torment me not. ²⁹ (For he had commanded the unclean spirit to come out of the man. For oftentimes it had caught him: and he was kept bound with chains and in fetters; and he brake the bands, and was driven of the devil into the wilderness.) ³⁰ And Jesus asked him, saying, What is thy name? And he said, Legion: because many devils were entered into him. ³¹ And they besought him that he would not command them to go out into the deep. ³² And there was there an herd of many swine feeding on the mountain: and they besought him that he would suffer them to enter into them. And he suffered them. ³³ Then went the devils out of the man, and entered into the swine: and the herd ran violently down a steep place into the lake, and were choked. (Luke 8:26-33)

²² And it came to pass, that the beggar died, and was carried by the angels into Abraham's bosom: the rich man also died, and was buried; ²³ And in hell he lift up his eyes, being in torments, and seeth Abraham afar off, and Lazarus in his bosom. ²⁴ And he cried and said, Father Abraham, have mercy on me, and send Lazarus, that he may dip the tip of his finger in water, and cool my tongue; for I am tormented in this flame. ²⁵ But Abraham said, Son, remember that thou in thy lifetime receivedst thy good things, and likewise Lazarus evil things: but now he is comforted, and thou art tormented. ²⁶ And beside all this, between us and you there is a great gulf fixed: so that they which would pass from hence to you cannot; neither can they pass to us, that would come from thence. (Luke 16:22-26)

²¹ And it shall come to pass in that day, that the LORD shall punish the host of the high ones that are on high, and the kings of the earth upon the earth. ²² And

Revelation

they shall be gathered together, as prisoners are gathered in the pit, and shall be shut up in the prison, and after many days shall they be visited. (Isaiah 24:21-22)

The demons prefer to roam the earth and not to be held captive in the abyss or bottomless pit. The beast also is one that comes out of the bottomless pit as noted in Revelation 11:

⁷ And when they shall have finished their testimony, the beast that ascendeth out of the bottomless pit shall make war against them, and shall overcome them, and kill them. (Revelation 11:7)

When the Fifth Trumpet sounds, the demon forces that have been kept locked up will now be free to roam the earth. When the angel with the key opens the bottomless pit, out will come demon locusts to bring havoc upon the earth as described in Joel 2:

¹Blow ye the trumpet in Zion, and sound an alarm in my holy mountain: let all the inhabitants of the land tremble: for the day of the Lord cometh, for it is nigh at hand; ²A day of darkness and of gloominess, a day of clouds and of thick darkness, as the morning spread upon the mountains: a great people and a strong; there hath not been ever the like, neither shall be any more after it, even to the years of many generations. ³A fire devoureth before them; and behind them a flame burneth: the land is as the garden of Eden before them, and behind them a desolate wilderness; yea, and nothing shall escape them. ⁴The appearance of them is as the appearance of horses; and as horsemen, so shall they run. ⁵Like the noise of chariots on the tops of mountains shall they leap, like the noise of a flame of fire that devoureth the stubble, as a strong people set in battle array. ⁶Before their face the people shall be much pained: all faces shall gather blackness. ⁷They shall run like mighty men; they shall climb the wall like men of war; and they shall march every one on his ways, and they shall not break their ranks: ⁸neither shall one thrust another; they shall walk every one in his path: and when they fall upon the sword, they shall not be wounded. ⁹They shall run to and fro in the city; they shall run upon the wall, they shall climb up upon the houses; they shall enter in at the windows like a thief. ¹⁰The earth shall quake before them; the heavens shall tremble: the sun and the moon shall be dark, and the stars shall withdraw their shining: ¹¹And the Lord shall utter his voice before his army: for his camp is very great: for he is strong that executeth his word: for the day of the LORD is great and very terrible; and who can abide it? (Joel 2:1-11)

This portion in Joel describes events that cover both the Fifth and Sixth Trumpet judgments. These locusts torture and drive men mad for five months. They are powerful and prepared for battle (horses), they are bold and independent (crowns), violent (lions' teeth), they show no pity and are

Trumpet Judgments - Part Two

prepared for battle (iron breastplate). It is noted in Proverbs 30:27 that locusts do not have a king, but these demon locusts do have a king. This indicates that they are intelligent and follow a chain of command.

The locusts that come out of the bottomless pit are not the locusts as we know today. They attack only men and do not touch plant life. The object of their attack is all mankind except for the 144,000 Israelites who have been sealed. Notice that the saints are still on the earth when this plague happens. The saints cannot be the church, as the church is not destined to experience the *orge* of God! These saints are the 144,000 Israelites who are protected and are not to come under attack by the locusts during this trumpet judgment. The locusts have tails with which they inflict pain and agony on their victims. Have you ever been in such a terrible pain and agony for an entire day that you wish you could die? The next morning you begin to recover and start feeling better. With this plague the pain and agony do not go away the next day, but linger for five months. What a terrible, painful judgment this would be as men are not able to die when they want to.

The two witnesses are also protected from the locusts. Their ministry continues into the Great Tribulation period. With their ministry lasting only 1,260 days, the start of their ministry must begin at least five months after the start of the seventieth week of Daniel. The conclusion of their ministry is provided during the Sixth Trumpet judgment.

The world has recently been fascinated with the possibility of a zombie apocalypse. The Fifth Trumpet judgment may resemble a zombie apocalypse that lasts for five months. This plague impacts men to such a degree that they wish they could die, but cannot. This is a horrible plague, but the events on the earth will get worse as there are two more woes to come.

Revelation 9:13-21
The Sixth Trumpet Judgment

And the sixth angel sounded, and I heard a voice from the four horns of the golden altar which is before God, Saying to the sixth angel which had the trumpet, Loose the four angels which are bound in the great river Euphrates. And the four angels were loosed, which were prepared for an hour, and a day, and a month, and a year, for to slay the third part of men. And the number of the army of the horsemen were two hundred thousand thousand: and I heard the number of them. And thus I saw the horses in the vision, and them that sat on them, having breastplates of fire, and of jacinth, and brimstone: and the heads of the horses were as the heads of lions; and out of their mouths issued fire and smoke and brimstone. By these three was the

Revelation

third part of men killed, by the fire, and by the smoke, and by the brimstone, which issued out of their mouths. For their power is in their mouth, and in their tails: for their tails were like unto serpents, and had heads, and with them they do hurt. And the rest of the men which were not killed by these plagues yet repented not of the works of their hands, that they should not worship devils, and idols of gold, and silver, and brass, and stone, and of wood: which neither can see, nor hear, nor walk: Neither repented they of their murders, nor of their sorceries, nor of their fornication, nor of their thefts.

The four demons that are released as part of the Sixth Trumpet are so evil that God has to keep them chained up. The Lord in His mercy does not let these four demons loose upon the earth. Now, as part of the *orge* of God, these four demons are loosed from their prison and they wreak havoc and death for 13 months. Jude refers to angels who did not keep their previous estate, but abandoned their place in heaven:

5 I will therefore put you in remembrance, though ye once knew this, how that the Lord, having saved the people out of the land of Egypt, afterward destroyed them that believed not. 6 And the angels which kept not their first estate, but left their own habitation, he hath reserved in everlasting chains under darkness unto the judgment of the great day. 7 Even as Sodom and Gomorrah, and the cities about them in like manner, giving themselves over to fornication, and going after strange flesh, are set forth for an example, suffering the vengeance of eternal fire. (Jude 5-7).

God, in His mercy, has kept these creatures bound until the judgment of the great Day of the Lord. These four demons are so evil and destructive that they make Satan appear as Mary Poppins. Today, we praise the Lord God Almighty for His mercy that the four demons are not loose upon the earth. The Greek language suggests that the four demons do their destructive work in just one hour near the end of the 13 months and not over a 13-month period.

The number two hundred thousand thousand (200 million) refers to a number not previously recorded in the Scriptures. This army of 200 million appears to be composed of supernatural beings. A third of mankind is killed by the fire, smoke, and brimstone from the mouths of this advancing army of supernatural creatures. The four angels are somehow related to this vast army that is reserved for the wrath of God upon the wicked men set in their rebellion against the Creator of all things.

The abomination of desolation has already taken place at this time as foretold in Daniel 9:27 and Matthew 24:15. The antichrist must now be punished as he has declared himself to be God and demands to be worshipped as God. The antichrist most likely has already set up the economic system whereby everyone who desires to work, buy, or sell, must agree to receive the mark of the beast and to bow down and worship the beast. Those who refuse are not permitted to buy or sell. For those who are retired, this may mean the loss of Social Security checks for refusing to take the mark of the beast. Homeowners will be refused utilities to their home unless they take the mark of the beast. It will be a time of great persecution. The Bible refers to this time as the Great Tribulation period.

Joel 2 appears to be descriptive of both the Fifth and Sixth Trumpet judgments. This is part of the dreadful Day of the Lord as the birth pangs are increasing in intensity toward the end as recorded in Joel 1:13-20. Verses 19 and 20 appear to be plagues from the Trumpet judgments.

> [13] *Gird yourselves, and lament, ye priests: howl, ye ministers of the altar: come, lie all night in sackcloth, ye ministers of my God: for the meat offering and the drink offering is withholden from the house of your God.* [14] *Sanctify ye a fast, call a solemn assembly, gather the elders and all the inhabitants of the land into the house of the LORD your God, and cry unto the LORD,* [15] *Alas for the day! For the day of the LORD is at hand, and as a destruction from the Almighty shall it come.* [16] *Is not the meat cut off before our eyes, yea, joy and gladness from the house of our God?* [17] *The seed is rotten under their clods, the garners are laid desolate, the barns are broken down; for the corn is withered.* [18] *How do the beasts groan! The herds of cattle are perplexed, because they have no pasture; yea, the flocks of sheep are made desolate.* [19] *O LORD, to thee will I cry: for the fire hath devoured the pastures of the wilderness, and the flame hath burned all the trees of the field.* [20] *The beasts of the field cry also unto thee: for the rivers of waters are dried up, and the fire hath devoured the pastures of the wilderness.* (Joel 1:13-20)

The effect of this plague is so great that even the animal life is impacted. The wicked people of the world continue in their wickedness as they do not repent of their sorceries (Revelation 9:21), which in the Greek language indicates drug usage. During the oppression of the Jews in Egypt, Pharaoh hardened his heart and would not allow the Jews to leave Egypt. Day after day Pharaoh continued to harden his heart and not let the people go. Later the Lord made firm Pharaoh's heart as Pharaoh continued to resist the Lord. As he resisted the Lord, he went from a state of mind and heart that he would not repent, to a state where he could not repent. This is a danger to any man who continues to resist the Lord over and over. The danger is that those who continue to live in sin, and live after the flesh, and continue to reject the Lord Jesus Christ, will transition from a state of will not repent, to where they cannot repent. Now all hope is gone, because as that person cannot repent, he is no longer responding to the call of the Creator in turning away from sin and the lifestyle of sin.

The events so far look devastating, as the planet earth has experienced many destructive plagues, and demons have been released from their prison to roam the earth. But the fiery indignation (*thumos*) of the Lord has not yet started. The earth is still experiencing *orge* at this time. The worst is yet to come as the wrath of God is going to intensify.

Chapter 10
The Mighty Angel and the Book
Revelation 10:1-11
The Event Between Trumpets Six and Seven

And I saw another mighty angel come down from heaven, clothed with a cloud: and a rainbow was upon his head, and his face was as it were the sun, and his feet as pillars of fire: And he had in his hand a little book open: and he set his right foot upon the sea, and his left foot on the earth, And cried with a loud voice, as when a lion roareth: and when he had cried, seven thunders uttered their voices. And when the seven thunders had uttered their voices, I was about to write: and I heard a voice from heaven saying unto me, Seal up those things which the seven thunders uttered, and write them not. And the angel which I saw stand upon the sea and upon the earth lifted up his hand to heaven, And sware by him that liveth for ever and ever, who created heaven, and the things that therein are, and the earth, and the things that therein are, and the sea, and the things which are therein, that there should be time no longer: But in the days of the voice of the seventh angel, when he shall begin to sound, the mystery of God should be finished, as he hath declared to his servants the prophets. And the voice which I heard from heaven spake unto me again, and said, Go and take the little book which is open in the hand of the angel which standeth upon the sea and upon the earth. And I went unto the angel, and said unto him, Give me the little book. And he said unto me, Take it, and eat it up; and it shall make thy belly bitter, but it shall be in thy mouth sweet as honey. And I took the little book out of the angel's hand, and ate it up; and it was in my mouth sweet as honey: and as soon as I had eaten it, my belly was bitter. And he said unto me, Thou must prophesy again before many peoples, and nations, and tongues, and kings.

Revelation

SOME BIBLE SCHOLARS see this angel as the Lord Jesus Christ. However, Jesus is not described as an angel in the Book of Revelation. He is the Lord over the angels. This angel is described as another mighty angel. Angels who are glorious in appearance do not have to be the Lord Jesus, as noted in the Book of Daniel:

⁴ And in the four and twentieth day of the first month, as I was by the side of the great river, which is Hiddekel; ⁵ Then I lifted up mine eyes, and looked, and behold a certain man clothed in linen, whose loins were girded with fine gold of Uphaz: ⁶ His body also was like the beryl, and his face as the appearance of lightning, and his eyes as lamps of fire, and his arms and his feet like in colour to polished brass, and the voice of his words like the voice of a multitude. (Daniel 10:4-6)

¹² Then said he unto me, Fear not, Daniel: for from the first day that thou didst set thine heart to understand, and to chasten thyself before thy God, thy words were heard, and I am come for thy words. ¹³ But the prince of the kingdom of Persia withstood me one and twenty days: but, lo, Michael, one of the chief princes, came to help me; and I remained there with the kings of Persia. (Daniel 10:12-13)

The mighty angel from the Book of Daniel cannot be the Lord Jesus, as this angel needed Michael's assistance. It is important not to confuse angels with the Lord Jesus every time an angel is mentioned in the Scriptures. The Lord created many angels before He created man. There are probably many types of angels, some of them glorious in appearance as described in the Book of Daniel and the Book of Revelation.

The sea and land are symbolic of Israel and the Gentile nations. The wrath (*thumos*) of God will greatly impact both Israel and the Gentile nations as recorded in the Psalms:

¹ Why do the heathen rage, and the people imagine a vain thing? ² The kings of the earth set themselves, and the rulers take counsel together, against the LORD, and against his anointed, saying, ³ Let us break their bands asunder, and cast away their cords from us. ⁴ He that sitteth in the heavens shall laugh: the LORD shall have them in derision. ⁵ Then shall he speak unto them in his wrath, and vex them in his sore displeasure. ⁶ Yet have I set my king upon my holy hill of Zion. ⁷ I will declare the decree: the LORD hath said unto me, Thou art my Son; this day have I begotten thee. ⁸ Ask of me, and I shall give thee the heathen for thine inheritance, and the uttermost parts of the earth for thy possession. ⁹ Thou shalt break them with a rod of iron; thou shalt dash them in pieces like a potter's vessel. ¹⁰ Be wise now therefore, O ye kings: be instructed, ye judges of the earth. ¹¹ Serve the LORD with fear, and rejoice with trembling. ¹² Kiss the Son, lest he be angry,

The Mighty Angel and the Book

and ye perish from the way, when his wrath is kindled but a little. Blessed are all they that put their trust in him. (Psalm 2:1-12)

⁴ The voice of the LORD is powerful; the voice of the LORD is full of majesty. ⁵ The voice of the LORD breaketh the cedars; yea, the LORD breaketh the cedars of Lebanon. ⁶ He maketh them also to skip like a calf; Lebanon and Sirion like a young unicorn. ⁷ The voice of the LORD divideth the flames of fire. ⁸ The voice of the LORD shaketh the wilderness; the LORD shaketh the wilderness of Kadesh. ⁹ The voice of the LORD maketh the hinds to calve, and discovereth the forests: and in his temple doth every one speak of his glory. (Psalm 24:4-9)

Before Jesus returns to the earth to reign as King of Kings and Lord of Lords, there will be heavy judgments from the Lord upon the earth during this seven-year period. The kingdom of antichrist must be punished as the beast is leading the world in rebellion against the Lord. Psalm 2 indicates that the antichrist will stir up other rulers of the world to unite in their rebellion against the Lord. Proverbs 21:30 declares that there is no wisdom, no understanding, and no counsel against the Lord. The antichrist is no doubt a great orator and will persuade men to rebel against the Lord, causing them to believe that united they can defeat God. This persuasion will lead the earth to ruin when the Seventh Trumpet sounds; when Jesus returns, righteousness will cover the earth.

When will the judgment be for the mass of people in this world who have rejected Jesus Christ? The answer is here. The mystery of God should be finished in the days of the seventh angel when he shall begin to sound as recorded in the Book of Revelation:

¹⁵ And the seventh angel sounded; and there were great voices in heaven, saying, the kingdoms of this world are become the kingdoms of our Lord, and of his Christ; and he shall reign for ever and ever. ¹⁶ And the four and twenty elders, which sat before God on their seats, fell upon their faces, and worshipped God, ¹⁷ Saying, We give thee thanks, O LORD God Almighty, which art, and wast, and art to come; because thou hast taken to thee thy great power, and hast reigned. ¹⁸ And the nations were angry, and thy wrath is come, and the time of the dead, that they should be judged, and that thou shouldest give reward unto thy servants the prophets, and to the saints, and them that fear thy name, small and great; and shouldest destroy them which destroy the earth. ¹⁹ And the temple of God was opened in heaven, and there was seen in his temple the ark of his testament: and there were lightnings, and voices, and thunderings, and an earthquake, and great hail. (Revelation 11:15-19)

Revelation

The God who created all things in the heavens, on the earth, and in the sea, is about to restore all things just as they were before the fall of man in the Garden of Eden. God will also create a new heaven and a new earth after the 1,000-year kingdom age has been completed.

Some Bible scholars see the little book that is in the angel's hand as the Title Deed to the earth, while others see this as the proclamation that the Lord Jesus is coming soon as King of Kings and Lord of Lords.

God has an interesting clock as noted in Daniel 9:24-27, and it deals only with the nation of Israel, not the church. God stopped the clock when Jesus rode into Jerusalem, signifying the first coming of the Messiah. Sixty-nine of the seventy weeks have been completed from Daniel 9:24-27 and there is only one seven-year period remaining (see appendix A). God will restart the clock once the man of sin makes a covenant with the nation of Israel. However, the last three-and-a-half years will be a time of Great Tribulation for the Jews. There is a promise to the Jews in the kingdom age that all Israel will be saved as noted in Romans 11:26:

[26] *And so all Israel shall be saved: as it is written, There shall come out of Sion the Deliverer, and shall turn away ungodliness from Jacob.* (Romans 11:26)

It was revealed to John that he will return to the earth, live out his days, and will die a natural death. From church history we know that John later went back to Ephesus. There are some who believe that John the apostle will be one of the two witnesses because of Revelation 10:11. If John is indeed one of the two witnesses, then he cannot be one of the 24 elders in heaven seated around the throne. If John is indeed one of the 24 elders, then he cannot be the other witness along with Elijah when Elijah returns to the earth.

Chapter 11
The Two Witnesses

Revelation 11:1-2
A Restored Temple and Altar

And there was given me a reed like unto a rod: and the angel stood, saying, Rise, and measure the temple of God, and the altar, and them that worship therein. But the court which is without the temple leave out, and measure it not; for it is given unto the Gentiles: and the holy city shall they tread under foot forty and two months.

JACOB PRASCH HAS revealed in his book, *Harpazo: the Intra-Seal Rapture of the Church*, that when God uses the number 1,260 days, it is for Israel and the two witnesses. When God uses the phrase "42 months," it is most often associated with apostasy or the antichrist. For example, there were 42 youths taunting Elisha over the rapture of Elijah. The unfaithful generation of Israel that Moses led through the wilderness stopped at 42 places in their wilderness journey for 40 years, and there were 42 sons of the unfaithful king of Israel who were killed by Jehu whom the Lord had called to be the next king. The holy city and the Temple will be trodden down by the Gentiles and the antichrist for 42 months. The number 42 signifies apostasy and this is the number of months that the beast or antichrist will reign, according to Revelation 13:

⁴And they worshipped the dragon which gave power unto the beast: and they worshipped the beast, saying, Who is like unto the beast? who is able to make war with him? ⁵And there was given unto him a mouth speaking great things and blasphemies; and power was given unto him to continue forty and two months. (Revelation 13:4-5)

Revelation

Chapter 11 is crucial to the various interpretations of the Book of Revelation. The events of chapter 11 are part of the Sixth Trumpet judgment, which is also called the second woe (Revelation 8:13). Before the Seventh Trumpet judgment sounds, John is given a picture of what is transpiring in Jerusalem. He sees a restored Jewish Temple and an altar. Outside and in the outer court could be the Al-Aqsa Mosque and the Dome of the Rock which are holy sites for the Muslims. Whatever is in the outer court, John is given instructions not to measure the outer court. Most Bible scholars agree and believe that one of the conditions of the covenant the antichrist will agree to with the nation of Israel is permission for the Jews to rebuild their Temple. This is something that many Jews today are looking to accomplish. We know that if the Jews started to rebuild their Temple today, the Muslim countries would start a holy war, and this is something that the nation of Israel wants to avoid. Bible scholars agree that some event will take place in the future that will grant permission to the Jews to rebuild their Temple.

The abomination of desolation spoken of in the Book of Daniel and in the Gospel of Matthew, refers to this coming world leader who makes a covenant with the nation of Israel to rebuild and to restore their Temple and their sacrifices. Then after three and a half years, the antichrist will break his covenant with the nation of Israel. After breaking his covenant with Israel, he will set up his image in the Jewish Temple, demanding that the entire world worship him as God. Once this event occurs, the Jews will recognize that they have been betrayed by the world leader who signed a covenant with them three-and-a-half years earlier. The time of great persecution of the Jews will begin after the desecration of the Temple by the antichrist. This is the start of the Great Tribulation period as spoken of in the Book of Zechariah and in the Gospel of Matthew:

⁵ And ye shall flee to the valley of the mountains; for the valley of the mountains shall reach unto Azal: yea, ye shall flee, like as ye fled from before the earthquake in the days of Uzziah king of Judah: and the LORD *my God shall come, and all the saints with thee.* (Zechariah 14:5)

¹⁵ When ye therefore shall see the abomination of desolation, spoken of by Daniel the prophet, stand in the holy place, (whoso readeth, let him understand:) ¹⁶ Then let them which be in Judaea flee into the mountains: ¹⁷ Let him which is on the housetop not come down to take any thing out of his house: ¹⁸ Neither let him which is in the field return back to take his clothes. ¹⁹ And woe unto them that are with child, and to them that give suck in those days! ²⁰ But pray ye that your flight be not in the winter, neither on the sabbath day: ²¹ *For then shall be great tribulation, such as was not since the beginning of the world to this time, no, nor ever shall be.* ²² *And except those days should be shortened, there should no flesh be saved: but for the elect's sake those days shall be shortened.* (Matthew 24:15-22)

This will indeed be a time of Great Tribulation because two out of every three Jews will be killed as revealed in Zechariah's prophecy:

⁸ *And it shall come to pass, that in all the land, saith the* LORD, *two parts therein shall be cut off and die; but the third shall be left therein.* ⁹ *And I will bring the third part through the fire, and will refine them as silver is refined, and will try them as gold is tried: they shall call on my name, and I will hear them: I will say, It is my people: and they shall say, The* LORD *is my God.* (Zechariah 13:8-9)

The Jews will flee into the wilderness for 1,260 days in order to escape antichrist's wrath when they realize that they were deceived and betrayed by him as revealed in Revelation 12:

⁶ *And the woman fled into the wilderness, where she hath a place prepared of God, that they should feed her there a thousand two hundred and threescore days.* (Revelation 12:6)

The God of Israel will nourish the remnant of Jews during this time as revealed in Revelation 12:

¹¹ *And to the woman were given two wings of a great eagle, that she might fly into the wilderness, into her place, where she is nourished for a time, and times, and half a time, from the face of the serpent.* (Revelation 12:14)

Jerusalem will be taken over by the Gentiles for 42 months. This is known as the "times of the Gentiles." The times of the Gentiles and the Great Tribulation will occur in the second half of the seventieth week of Daniel. This terrible time is revealed in Zechariah and the Gospel of Luke:

¹*Behold, the day of the* LORD *cometh, and thy spoil shall be divided in the midst of thee.* ² *For I will gather all nations against Jerusalem to battle; and the city shall be taken, and the houses rifled, and the women ravished; and half of the city shall go forth into captivity, and the residue of the people shall not be cut off from the city.* (Zechariah 14:1-2)

²⁰ *And when ye shall see Jerusalem compassed with armies, then know that the desolation thereof is nigh.* ²¹ *Then let them which are in Judaea flee to the mountains; and let them which are in the midst of it depart out; and let not them that are in the countries enter thereinto.* ²² *For these be the days of vengeance, that all things which*

are written may be fulfilled. ²³ But woe unto them that are with child, and to them that give suck, in those days! For there shall be great distress in the land, and wrath upon this people. ²⁴ And they shall fall by the edge of the sword, and shall be led away captive into all nations: and Jerusalem shall be trodden down of the Gentiles, until the times of the Gentiles be fulfilled. (Luke 21:20-24)

Just like the events that occurred in AD 70 when the true and faithful church fled Jerusalem when the Roman armies were surrounding the city, many Jews will flee Jerusalem when the antichrist breaks his treaty and begins to come against Israel. The Jews will still be blinded concerning who their Messiah is. They thought that the antichrist was their Messiah when he signed the agreement with the nation of Israel and granted them permission to rebuild their Temple. Today if one would ask the Jews how they would recognize their Messiah, they would respond that the Messiah will be the one who helps them rebuild their Temple. The rejection of Jesus Christ has blinded the eyes of the nation of Israel to whom their Messiah truly is. At the end of the Great Tribulation, when Jesus returns to the earth, all Israel shall be saved and the blindness will be removed as revealed in the Book of Romans 11:25-26.

The deception of the antichrist and his evil reign is foretold in the Book of Daniel:

²³ Thus he said, the fourth beast shall be the fourth kingdom upon earth, which shall be diverse from all kingdoms, and shall devour the whole earth, and shall tread it down, and break it in pieces. ²⁴ And the ten horns out of this kingdom are ten kings that shall arise: and another shall rise after them; and he shall be diverse from the first, and he shall subdue three kings. ²⁵ And he shall speak great words against the most High, and shall wear out the saints of the most High, and think to change times and laws: and they shall be given into his hand until a time and times and the dividing of time. (Daniel 7:23-25)

The beast will arise after the kingdom of the ten nations or ten kingdoms have been set up. The beast will not tolerate any resistance to his reign and will subdue three kings as the prophet Daniel foretells. The beast will be a blasphemer as he will speak great words against the Creator of all things. He will even dare to change the times and the laws. This may indicate that he may even dare to change the calendar of the world. For example, the year 2017 represents 2017 years of our Lord Jesus Christ. He may desire to change the calendars of the world to his birth date.

The antichrist scatters the nation of Israel as revealed also in Daniel:

The Two Witnesses

⁷ And I heard the man clothed in linen, which was upon the waters of the river, when he held up his right hand and his left hand unto heaven, and sware by him that liveth for ever that it shall be for a time, times, and an half; and when he shall have accomplished to scatter the power of the holy people, all these things shall be finished. (Daniel 12:7)

The breaking of the covenant with the nation of Israel says much about the true character of the antichrist, indicating that he is a man who cannot be trusted. It is from the Book of Daniel that we see the characteristics of the antichrist. There certainly is a prophetic and historical connection between the three-and-a-half years of the temple-defiling antics of Antiochus Epiphanes IV and the 42 months of Revelation 11:1-2, where the antichrist sets up an image in the rebuilt Jewish Temple just as Antiochus Epiphanes did earlier in history.

There is a resemblance which is also obvious between the function of the two witnesses of chapter 11 and during the time of the Maccabees, particularly Eliezer and Yehuda as they resisted the Temple-defiling antics of Antiochus Epiphanes IV. Just as two of the Maccabees were martyred for their efforts opposing the satanic defilement of the Temple, the two witnesses of chapter 11 will be martyred for opposing the antichrist. The Maccabean and Hanukkah connection from Daniel's prophecies (Daniel 8:9-14), the teachings of Jesus in the Olivet Discourse and John 10 where Jesus came to Jerusalem for the Feast of Dedication in the winter, have for too long been all but ignored.

From the Book of Daniel we learn that the abomination of desolation will last 1,290 days and that Jesus will return to judge the nations:

¹¹ And from the time that the daily sacrifice shall be taken away, and the abomination that maketh desolate set up, there shall be a thousand two hundred and ninety days. ¹² Blessed is he that waiteth, and cometh to the thousand three hundred and five and thirty days. (Daniel 12:11-12)

Following the period of 1,290 days there will be a period of 45 days which will see the judgment of the nations to determine who is worthy to enter into the kingdom age. Jesus will return as King and there will be a 45-day judgment period known as the "judgment of the sheep and goats" as described in Matthew 25. Surviving until the end of the seventieth week of Daniel does not guarantee that someone will be granted permission to enter the 1,000-year reign of Jesus Christ after He returns. Anyone who has the mark of the beast will not be able to enter into the 1,000-year kingdom.

Revelation

Instead, they will be sent to the everlasting fire that was prepared for the Devil and his angels. Those who were merciful to the Jews as noted in Matthew 25 will be granted permission to enter the 1,000-year kingdom.

Revelation 11:3-12
The Two Witnesses

And I will give power unto my two witnesses, and they shall prophesy a thousand two hundred and threescore days, clothed in sackcloth. These are the two olive trees, and the two candlesticks standing before the God of the earth. And if any man will hurt them, fire proceedeth out of their mouth, and devoureth their enemies: and if any man will hurt them, he must in this manner be killed. These have power to shut heaven, that it rain not in the days of their prophecy: and have power over waters to turn them to blood, and to smite the earth with all plagues, as often as they will. And when they shall have finished their testimony, the beast that ascendeth out of the bottomless pit shall make war against them, and shall overcome them, and kill them. And their dead bodies shall lie in the street of the great city, which spiritually is called Sodom and Egypt, where also our Lord was crucified. And they of the people and kindreds and tongues and nations shall see their dead bodies three days and an half, and shall not suffer their dead bodies to be put in graves. And they that dwell upon the earth shall rejoice over them, and make merry, and shall send gifts one to another; because these two prophets tormented them that dwelt on the earth. And after three days and an half the spirit of life from God entered into them, and they stood upon their feet; and great fear fell upon them which saw them. And they heard a great voice from heaven saying unto them, Come up hither. And they ascended up to heaven in a cloud; and their enemies beheld them.

The two olive trees are symbolic and are mentioned in the Book of Zechariah. In the time of Zechariah and Zerubbabel, as the restoration of the Temple began Zerubbabel was one of the two olive trees in Zechariah's vision:

¹And the angel that talked with me came again, and waked me, as a man that is wakened out of his sleep. ² And said unto me, What seest thou? And I said, I have looked, and behold a candlestick all of gold, with a bowl upon the top of it, and his seven lamps thereon, and seven pipes to the seven lamps, which are upon the top thereof: ³ And two olive trees by it, one upon the right side of the bowl, and the other upon the left side thereof. ⁴ So I answered and spake to the angel that talked with me, saying, What are these, my lord? ⁵ Then the angel that talked with me answered and said unto me, Knowest thou not what these be? And I said, No, my lord. ⁶ Then he answered and spake unto me, saying, This is the word of the LORD unto

The Two Witnesses

Zerubbabel, saying, Not by might, nor by power, but by my spirit, saith the LORD of hosts. (Zechariah 4:1-6)

The two witnesses in the vision of Zechariah will be anointed and empowered by the Holy Spirit during the days of their prophecy. According to the Scriptures, Elijah will be one of the two witnesses as revealed in Malachi:

⁵ Behold, I will send you Elijah the prophet before the coming of the great and dreadful day of the LORD: ⁶ And he shall turn the heart of the fathers to the children, and the heart of the children to their fathers, lest I come and smite the earth with a curse. (Malachi 4:5-6)

Malachi's prophecy reveals two important truths. First is that Elijah is one of the two witnesses. The second is that Elijah will return before the Day of the Lord. Since the Day of the Lord commences after the harpazo, the two witnesses may be upon the earth at the time when the Lord Jesus comes for His church. This concludes that the Day of the Lord will begin sometime after the beginning of the seventieth week of Daniel. This also provides strong scriptural support that the harpazo will occur during the seventieth week of Daniel and not before.

Our Lord Jesus revealed that Elijah was on the earth during the time of His first coming and that John the Baptist came in the same spirit as Elijah – heralding the coming of the Messiah. Elijah will return to the earth as one of the two witnesses to herald His second coming (Malachi 4:5-6).

¹ Behold, I will send my messenger, and he shall prepare the way before me: and the LORD, whom ye seek, shall suddenly come to his temple, even the messenger of the covenant, whom ye delight in: behold, he shall come, saith the LORD of hosts. ² But who may abide the day of his coming? And who shall stand when he appeareth? for he is like a refiner's fire, and like fullers' soap: ³ And he shall sit as a refiner and purifier of silver: and he shall purify the sons of Levi, and purge them as gold and silver, that they may offer unto the LORD an offering in righteousness. ⁴ Then shall the offering of Judah and Jerusalem be pleasant unto the LORD, as in the days of old, and as in former years. ⁵ And I will come near to you to judgment; and I will be a swift witness against the sorcerers, and against the adulterers, and against false swearers, and against those that oppress the hireling in his wages, the widow, and the fatherless, and that turn aside the stranger from his right, and fear not me, saith the LORD of hosts. ⁶ For I am the LORD, I change not; therefore ye sons of Jacob are not consumed. (Malachi 3:1-6)

Revelation

¹³ For all the prophets and the law prophesied until John. ¹⁴ And if ye will receive it, this is Elias, which was for to come. (Matthew 11:13-14)

¹⁰ And his disciples asked him, saying, Why then say the scribes that Elias must first come? ¹¹ And Jesus answered and said unto them, Elias truly shall first come, and restore all things. ¹² But I say unto you, That Elias is come already, and they knew him not, but have done unto him whatsoever they listed. Likewise shall also the Son of man suffer of them. ¹³ Then the disciples understood that he spake unto them of John the Baptist. (Matthew 17:10-13)

Elias is the old King James word for Elijah. The Lord Jesus declared that Elijah did indeed return to the earth the second time as recorded in Malachi. The Lord has a special ministry for the prophet Elijah. When Elijah was upon the earth he prayed that it would not rain for three-and-a-half years and there was no rain upon the land of Israel for three and a half years. In addition to having power over the rain, these witnesses can call fire down from heaven, similar to what Elijah did when he walked upon the earth.

¹And Elijah the Tishbite, who was of the inhabitants of Gilead, said unto Ahab, As the LORD God of Israel liveth, before whom I stand, there shall not be dew nor rain these years, but according to my word. (I Kings 17:1)

¹⁷ Elias was a man subject to like passions as we are, and he prayed earnestly that it might not rain: and it rained not on the earth by the space of three years and six months. (James 5:17)

⁶ And they said unto him, There came a man up to meet us, and said unto us, Go, turn again unto the king that sent you, and say unto him, Thus saith the LORD, Is it not because there is not a God in Israel, that thou sendest to enquire of Baalzebub the god of Ekron? therefore thou shalt not come down from that bed on which thou art gone up, but shalt surely die. ⁷ And he said unto them, What manner of man was he which came up to meet you, and told you these words? ⁸ And they answered him, He was an hairy man, and girt with a girdle of leather about his loins. And he said, It is Elijah the Tishbite. ⁹ Then the king sent unto him a captain of fifty with his fifty. And he went up to him: and, behold, he sat on the top of an hill. And he spake unto him, Thou man of God, the king hath said, Come down. ¹⁰ And Elijah answered and said to the captain of fifty, If I be a man of God, then let fire come down from heaven, and consume thee and thy fifty. And there came down fire from heaven, and consumed him and his fifty. ¹¹ Again also he sent unto him another captain of fifty with his fifty. And he answered and said unto him, O man of God, thus hath the king said, Come down quickly. ¹² And Elijah answered and said unto them, If I be a man of God, let fire

The Two Witnesses

come down from heaven, and consume thee and thy fifty. And the fire of God came down from heaven, and consumed him and his fifty. (II Kings 1:6-12)

It is very clear from the Scriptures that Elijah will be one of the two witnesses. There has been much debate as to the identity of the second witness. Will John the apostle be the other witness as some Bible scholars suggest because of Revelation 10:11? Did John fulfill this prophecy when he came back to the earth? If it is not John, then some other options are Moses, Enoch, or someone else. If John is one of the 24 elders around the Throne in Revelation 4 and Revelation 5, then he cannot be one of the two witnesses.

The beast mentioned in Revelation 11 is from the bottomless pit. The opening of the pit commences with the Fifth Trumpet judgment. He ascends out of the bottomless pit along with the demon locusts. Until the ministry of the two witnesses is complete, they cannot be harmed by the beast or by man.

The 1,260 days is the duration of the time that the two witnesses will be preaching and witnessing upon the earth, but the start of their ministry is not provided. Their ministry is finished after the announcement of the Sixth Trumpet, sometime during the seventieth week of Daniel. It is clear that the time of their testimony covers some of the first three-and-a-half years and part of the second three and a half years. The starting point of their ministry cannot be the first day of the seventieth week of Daniel as some Bible scholars believe. The two witnesses are martyred in the second half of the seventieth week of Daniel after the commencement of the Sixth Trumpet judgment. This clearly indicates that their death occurs many months into the second half of the seventieth week of Daniel. Their ministry starts before the Day of the Lord, which immediately follows the harpazo (Malachi 4:5). Many Bible scholars believe that the two witnesses may be upon the earth before Christ comes for His church.

The ministry of the two witnesses covers 1,260 days. They are martyred after the start of the Sixth Trumpet which is in the second half of the three-and-a-half years of the seventieth week of Daniel. The starting point of the ministry of the two witnesses will be at least five months (most likely more) after the start of the seventieth week of Daniel. Since the Day of the Lord follows the harpazo, there must be a time period of at least five months from the starting point of the seventieth week of Daniel until the Day of the Lord. For those who believe that the harpazo will occur Before the First Seal is opened, they must accept that it would be at least five months from the start of the seventieth week of Daniel until the First Seal is opened.

Revelation

When the time of the two witnesses' ministry is completed, the beast will have the authority to kill them. However, the world will not allow their dead bodies to be placed into the ground. The people of the world will desire to gloat over their dead bodies for a time. The entire world will see their dead bodies for three-and-a-half days. This could not be possible without the technology of today, such as the Internet, cell phones and television. With today's technology the entire world will be watching this event and quite possibly replaying the death of these two witnesses by the hand of the beast. Their broadcast will be interrupted when the Lord brings the two witnesses back to life and they ascend into heaven.

Below is a graph illustrating the 1,260 days of the ministry of the two witnesses.

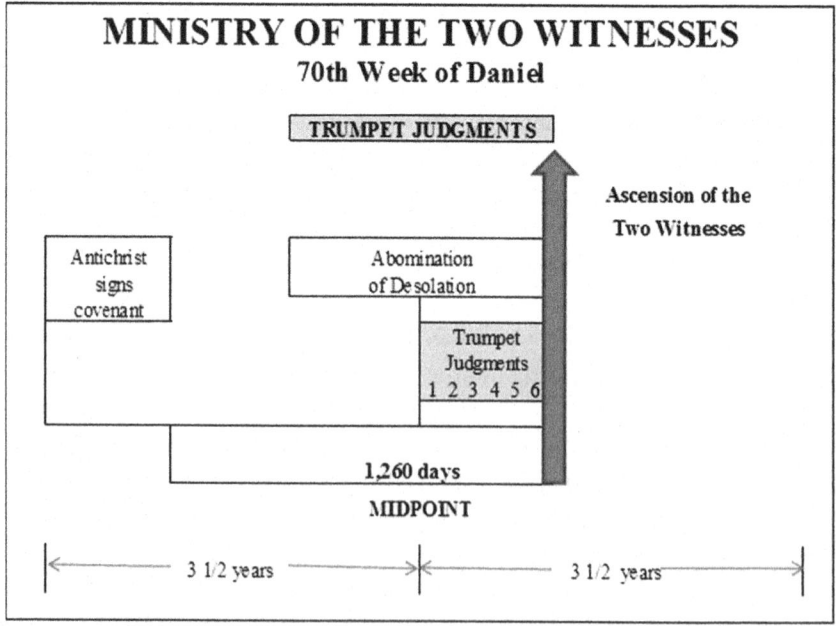

The power behind the beast is Satan or Lucifer. Lucifer was the covering cherub as revealed in Ezekiel:

[11] *Moreover the word of the LORD came unto me, saying,* [12] *Son of man, take up a lamentation upon the king of Tyrus, and say unto him, Thus saith the Lord GOD; Thou sealest up the sum, full of wisdom, and perfect in beauty.* [13] *Thou hast been in Eden the garden of God; every precious stone was thy covering, the sardius, topaz, and the diamond, the beryl, the onyx, and the jasper, the sapphire, the emerald,*

*and the carbuncle, and gold: the workmanship of thy tabrets and of thy pipes was prepared in thee in the day that thou wast created. *[14]* Thou art the anointed cherub that covereth; and I have set thee so: thou wast upon the holy mountain of God; thou hast walked up and down in the midst of the stones of fire. *[15]* Thou wast perfect in thy ways from the day that thou wast created, till iniquity was found in thee. *[16]* By the multitude of thy merchandise they have filled the midst of thee with violence, and thou hast sinned: therefore I will cast thee as profane out of the mountain of God: and I will destroy thee, O covering cherub, from the midst of the stones of fire. *[17]* Thine heart was lifted up because of thy beauty, thou hast corrupted thy wisdom by reason of thy brightness: I will cast thee to the ground, I will lay thee before kings, that they may behold thee.* (Ezekiel 28:11-17)

Lucifer was called the anointed cherub and had a unique ministry for the God of heaven. He spoke for God to the universe. He took the worship of the universe to God as a priest. This was a powerful and unique ministry. Satan's sin and fall is described in Isaiah:

[12] How art thou fallen from heaven, O Lucifer, son of the morning! How art thou cut down to the ground, which didst weaken the nations! [13] For thou hast said in thine heart, I will ascend into heaven, I will exalt my throne above the stars of God: I will sit also upon the mount of the congregation, in the sides of the north: [14] I will ascend above the heights of the clouds; I will be like the most High. [15] Yet thou shalt be brought down to hell, to the sides of the pit. (Isaiah 14:12-15)

Lucifer desired to be like the Most High. He wanted to sit on God's Throne and exalt himself. Just as Lucifer desired to overthrow the Father, the beast will desire to overthrow the two witnesses and anyone who has the testimony of Jesus Christ. The antichrist, just like Lucifer, will battle God and his armies. This battle is foretold in the Psalms:

[1]Why do the heathen rage, and the people imagine a vain thing? [2] The kings of the earth set themselves, and the rulers take counsel together, against the LORD, and against his anointed, saying, [3] Let us break their bands asunder, and cast away their cords from us. [4] He that sitteth in the heavens shall laugh: the LORD shall have them in derision. [5] Then shall he speak unto them in his wrath, and vex them in his sore displeasure. (Psalm 2:1-5)

The antichrist will be guilty of the same sin—the belief that the God of heaven can be defeated and that Lucifer would be a better ruler over the universe. After the beast has defeated the two witnesses, he will persuade men of the world that they can defeat God with the technology of man. This was the sin of Lucifer and this will be the sin of the antichrist when he is empowered by Lucifer.

Revelation 11:13-19
The Seventh Trumpet is About to Sound

And the same hour was there a great earthquake, and the tenth part of the city fell, and in the earthquake were slain of men seven thousand: and the remnant were affrighted, and gave glory to the God of heaven. The second woe is past; and, behold, the third woe cometh quickly. And the seventh angel sounded; and there were great voices in heaven, saying, The kingdoms of this world are become the kingdoms of our Lord, and of his Christ; and he shall reign for ever and ever. And the four and twenty elders, which sat before God on their seats, fell upon their faces, and worshipped God, Saying, We give thee thanks, O LORD God Almighty, which art, and wast, and art to come; because thou hast taken to thee thy great power, and hast reigned. And the nations were angry, and thy wrath is come, and the time of the dead, that they should be judged, and that thou shouldest give reward unto thy servants the prophets, and to the saints, and them that fear thy name, small and great; and shouldest destroy them which destroy the earth. And the temple of God was opened in heaven, and there was seen in his temple the ark of his testament: and there were lightnings, and voices, and thunderings, and an earthquake, and great hail.

Even at this late stage in the seventieth week of Daniel there are people who will recognize that the resurrection of the two witnesses was of the Lord. There is a remnant that will praise Him (Revelation 11:13).

The Seventh Trumpet sounds in Revelation 11:15. The Trumpet signifies that the wrath (*orge*) of God is to continue. *Orge* means punishment, anger, and it is the same Greek word that is used in the Sixth Seal judgment to signify the wrath of the Lamb has come. There is great rejoicing in heaven when the Seventh Trumpet sounds. Soon the Father and the Son will reign forever and ever. Satan's reign as the prince of this world is coming to a close. The dead will soon be judged. The righteous will receive rewards.

The Seventh Trumpet is not to be confused with the last trump of God which signifies the harpazo of the church. As we learned earlier, the church is not destined to the Sixth Seal.

The Temple of God is opened and all see the Ark within the heavenly tabernacle. Now the world will see from where the *thumos* of God is originating.

Chapter 12

War In Heaven

Revelation 12:1-2
Israel, the Woman Clothed With the Sun

And there appeared a great wonder in heaven; a woman clothed with the sun, and the moon under her feet, and upon her head a crown of twelve stars: And she being with child cried, travailing in birth, and pained to be delivered.

THE WOMAN DESCRIBED in Revelation 12:1-2 is not the Virgin Mary. The woman is not the church; the church is the virgin bride of Christ. This woman is pregnant and therefore she cannot represent the church, the virgin bride of Christ. It is clear that this woman represents the nation of Israel as revealed in Genesis 37:9-11:

> ⁹ *And he dreamed yet another dream, and told it his brethren, and said, Behold, I have dreamed a dream more; and, behold, the sun and the moon and the eleven stars made obeisance to me.* ¹⁰ *And he told it to his father, and to his brethren: and his father rebuked him, and said unto him, What is this dream that thou hast dreamed? Shall I and thy mother and thy brethren indeed come to bow down ourselves to thee to the earth?* ¹¹ *And his brethren envied him; but his father observed the saying.* (Genesis 37:9-11)

The woman does indeed appear to represent the nation of Israel especially with the description of the woman within the rest of chapter 12.

Revelation

Revelation 12:3-6
Satan and His Persecution of Israel

And there appeared another wonder in heaven; and behold a great red dragon, having seven heads and ten horns, and seven crowns upon his heads. And his tail drew the third part of the stars of heaven, and did cast them to the earth: and the dragon stood before the woman which was ready to be delivered, for to devour her child as soon as it was born. And she brought forth a man child, who was to rule all nations with a rod of iron: and her child was caught up unto God, and to his throne. And the woman fled into the wilderness, where she hath a place prepared of God, that they should feed her there a thousand two hundred and threescore days.

Satan is described as having seven heads, ten horns and seven crowns on his heads. The antichrist in Revelation 13 is described as having seven heads and ten horns, but having ten crowns upon his horns. The crowns on his seven heads show Satan's power and authority over the major empires of the world. The heads represent the empires of world history. The ten kings or kingdoms ruling over the earth during the seventieth week of Daniel represent the seventh empire (the seventh head). The beast that ascends out of the bottomless pit is the eighth king as noted in Revelation 17:

⁷ And the angel said unto me, Wherefore didst thou marvel? I will tell thee the mystery of the woman, and of the beast that carrieth her, which hath the seven heads and ten horns. ⁸ The beast that thou sawest was, and is not; and shall ascend out of the bottomless pit, and go into perdition: and they that dwell on the earth shall wonder, whose names were not written in the book of life from the foundation of the world, when they behold the beast that was, and is not, and yet is. ⁹ And here is the mind which hath wisdom. The seven heads are seven mountains, on which the woman sitteth. ¹⁰ And there are seven kings: five are fallen, and one is, and the other is not yet come; and when he cometh, he must continue a short space. ¹¹ And the beast that was, and is not, even he is the eighth, and is of the seven, and goeth into perdition. ¹² And the ten horns which thou sawest are ten kings, which have received no kingdom as yet; but receive power as kings one hour with the beast. ¹³ These have one mind, and shall give their power and strength unto the beast. (Revelation 17:7-13)

Angels are often referred to as stars in the Scriptures. Satan was able to persuade a third of the angels to follow him in his rebellion. They were removed from heaven and now dwell upon the earth, but apparently they have visiting privileges to heaven as noted in the Book of Job:

⁶ Now there was a day when the sons of God came to present themselves before the LORD, and Satan came also among them. ⁷ And the LORD said unto Satan,

War in Heaven

Whence comest thou? Then Satan answered the LORD, *and said, From going to and fro in the earth, and from walking up and down in it.* ⁸ *And the* LORD *said unto Satan, Hast thou considered my servant Job, that there is none like him in the earth, a perfect and an upright man, one that feareth God, and escheweth evil?* ⁹ *Then Satan answered the* LORD, *and said, Doth Job fear God for nought?* ¹⁰ *Hast not thou made an hedge about him, and about his house, and about all that he hath on every side? Thou hast blessed the work of his hands, and his substance is increased in the land.* ¹¹ *But put forth thine hand now, and touch all that he hath, and he will curse thee to thy face.* ¹² *And the* LORD *said unto Satan, Behold, all that he hath is in thy power; only upon himself put not forth thine hand. So Satan went forth from the presence of the* LORD. (Job 1:6-12)

We can see that even Satan has to obey the Lord. Satan had a limitation put on him. He was permitted at this time to touch Job's possessions, but could not touch Job.

Just as King Saul tried to kill David, the rightful king, Satan has tried to kill the Messiah (using King Herod). Satan has also persecuted the Jews in an attempt to prevent the prophecies of the Old Testament from being fulfilled. One of Satan's goals is to eliminate the Jews as a race, thus preventing the fulfillment of the prophecy of Jesus returning to the earth, reigning as King and sitting upon the throne of David. Satan will once again try to exterminate the Jews when the abomination of desolation is set up. The Jews will reject the claim of the antichrist that he is God. Their eyes will be opened to the deception of this man as recorded in Matthew 24.

Revelation 12:3-5 are historical and have already been fulfilled. Revelation 12:6 is destined for the future once the abomination is set up and the Jews realize that they have been deceived by the antichrist.

Revelation 12:7-12
Expulsion of Satan from Heaven

And there was war in heaven: Michael and his angels fought against the dragon; and the dragon fought and his angels, and prevailed not; neither was their place found any more in heaven. And the great dragon was cast out, that old serpent, called the Devil, and Satan, which deceiveth the whole world: he was cast out into the earth, and his angels were cast out with him. And I heard a loud voice saying in heaven, now is come salvation, and strength, and the kingdom of our God, and the power of his Christ: for the accuser of our brethren is cast down, which accused them before our God day and night. And they overcame him by the blood of the Lamb, and by the word of their testimony; and they loved not their lives unto the death. Therefore

Revelation

rejoice, ye heavens, and ye that dwell in them. Woe to the inhabiters of the earth and of the sea! For the devil is come down unto you, having great wrath, because he knoweth that he hath but a short time.

Satan and his angels have been removed from dwelling in heaven as noted in Ezekiel:

¹² Son of man, take up a lamentation upon the king of Tyrus, and say unto him, Thus saith the Lord GOD; Thou sealest up the sum, full of wisdom, and perfect in beauty. ¹³ Thou hast been in Eden the garden of God; every precious stone was thy covering, the sardius, topaz, and the diamond, the beryl, the onyx, and the jasper, the sapphire, the emerald, and the carbuncle, and gold: the workmanship of thy tabrets and of thy pipes was prepared in thee in the day that thou wast created. ¹⁴ Thou art the anointed cherub that covereth; and I have set thee so: thou wast upon the holy mountain of God; thou hast walked up and down in the midst of the stones of fire. ¹⁵ Thou wast perfect in thy ways from the day that thou wast created, till iniquity was found in thee. ¹⁶ By the multitude of thy merchandise they have filled the midst of thee with violence, and thou hast sinned: therefore I will cast thee as profane out of the mountain of God: and I will destroy thee, O covering cherub, from the midst of the stones of fire. ¹⁷ Thine heart was lifted up because of thy beauty, thou hast corrupted thy wisdom by reason of thy brightness: I will cast thee to the ground, I will lay thee before kings, that they may behold thee. (Ezekiel 28:12-17)

The day is coming when Satan and his angels will be thrown out of heaven and all visiting rights will be revoked. There is no Scripture to show that Satan has ever been to hell, nor does he rule there:

¹² How art thou fallen from heaven, O Lucifer, son of the morning! How art thou cut down to the ground, which didst weaken the nations! ¹³ For thou hast said in thine heart, I will ascend into heaven, I will exalt my throne above the stars of God: I will sit also upon the mount of the congregation, in the sides of the north: ¹⁴ I will ascend above the heights of the clouds; I will be like the most High. ¹⁵ Yet thou shalt be brought down to hell, to the sides of the pit. (Isaiah 14:12-15)

Daniel 12 speaks of the day when the battle in the heavens will take place:

¹ And at that time shall Michael stand up, the great prince which standeth for the children of thy people: and there shall be a time of trouble, such as never was since there was a nation even to that same time: and at that time thy people shall be delivered, every one that shall be found written in the book. ² And many of them that sleep in the dust of the earth shall awake, some to everlasting life, and some to shame and everlasting contempt. (Daniel 12:1-2)

War in Heaven

The event of Satan and his angels being cast out of heaven for good takes place at the Sixth Seal judgment as noted in Revelation 6:

12 And I beheld when he had opened the sixth seal, and, lo, there was a great earthquake; and the sun became black as sackcloth of hair, and the moon became as blood; 13 And the stars of heaven fell unto the earth, even as a fig tree casteth her untimely figs, when she is shaken of a mighty wind. (Revelation 6:12-13)

The stars of heaven falling to the earth are symbolic of Satan and his angels being cast out of heaven. This event is tied to the Sixth Seal. The root sin of Satan was pride, as his heart was lifted up with his desire to be like God and to sit on His throne. Pride is the root of all sin as it leads to rebellion against the Lord God Almighty.

Satan is a defeated enemy. Our Lord Jesus has won the victory. Those who belong to Jesus are victorious as declared elsewhere in the New Testament:

38 For I am persuaded, that neither death, nor life, nor angels, nor principalities, nor powers, nor things present, nor things to come, 39 Nor height, nor depth, nor any other creature, shall be able to separate us from the love of God, which is in Christ Jesus our Lord. (Romans 8:38-39)

8 He that committeth sin is of the devil; for the devil sinneth from the beginning. For this purpose the Son of God was manifested, that he might destroy the works of the devil. (I John 3:8)

14 Forasmuch then as the children are partakers of flesh and blood, he also himself likewise took part of the same; that through death he might destroy him that had the power of death, that is, the devil. (Hebrews 2:14)

25 Wherefore he is able also to save them to the uttermost that come unto God by him, seeing he ever liveth to make intercession for them. (Hebrews 7:25)

Satan was defeated by the blood of the Lamb. The Lord Jesus paid the price by shedding His own blood to defeat Satan and his attempt to destroy mankind. God has completed His part and now the children of God are called upon to do their part. The saints of God overcome Satan and eternal death by the word of their testimony and by their desire for death over love for their lives. The saints display to the lost world that they are different by the word of their testimony that Jesus Christ is the Son of God and is coming back again.

Today the children of God are in a spiritual warfare as they wrestle against Satan and his forces while living on the earth in this body of flesh.

Revelation

In order to overcome the evil ones, the children of God will need spiritual weapons to overcome Satan and his angels. Man-made weapons will not work as noted in Ephesians:

¹² For we wrestle not against flesh and blood, but against principalities, against powers, against the rulers of the darkness of this world, against spiritual wickedness in high places. ¹³ Wherefore take unto you the whole armour of God, that ye may be able to withstand in the evil day, and having done all, to stand. ¹⁴ Stand therefore, having your loins girt about with truth, and having on the breastplate of righteousness; ¹⁵ and your feet shod with the preparation of the gospel of peace; ¹⁶ Above all, taking the shield of faith, wherewith ye shall be able to quench all the fiery darts of the wicked. ¹⁷ And take the helmet of salvation, and the sword of the Spirit, which is the word of God: ¹⁸ Praying always with all prayer and supplication in the Spirit, and watching thereunto with all perseverance and supplication for all saints. (Ephesians 6:12-18)

The children of God will need to put on all of the armor of God to stand against an enemy that cannot be seen with physical eyes. One cannot go into battle with only a few pieces of armor and expect to come out of the battle victorious.

It is interesting to note that the first time the Greek word *thumos* is mentioned in Revelation is in verse 12. Satan knows his time is short and he is filled with intense rage against all humanity. It is here that Satan is filled with great wrath, and he will begin to persecute the Jews. This event appears to be tied to the start of the Great Tribulation period.

Revelation 12:13-17
Satan's Wrath Against the Jews and Those Who Have the Testimony of Jesus

And when the dragon saw that he was cast unto the earth, he persecuted the woman which brought forth the man child. And to the woman were given two wings of a great eagle, that she might fly into the wilderness, into her place, where she is nourished for a time, and times, and half a time, from the face of the serpent. And the serpent cast out of his mouth water as a flood after the woman, that he might cause her to be carried away of the flood. And the earth helped the woman, and the earth opened her mouth, and swallowed up the flood which the dragon cast out of his mouth. And the dragon was wroth with the woman, and went to make war with the remnant of her seed, which keep the commandments of God, and have the testimony of Jesus Christ.

War in Heaven

Satan, in his great wrath, will persecute the Jews for three-and-a-half years and will attempt to exterminate them as a race as Jesus prophesied would happen:

15 When ye therefore shall see the abomination of desolation, spoken of by Daniel the prophet, stand in the holy place, (whoso readeth, let him understand:) 16 Then let them which be in Judaea flee into the mountains: 17 Let him which is on the housetop not come down to take any thing out of his house: 18 Neither let him which is in the field return back to take his clothes. 19 And woe unto them that are with child, and to them that give suck in those days! 20 But pray ye that your flight be not in the winter, neither on the sabbath day: 21 For then shall be great tribulation, such as was not since the beginning of the world to this time, no, nor ever shall be. 22 And except those days should be shortened, there should no flesh be saved: but for the elect's sake those days shall be shortened. (Matthew 24:15-22)

20 And when ye shall see Jerusalem compassed with armies, then know that the desolation thereof is nigh. 21 Then let them which are in Judaea flee to the mountains; and let them which are in the midst of it depart out; and let not them that are in the countries enter thereinto. 22 For these be the days of vengeance, that all things which are written may be fulfilled. 23 But woe unto them that are with child, and to them that give suck, in those days! For there shall be great distress in the land, and wrath upon this people. 24 And they shall fall by the edge of the sword, and shall be led away captive into all nations: and Jerusalem shall be trodden down of the Gentiles, until the times of the Gentiles be fulfilled. (Luke 21:20-24)

What happened in the past will be played out again in the future. Satan has tried to exterminate the Jews many times throughout history. A recent attempt was by Adolf Hitler and Nazi Germany. Today, many Middle East nations that surround Israel have tried, and will continue to try, to destroy all the Jews they can. Ultimately, Satan will use the antichrist in the final attempt to exterminate the Jews. The persecution that the Jews will receive from the beast will be greater than the persecution they experienced from Nazi Germany, and it will be worldwide as prophesied in Daniel:

9 And out of one of them came forth a little horn, which waxed exceeding great, toward the south, and toward the east, and toward the pleasant land. 10 And it waxed great, even to the host of heaven; and it cast down some of the host and of the stars to the ground, and stamped upon them. 11 Yea, he magnified himself even to the prince of the host, and by him the daily sacrifice was taken away, and the place of the sanctuary was cast down. 12 And an host was given him against the daily sacrifice

Revelation

by reason of transgression, and it cast down the truth to the ground; and it practised, and prospered. (Daniel 8:9-12)

²⁷ And he shall confirm the covenant with many for one week: and in the midst of the week he shall cause the sacrifice and the oblation to cease, and for the overspreading of abominations he shall make it desolate, even until the consummation, and that determined shall be poured upon the desolate. (Daniel 9:27)

The antichrist will rule and devour the whole earth as revealed in Daniel. He will set up himself as God and persecute all who oppose him. He will be a conquering king, and his conquests are noted in Daniel 11, but the lands of Edom, Moab, and Ammon will escape out of his hand:

³⁶ And the king shall do according to his will; and he shall exalt himself, and magnify himself above every god, and shall speak marvellous things against the God of gods, and shall prosper till the indignation be accomplished: for that that is determined shall be done. ³⁷ Neither shall he regard the God of his fathers, nor the desire of women, nor regard any god: for he shall magnify himself above all. ³⁸ But in his estate shall he honour the God of forces: and a god whom his fathers knew not shall he honour with gold, and silver, and with precious stones, and pleasant things. ³⁹ Thus shall he do in the most strong holds with a strange god, whom he shall acknowledge and increase with glory: and he shall cause them to rule over many, and shall divide the land for gain. ⁴⁰ And at the time of the end shall the king of the south push at him: and the king of the north shall come against him like a whirlwind, with chariots, and with horsemen, and with many ships; and he shall enter into the countries, and shall overflow and pass over. ⁴¹ He shall enter also into the glorious land, and many countries shall be overthrown: but these shall escape out of his hand, even Edom, and Moab, and the chief of the children of Ammon. ⁴² He shall stretch forth his hand also upon the countries: and the land of Egypt shall not escape. ⁴³ But he shall have power over the treasures of gold and of silver, and over all the precious things of Egypt: and the Libyans and the Ethiopians shall be at his steps. ⁴⁴ But tidings out of the east and out of the north shall trouble him: therefore he shall go forth with great fury to destroy, and utterly to make away many. ⁴⁵ And he shall plant the tabernacles of his palace between the seas in the glorious holy mountain; yet he shall come to his end, and none shall help him. (Daniel 11:36-45)

The antichrist will prosper until all that the Lord has determined will be accomplished. It will be a horrible time on the earth as evil will have a license to prosper for seven years. The last three-and-a-half years will be the most dreadful as the wrath of the Lamb will begin. It will be a time of Great Tribulation for the Jews and all who oppose the antichrist.

Chapter 13

The Two Beasts

Revelation 13:1-10
The Beast

And I stood upon the sand of the sea, and saw a beast rise up out of the sea, having seven heads and ten horns, and upon his horns ten crowns, and upon his heads the name of blasphemy. And the beast which I saw was like unto a leopard, and his feet were as the feet of a bear, and his mouth as the mouth of a lion: and the dragon gave him his power, and his seat, and great authority. And I saw one of his heads as it were wounded to death; and his deadly wound was healed: and all the world wondered after the beast. And they worshipped the dragon which gave power unto the beast: and they worshipped the beast, saying, Who is like unto the beast? Who is able to make war with him? And there was given unto him a mouth speaking great things and blasphemies; and power was given unto him to continue forty and two months. And he opened his mouth in blasphemy against God, to blaspheme his name, and his tabernacle, and them that dwell in heaven. And it was given unto him to make war with the saints, and to overcome them: and power was given him over all kindreds, and tongues, and nations. And all that dwell upon the earth shall worship him, whose names are not written in the book of life of the Lamb slain from the foundation of the world. If any man have an ear, let him hear. He that leadeth into captivity shall go into captivity: he that killeth with the sword must be killed with the sword. Here is the patience and the faith of the saints.

Revelation

SATAN, CAST OUT of heaven, looks for an instrument through whom he can carry on his warfare against his Creator. Satan finds a man among the nations as first noted in Daniel 2:31-45. The symbols of the seven heads and the ten horns are described in the Book of Daniel. The Book of Daniel reveals much concerning the antichrist and the kingdom that will rule the world in the last days. The kingdom of the antichrist will have the boldness of a lion, the crushing power of a bear, and the swiftness of a leopard, and we see this in the Book of Daniel:

² Daniel spake and said, I saw in my vision by night, and, behold, the four winds of the heaven strove upon the great sea. ³ And four great beasts came up from the sea, diverse one from another. ⁴ The first was like a lion, and had eagle's wings: I beheld till the wings thereof were plucked, and it was lifted up from the earth, and made stand upon the feet as a man, and a man's heart was given to it. ⁵ And behold another beast, a second, like to a bear, and it raised up itself on one side, and it had three ribs in the mouth of it between the teeth of it: and they said thus unto it, Arise, devour much flesh. ⁶ After this I beheld, and lo another, like a leopard, which had upon the back of it four wings of a fowl; the beast had also four heads; and dominion was given to it. ⁷ After this I saw in the night visions, and behold a fourth beast, dreadful and terrible, and strong exceedingly; and it had great iron teeth: it devoured and brake in pieces, and stamped the residue with the feet of it: and it was diverse from all the beasts that were before it; and it had ten horns. ⁸ I considered the horns, and, behold, there came up among them another little horn, before whom there were three of the first horns plucked up by the roots: and, behold, in this horn were eyes like the eyes of man, and a mouth speaking great things. (Daniel 7:2-8)

¹⁷ These great beasts, which are four, are four kings, which shall arise out of the earth. ¹⁸ But the saints of the most High shall take the kingdom, and possess the kingdom for ever, even for ever and ever. ¹⁹ Then I would know the truth of the fourth beast, which was diverse from all the others, exceeding dreadful, whose teeth were of iron, and his nails of brass; which devoured, brake in pieces, and stamped the residue with his feet; ²⁰ And of the ten horns that were in his head, and of the other which came up, and before whom three fell; even of that horn that had eyes, and a mouth that spake very great things, whose look was more stout than his fellows. ²¹ I beheld, and the same horn made war with the saints, and prevailed against them; ²² Until the Ancient of days came, and judgment was given to the saints of the most High; and the time came that the saints possessed the kingdom. ²³ Thus he said, The fourth beast shall be the fourth kingdom upon earth, which shall be diverse from all kingdoms, and shall devour the whole earth, and shall tread it down, and break it in pieces. ²⁴ And the ten horns out of this kingdom are ten kings that shall arise: and another

The Two Beasts

shall rise after them; and he shall be diverse from the first, and he shall subdue three kings. ²⁵ And he shall speak great words against the most High, and shall wear out the saints of the most High, and think to change times and laws: and they shall be given into his hand until a time and times and the dividing of time. ²⁶ But the judgment shall sit, and they shall take away his dominion, to consume and to destroy it unto the end. (Daniel 7:17-26)

The Lord showed to Daniel the empires that would arise and rule the world. Bible scholars agree that the first beast representing the lion was Babylon. The second beast representing the bear was the kingdom of the Medes and Persians which conquered Babylon. The third beast representing the leopard was the Empire of Greece. Under King Alexander the Great, Greece conquered the Medes and Persians. The fourth empire was Rome, and the Roman Empire devoured the known world until it collapsed in the fourth century.

The Lord revealed to Daniel that there will be a fifth empire that will arise out of the Roman Empire. This empire will consist of ten kingdoms or ten kings. Once the fifth empire is set up, a man shall arise and become the ruler over this vast empire. This man is described as the little horn in the Book of Daniel and in the New Testament. He has many names: antichrist, the beast, the man of sin, and the son of perdition. The antichrist will be a mighty orator, gifted with the power of persuasion when he speaks. He will oppose and speak out against the God of heaven and those who dwell in heaven. The world will choose to follow him.

In Revelation 17, additional detail is provided concerning the beast with seven heads and ten horns:

¹And there came one of the seven angels which had the seven vials, and talked with me, saying unto me, Come hither; I will shew unto thee the judgment of the great whore that sitteth upon many waters: ² With whom the kings of the earth have committed fornication, and the inhabitants of the earth have been made drunk with the wine of her fornication. ³ So he carried me away in the spirit into the wilderness: and I saw a woman sit upon a scarlet coloured beast, full of names of blasphemy, having seven heads and ten horns. ⁴ And the woman was arrayed in purple and scarlet colour, and decked with gold and precious stones and pearls, having a golden cup in her hand full of abominations and filthiness of her fornication: ⁵ And upon her forehead was a name written, MYSTERY, BABYLON THE GREAT, THE MOTHER OF HARLOTS AND ABOMINATIONS OF THE EARTH. (Revelation 17:1-5)

Revelation

    ⁹ *And here is the mind which hath wisdom. The seven heads are seven mountains, on which the woman sitteth.* ¹⁰ *And there are seven kings: five are fallen, and one is, and the other is not yet come; and when he cometh, he must continue a short space.* ¹¹ *And the beast that was, and is not, even he is the eighth, and is of the seven, and goeth into perdition.* ¹² *And the ten horns which thou sawest are ten kings, which have received no kingdom as yet; but receive power as kings one hour with the beast.* ¹³ *These have one mind, and shall give their power and strength unto the beast.* ¹⁴ *These shall make war with the Lamb, and the Lamb shall overcome them: for he is Lord of lords, and King of kings: and they that are with him are called, and chosen, and faithful.* ¹⁵ *And he saith unto me, The waters which thou sawest, where the whore sitteth, are peoples, and multitudes, and nations, and tongues.* ¹⁶ *And the ten horns which thou sawest upon the beast, these shall hate the whore, and shall make her desolate and naked, and shall eat her flesh, and burn her with fire.* (Revelation 17:9-16)

    The seven heads are seven mountains. A mountain is symbolic of a nation or a kingdom in the Scriptures as declared in Revelation 17:9. In Revelation 17:15 the word "waters" represents the sea of humanity. The beast is ruling over the sea of humanity. However, the language describing this beast more accurately is reflected in Daniel 7 where the sea refers to the Mediterranean Sea. The countries or nations around the Mediterranean Sea made up the nations over which the Roman Empire ruled. In the Book of Daniel and in the Book of Revelation, it is recorded that the antichrist will be defeated by the Lord Jesus when He returns to the earth the second time, to reign as King of Kings and Lord of Lords. Hosea, just like Daniel, prophesied of the lion, bear, leopard, and the dreadful beast (Hosea 13:7-8).

    The woman sitting on the beast in Revelation 17:1-5 and Revelation 17:9-16 is the religious system that the beast will use to obtain power and authority over the kingdoms of the world. The religious system will be covered in greater detail later.

    There has been much speculation as to the identity of the antichrist. Hollywood has produced movies concerning this coming ruler. In the Book of Daniel and in the Book of Revelation we see the characteristics of this man, and quite possibly a clue to his lineage. His possible lineage appears to be revealed in verse 2. The antichrist may have his lineage from Iraq (lion), Iran (bear), and from Greece (leopard). We know from the Book of Daniel what nations these animals represent. If this assumption is correct, then this would make the antichrist a man who would be approved by both eastern and western cultures. Since all who dwell on the earth will worship the beast, could he not be all things to all people and religions? Buddhists await the

Fifth Buddha; New Agers await their Maitreya; Jews await the Messiah; Muslims await the Mahdi; but Christians await the glorious appearing of Jesus. It is possible that this one man may be what everyone is looking for—a man who can unite west and east and solve the economic problems of the world.

The antichrist is described in chapter 13 as having crowns on his horns, whereas Satan in Revelation 12 has crowns on his heads. This signifies that Satan is the power behind this man who deceives the world. In order for Satan to persuade one third of the angels to follow him in his rebellion against God, he must have a very persuasive character. He must be a mighty orator. These characteristics were seen in Nimrod when he persuaded men to rebel against the God of Noah and to follow after him. The antichrist will also be very persuasive as he deceives the whole world, and even the leaders of the world. We saw this character in Adolf Hitler as he persuaded the German people to follow him. Those who were close to Adolf Hitler revealed his very dynamic and persuasive character. The character of Adolf Hitler deceived many and resulted in millions of people being killed and many others suffering greatly. Adolf Hitler is just one example of what the antichrist will be like.

Both Daniel and John saw the empires of the future. The five kingdoms that preceded John were:

- Egypt
- Assyria
- Babylon
- Medes and Persians
- Greece

The sixth kingdom was the kingdom during John's lifetime, which was Rome as revealed in Revelation 17:10. John sees the complete picture where Daniel did not see Egypt and Assyria, since they had been overthrown prior to the time of Daniel. Daniel was given the view from his present to the future, whereas John was presented with the view starting from the last empire and then back to the first empire that ruled the world which was Egypt.

The seventh kingdom that John saw was the fifth beast that Daniel saw with the ten horns. The realm of the antichrist will consist of ten parts, with each part having a ruler. There are three kings who will be put down as prophesied in Daniel 7:24-25. It is possible that three of the ten kingdoms have second thoughts about giving their power and authority over to the antichrist, and the antichrist moves swiftly against them. Another interpretation is that the antichrist will subdue three other kingdoms as part of his conquests.

We must take into account that the antichrist will replay the actions of Antiochus Epiphanes IV (who set up the abomination of desolation as recorded in Daniel 8:11-14) and his successor Demetrius I (that is Demetrius I Soter who is recorded in Daniel 11). The antichrist will also replay the character of Nimrod. We can say in a sense that Nimrod was the first major type of the antichrist. These evil men are types of what the antichrist will be like. The Jews refer to this as Pesher Midrash. It was Nimrod at the tower of Babel who persuaded men to rebel against the God of Noah. Nimrod became a king and ruler over the area around Shinar and persuaded men to follow after him. That evil spirit of Nimrod continues to permeate religious thinking not only in the long-recognized neo-Babylonian character of Roman Catholicism and Eastern Orthodoxy, but also now is in the modern New Age Movement that has so aptly infiltrated much of Evangelicalism through the Ecumenical Movement and in the form of the Emergent Church. Nimrod died a long time ago, but his legacy lives on.

The antichrist will appear to have a deadly wound, but this wound will not end his life. The entire world will be amazed at his recovery. Many Bible scholars see the prophecy in Zechariah 11:16-17 as pertaining to the antichrist:

16 For, lo, I will raise up a shepherd in the land, which shall not visit those that be cut off, neither shall seek the young one, nor heal that that is broken, nor feed that that standeth still: but he shall eat the flesh of the fat, and tear their claws in pieces. 17 Woe to the idol shepherd that leaveth the flock! The sword shall be upon his arm, and upon his right eye: his arm shall be clean dried up, and his right eye shall be utterly darkened. (Zechariah 11:16-17)

Perhaps part of the deception that the antichrist will use to deceive the world will be the sign of his recovery from a deadly wound. He may point to the wounds in his body as proof that he is the Messiah. It could be that the antichrist will attempt to counterfeit the wounds of Jesus Christ.

As the ministry of the Lord Jesus was three-and-a-half years on the earth, so Satan will demand equal time. Satan will have his three-and-a-half years (or 42 months) to persuade mankind to follow him. The antichrist will deceive the world and many will follow after him as noted in Thessalonians:

1Now we beseech you, brethren, by the coming of our Lord Jesus Christ, and by our gathering together unto him, 2 That ye be not soon shaken in mind, or be troubled, neither by spirit, nor by word, nor by letter as from us, as that the day of Christ is at hand. ³ *Let no man deceive you by any means: for that day shall not come, except there come a falling away first, and that man of sin be revealed, the son of perdition;* ⁴ *Who opposeth and exalteth himself above all that is called God, or that is worshipped; so that he as God sitteth in the temple of God, shewing himself that he is God.* ⁵ *Remember ye not, that, when I was yet with you, I told you these things?* ⁶ *And now ye know what withholdeth that he might be revealed in his time.* ⁷ *For the mystery of iniquity doth already work: only he who now letteth will let, until he be taken out of the way.* ⁸ *And then shall that Wicked be revealed, whom the Lord shall consume with the spirit of his mouth, and shall destroy with the brightness of his coming:* ⁹ *Even him, whose coming is after the working of Satan with all power and signs and lying wonders,* ¹⁰ *And with all deceivableness of unrighteousness in them that perish; because they received not the love of the truth, that they might be saved.* ¹¹ *And for this cause God shall send them strong delusion, that they should believe a lie:* ¹² *That they all might be damned who believed not the truth, but had pleasure in unrighteousness.* (II Thessalonians 2:1-12)

If people today cannot see through the deception and lies of those evangelists on the Internet or television who place their emphasis on money and prosperity, those same people will never see through the deception of the antichrist. People who follow signs and wonders, and believe that signs and wonders are an indication that a man is anointed by the Lord, are opening themselves up to deception as the antichrist and his false prophet will put on a show, second to none. They will not see through the deception when the false prophet makes it a law that in order to buy or sell, one must take the mark of the beast and worship him. It is very unlikely that these people will choose to die for Jesus in the future when they are not living for Jesus today.

Today there are many different English translations of the Bible. The author has noted that since the 1970's the English translations that appear in Christian bookstores have become watered down. The times are getting ripe for the antichrist to arrive on the scene as he will most likely have his own translation of the Scriptures—a Bible that he will approve and use as a substitute in place of the true Word of God. Satan's aim is to have his word in place of God's word. The Bible of choice of mainstream Protestant denominations is increasingly becoming more watered down as the newer translations are filtering out passages with which they disagree, such as portions of Deuteronomy and Romans that warn against homosexuality.

Revelation

The antichrist will be similar to men of the past. A man of persuasion and deception, he will be like the prince of Tyre who possesses wisdom, but his heart is lifted up in pride as declared in Ezekiel:

¹The word of the LORD came again unto me, saying, ² Son of man, say unto the prince of Tyrus, Thus saith the Lord GOD; Because thine heart is lifted up, and thou hast said, I am a God, I sit in the seat of God, in the midst of the seas; yet thou art a man, and not God, though thou set thine heart as the heart of God: ³ Behold, thou art wiser than Daniel; there is no secret that they can hide from thee: ⁴ With thy wisdom and with thine understanding thou hast gotten thee riches, and hast gotten gold and silver into thy treasures: ⁵ By thy great wisdom and by thy traffick hast thou increased thy riches, and thine heart is lifted up because of thy riches: ⁶ Therefore thus saith the Lord GOD; Because thou hast set thine heart as the heart of God; ⁷ Behold, therefore I will bring strangers upon thee, the terrible of the nations: and they shall draw their swords against the beauty of thy wisdom, and they shall defile thy brightness. ⁸ They shall bring thee down to the pit, and thou shalt die the deaths of them that are slain in the midst of the seas. ⁹ Wilt thou yet say before him that slayeth thee, I am God? But thou shalt be a man, and no God, in the hand of him that slayeth thee. ¹⁰ Thou shalt die the deaths of the uncircumcised by the hand of strangers: for I have spoken it, saith the Lord GOD. (Ezekiel 28:1-10)

Beauty, wealth and greatness are characteristics that rulers desire for their kingdoms. Rulers desire wisdom and understanding. All of these blessings can lead to one's heart being lifted up in pride. King David remembered that it was the Lord who blessed him and he never forgot God when the nation of Israel was blessed during his reign. The people who forget God can easily fall into sin. They can become deceived and believe that because of their own righteousness, all of these great blessings have appeared.

The beauty, wealth, and greatness of antichrist's kingdom will also be like the kingdom of Assyria and Babylon as declared in Ezekiel 31:

¹And it came to pass in the eleventh year, in the third month, in the first day of the month, that the word of the LORD came unto me, saying, ² Son of man, speak unto Pharaoh king of Egypt, and to his multitude; Whom art thou like in thy greatness? ³ Behold, the Assyrian was a cedar in Lebanon with fair branches, and with a shadowing shroud, and of an high stature; and his top was among the thick boughs. ⁴ The waters made him great, the deep set him up on high with her rivers running round about his plants, and sent her little rivers unto all the trees of the field. ⁵ Therefore his height was exalted above all the trees of the field, and his boughs were multiplied, and his branches became long because of the multitude of waters, when he shot forth. *6 All the fowls of heaven made their nests in his boughs, and under his branches did all the beasts of the field bring forth their young, and under his shadow dwelt all great nations. 7 Thus was he fair in his greatness, in the length of his branches: for his root was by great waters. 8 The cedars in the garden of God could not hide him: the fir trees were not like his boughs, and the chestnut trees were not like his branches; nor any tree in the garden of God was like unto him in his beauty. 9 I have made him fair by the multitude of his branches: so that all the trees of Eden, that were in the garden of God, envied him.* (Ezekiel 31:1-9)

The antichrist will be similar to General Pompeii who represented the triumvirate of Rome. He made a treaty with the Jews, and then he double-crossed them when he entered the Holy of Holies. He is a type of the antichrist that many people overlook.

The antichrist will come into judgment just as Pharaoh of Egypt and the Assyrian were judged because of their pride and exalting of their kingdoms as noted again in Ezekiel:

10 Therefore thus saith the Lord GOD; Because thou hast lifted up thyself in height, and he hath shot up his top among the thick boughs, and his heart is lifted up in his height; 11 I have therefore delivered him into the hand of the mighty one of the heathen; he shall surely deal with him: I have driven him out for his wickedness. 12 And strangers, the terrible of the nations, have cut him off, and have left him: upon the mountains and in all the valleys his branches are fallen, and his boughs are broken by all the rivers of the land; and all the people of the earth are gone down from his shadow, and have left him. 13 Upon his ruin shall all the fowls of the heaven remain, and all the beasts of the field shall be upon his branches: 14 To the end that none of all the trees by the waters exalt themselves for their height, neither shoot up their top among the thick boughs, neither their trees stand up in their height, all that drink water: for they are all delivered unto death, to the nether parts of the earth, in the midst of the children of men, with them that go down to the pit. 15 Thus saith the Lord GOD; In the day when he went down to the grave I caused a mourning: I covered the deep for him, and I restrained the floods thereof, and the great waters were stayed: and I caused Lebanon to mourn for him, and all the trees of the field fainted for him. 16 I made the nations to shake at the sound of his fall, when I cast him down to hell with them that descend into the pit: and all the trees of Eden, the choice and best of Lebanon, all that drink water, shall be comforted in the nether parts of the earth. 17 They also went down into hell with him unto them that be slain with the sword; and they that were his arm, that dwelt under his shadow in the midst of the heathen. 18 To whom art thou thus like in glory and in greatness among the trees of Eden? Yet shalt thou be brought down with the trees of Eden unto the nether parts of the earth:

Revelation

thou shalt lie in the midst of the uncircumcised with them that be slain by the sword. This is Pharaoh and all his multitude, saith the Lord GOD. (Ezekiel 31:10-18)

The prophecy against Egypt and Babylon is an example of a Midrash or double fulfillment as it describes the destruction of Egypt, the destruction of the king of Babylon, and the kingdom of antichrist.

There are many parallels between Judas Iscariot and the antichrist. Judas Iscariot was referred to as a false brother going out from among the other disciples. He became a type of antichrist. There are many antichrists in the world and there is the spirit of antichrist. The spirit of antichrist is already in the world; he has always been there. The spirit of antichrist that denies the Father-Son relationship is by definition, antichrist. The false prophet and the beast of Revelation 13 are co-equally antichrist, and likewise will have the same spirit of antichrist. The false prophet is the satanic counterfeit of the Holy Spirit.

There are thirteen different titles for the antichrist. The antichrist is the second person in the unholy trinity. The first belongs to Satan and the third person would be the false prophet. The thirteen titles that are given to the antichrist are:

1. King of Babylon, Isaiah 14:4
2. Lucifer, son of the morning, Isaiah 14:12
3. The Assyrian, Isaiah 14:25
4. The little horn, Daniel 7:25
5. King of fierce countenance, Daniel 8:23
6. Prince that shall come, Daniel 9:26
7. Vile person, Daniel 11:21
8. Willful king, Daniel 11:36
9. The one that shall come in his own name, John 5:43
10. Man of sin, II Thessalonians 2:3
11. Son of perdition, II Thessalonians 2:7
12. Lawless one, II Thessalonians 2:8
13. The beast, Revelation 13:18

The wounding of one of the heads of the beast – an alternative view

There are some Bible scholars that believe the wounding and reviving of one of the heads of the beast refers to a nation and not a man (Revelation 13:1-4). The heads of this beast represent nations that have either conquered Jerusalem or have oppressed God's people (the Jews).

The Two Beasts

The six kingdoms that conquered Israel/Judah throughout history and the last-days kingdom of the future that the prophet Daniel saw in his vision were:

1. Egypt: prior to Daniel;
2. Assyria: prior to Daniel;
3. Babylon: head of gold;
4. Medes and Persians: chest and arms of silver;
5. Greece: stomach and thighs of brass;
6. Rome: legs of iron;
7. The last-days kingdom: feet and toes of iron and clay.

The kingdom that best fits the description of receiving a deadly wound and was healed would be the Roman Empire. The Roman Empire was depicted with legs of iron, and the future last-days kingdom is described with feet and toes of iron and clay.

The Roman Empire is always referred to by iron. Therefore, the feet and toes of iron and clay represent the last-days kingdom of antichrist comprised of Rome, which seemingly was wounded to death, but will rise in the last days to be united with other nations (the clay). The scholars that follow this alternate view will point out that only one of the heads of the beast contains all ten horns (Daniel 7:6-8) and the best fit appears to be the Roman Empire. This view is clearly detailed in Albert James Dager's book, *The Day of Yahweh*.

The alternate view does not negate the prophecy in Zechariah describing the antichrist having his eye dark and his arm withered. The prophecy in Zechariah is descriptive of a man and not a nation.

Revelation 13:11-15
The False Prophet

And I beheld another beast coming up out of the earth; and he had two horns like a lamb, and he spake as a dragon. And he exerciseth all the power of the first beast before him, and causeth the earth and them which dwell therein to worship the first beast, whose deadly wound was healed. And he doeth great wonders, so that he maketh fire come down from heaven on the earth in the sight of men, And deceiveth them that dwell on the earth by the means of those miracles which he had power to do in the sight of the beast; saying to them that dwell on the earth, that they should make an image to the beast, which had the wound by a sword, and did live. And he had power to give life unto the image of the beast, that the image of the beast should

Revelation

both speak, and cause that as many as would not worship the image of the beast should be killed.

The false prophet is the third member of the unholy satanic trinity. Some scholars believe that the false prophet will be a Jew (his likeness is as a lamb). He looks harmless, but he leads the world into worshipping the antichrist. He directs worship to Satan and to the beast. He commands an image of the beast to be made. Once the image is completed, all mankind will be commanded to worship the image or be killed. The false prophet has authority to enforce the worship of the beast whose deadly wound was healed as prophesied in Zechariah:

16 For, lo, I will raise up a shepherd in the land, which shall not visit those that be cut off, neither shall seek the young one, nor heal that that is broken, nor feed that that standeth still: but he shall eat the flesh of the fat, and tear their claws in pieces. 17 Woe to the idol shepherd that leaveth the flock! The sword shall be upon his arm, and upon his right eye: his arm shall be clean dried up, and his right eye shall be utterly darkened. (Zechariah 11:16-17)

The world government will be under the control of the world religion at this stage of world history. This event happened in the past and is predicted to occur once again in the future. This is a Midrash of what occurred in Babylon in Daniel 3 when the three Hebrew men were cast into the fiery furnace for refusing to bow down to the king of Babylon. In Daniel 3 the herald is a type of the false prophet who declares that everyone is to worship the golden image or they will be destroyed:

1Nebuchadnezzar the king made an image of gold, whose height was threescore cubits, and the breadth thereof six cubits: he set it up in the plain of Dura, in the province of Babylon. 2 Then Nebuchadnezzar the king sent to gather together the princes, the governors, and the captains, the judges, the treasurers, the counsellors, the sheriffs, and all the rulers of the provinces, to come to the dedication of the image which Nebuchadnezzar the king had set up. 3 Then the princes, the governors, and captains, the judges, the treasurers, the counsellors, the sheriffs, and all the rulers of the provinces, were gathered together unto the dedication of the image that Nebuchadnezzar the king had set up; and they stood before the image that Nebuchadnezzar had set up. 4 Then an herald cried aloud, To you it is commanded, O people, nations, and languages, 5 That at what time ye hear the sound of the cornet, flute, harp, sackbut, psaltery, dulcimer, and all kinds of musick, ye fall down and worship the golden image that Nebuchadnezzar the king hath set up: 6 And whoso falleth not down and worshippeth shall the same hour be cast into the midst of a burning fiery furnace. (Daniel 3:1-6)

As the king of Babylon had his herald, the beast will have his herald who will force the entire world to worship him. This is an example of Pesher Midrash according to the Jews. The false prophet will be like the herald. In order to buy or sell, and to provide for their families, everyone will be commanded to worship the beast as noted in II Thessalonians:

⁸ And then shall that Wicked be revealed, whom the Lord shall consume with the spirit of his mouth, and shall destroy with the brightness of his coming: ⁹ Even him, whose coming is after the working of Satan with all power and signs and lying wonders, ¹⁰ And with all deceivableness of unrighteousness in them that perish; because they received not the love of the truth, that they might be saved. ¹¹ And for this cause God shall send them strong delusion, that they should believe a lie: ¹² That they all might be damned who believed not the truth, but had pleasure in unrighteousness (II Thessalonians 2:8-12).

Signs and wonders are NOT proof that the Lord is behind this man. For those who follow signs and wonders and want to see the latest show, the false prophet will put on a show second to none, and many will follow after him. The prophecies of Fatima and alleged solar phenomena are debunked as false because so many of these predictions, such as the end of WWI on a specific date, simply did not come true. Some have predicted the elimination of homosexuals; others predicted that Zimbabwe would blossom in the 1990s just before the opposite took place. A Baptist preacher, William Miller, proclaimed that Jesus Christ would come for His church on October 22, 1844. When this did not happen, some of the leaders and followers revised the dates of Christ's return to 1845, but as we know Jesus did not come for His church in 1845.

Jesus warned about false prophets in the last days. If people are unable to see through those who by scriptural definition are obviously false prophets, there is no way they will be able to recognize the false prophet who is to come as the precursor to the beast.

There have been many false prophets throughout the history of the world. The false prophet in Revelation 13, although a religious leader, speaks as a dragon as did Caiaphas, and as did the medieval popes. Caiaphas and the Sanhedrin managed to seduce the people, and Jesus referred to them as a generation of vipers (Matthew 23:33).

Revelation

Rabshakeh also typifies the false prophet in II Kings 18 and 19, and II Chronicles 32, and Isaiah 36 and 37. Rabshakeh delivers a religious message to order God's people under King Hezekiah to follow the king of Assyria. Rabshakeh makes a false claim to be speaking for the God of Israel, and appeals to the people to swear allegiance to the king of Assyria.

The false prophet will be to the beast as John the Baptist was to Jesus Christ—the one who points to another who shall come, and who prepares the way for his coming. John the Baptist operated under the Holy Spirit to point men to Jesus Christ. The false prophet will operate under the spirit of antichrist and will point men to the beast that shall come (I John 4:3).

Revelation 13:16-18
The Number of the Beast

And he causeth all, both small and great, rich and poor, free and bond, to receive a mark in their right hand, or in their foreheads: And that no man might buy or sell, save he that had the mark, or the name of the beast, or the number of his name. Here is wisdom. Let him that hath understanding count the number of the beast: for it is the number of a man; and his number is Six hundred threescore and six.

Starting in Revelation 11, when the Lord refers to the antichrist, He uses the word "beast." The Lord refers to this man as the beast and deals with him as a beast. Gone are freedom and democracy, and now a bloody dictator rules. The false prophet will deceive the world into taking the mark of the beast. The Lord will send His angels as messengers to warn mankind of the eternal punishment that will come upon those who take the mark of the beast and worship his image as prophesied in Revelation 14:

[9] And the third angel followed them, saying with a loud voice, If any man worship the beast and his image, and receive his mark in his forehead, or in his hand, [10] The same shall drink of the wine of the wrath of God, which is poured out without mixture into the cup of his indignation; and he shall be tormented with fire and brimstone in the presence of the holy angels, and in the presence of the Lamb: [11] And the smoke of their torment ascendeth up for ever and ever: and they have no rest day nor night, who worship the beast and his image, and whosoever receiveth the mark of his name. (Revelation 14:9-11)

Many of the heathen gods had names that, when translated to numbers, would equal 666. The early church fathers believed that Nero was the antichrist and many referred to Nero as a beast. The number of his name came to 666. The Protestant churches during the Reformation believed that the pope was the antichrist as the popes ordered the persecution of Christians who were leaving the Roman Catholic Church.

People have a choice of either life or death. Unfortunately, many people choose not to follow after the Lord and His righteousness. Their eyes are on the present things of this world and not on the heavenly eternal things. Their eyes are on signs and wonders and not on truth. These people love the world and the things that are of the world, and the love of the Creator is not in them. They choose to ignore and even reject His commandments.

The Lord will make sure that everyone is warned before choosing to take the mark of the beast and worshiping him. The Lord will send His angels to warn everyone regardless of race and nationality. Everyone will be warned. Those who take the mark of the beast and worship his image will experience the wrath of God, the fiery indignation of the Lord. The Greek word for wrath used in Revelation 14 is *thumos*. God in His mercy warns everyone beforehand. Therefore, no one will be able to say that they did not know.

It is interesting to note that King Nebuchadnezzar's image was sixty cubits by six cubits in Daniel 3. The image of Nebuchadnezzar carries the dimension of 666 calculated from the use of the term *sheth* in the original Aramaic text. The statue that was set up in Babylon, and what it represented, will be a type of what is to come in the future. Everyone had to bow to the golden statue to live, and one day the beast will require the same. Everyone who wants to buy or sell and provide for their family must bow the knee to the image of the beast and take his mark.

If people cannot live for Jesus Christ today, how will they live for Him later when in order to eat and work, they must receive the mark of the beast and bow the knee to worship him? Once a person makes the decision to receive the mark of the beast and to worship him, there is no going back. That person's fate is sealed. There is no repentance for that person. That person will be eternally separated from God (Revelation 14:9-11).

History had many heralds who were in league with dictators. Some heralds have even come from the Vatican. Pope Pius XXII was in league with Benito Mussolini. Hitler made a concordat with the Roman Catholic bishops of Bavaria. The Roman Catholic hierarchy directly participated in the genocidal extermination of the Serbs and Jews by the Ustashi Nazis in the former Yugoslavia at the behest of Archbishop Stepinac. (Stepinac was beatified as a candidate for possible sainthood by Pope John Paul II).

Some Bible scholars believe that the antichrist will not be revealed to the faithful church until the mark of the beast has been established. The views below support this teaching:

Revelation

- Mid-Tribulational view
- The Intra-Seal view
- Pre-Wrath view
- Post-Tribulation view but earlier
- Post-Tribulation view

The scholars who believe that the harpazo will occur after the beast sets up his image in the rebuilt Jewish Temple and establishes the mark of the beast that is required in order to buy or sell will quote the uniform body of evidence from the early church fathers of the 1st, 2nd, and 3rd centuries. The early church fathers held to the belief that the apostles taught that the antichrist would be clearly identified to the faithful church prior to the coming of Jesus for His church. Irenaeus, the disciple of Polycarp, who was a disciple of John, believed that the church would see the abomination of desolation spoken of by Daniel the prophet. Some scholars believe this is questionable.

There will be many Muslims who will come to believe in the God of Abraham when the beast establishes his image and demands that all men must worship him. There is a hint from the Book of Isaiah that people from Egypt and Assyria will refuse to worship the beast. Many will survive the plagues during the Great Tribulation and will enter into the glorious 1,000-year kingdom reign as declared in Isaiah:

^{23} In that day shall there be a highway out of Egypt to Assyria, and the Assyrian shall come into Egypt, and the Egyptian into Assyria, and the Egyptians shall serve with the Assyrians. ^{24} In that day shall Israel be the third with Egypt and with Assyria, even a blessing in the midst of the land: ^{25} Whom the LORD of hosts shall bless, saying, Blessed be Egypt my people, and Assyria the work of my hands, and Israel mine inheritance. (Isaiah 19:23-25)

The people of Egypt are referred to as God's people, and the people of the land of Assyria as the work of His hands.

Chapter 14

The *Thumos* of God

Revelation 14:1-5
The Lamb and the 144,000

And I looked, and, lo, a Lamb stood on the mount Sion, and with him an hundred forty and four thousand, having his Father's name written in their foreheads. And I heard a voice from heaven, as the voice of many waters, and as the voice of a great thunder: and I heard the voice of harpers harping with their harps: And they sung as it were a new song before the throne, and before the four beasts, and the elders: and no man could learn that song but the hundred and forty and four thousand, which were redeemed from the earth. These are they which were not defiled with women; for they are virgins. These are they which follow the Lamb whithersoever he goeth. These were redeemed from among men, being the firstfruits unto God and to the Lamb. And in their mouth was found no guile: for they are without fault before the throne of God.

THE SCENE NOW shifts to events that will take place after Jesus has returned to the earth. We now see Jesus, the Lamb of God, standing upon Mount Zion with the 144,000 Israelites. There is great rejoicing in heaven. The creation of God in heaven sings a new song that only the 144,000 Israelites can sing. On the earth the Lord has chosen Mount Zion to rule from:

¹³ *For the* LORD *hath chosen Zion; he hath desired it for his habitation.* ¹⁴ *This is my rest for ever: here will I dwell; for I have desired it.* (Psalm 132:13-14)

Revelation

> ² And it shall come to pass in the last days, that the mountain of the LORD's house shall be established in the top of the mountains, and shall be exalted above the hills; and all nations shall flow unto it. ³ And many people shall go and say, Come ye, and let us go up to the mountain of the LORD, to the house of the God of Jacob; and he will teach us of his ways, and we will walk in his paths: for out of Zion shall go forth the law, and the word of the LORD from Jerusalem. ⁴ And he shall judge among the nations, and shall rebuke many people: and they shall beat their swords into plowshares, and their spears into pruninghooks: nation shall not lift up sword against nation, neither shall they learn war any more. (Isaiah 2:2-4)

The Lord will choose to dwell at Mount Zion when He returns to the earth as noted in the Psalms and in the prophets. The 144,000 had endured much, and now their place is to be with the Lamb of God as they follow Him wherever He goes. They have a unique ministry before the Lord.

The 144,000 are sealed before the Seventh Seal is opened. This event in Revelation 14 appears to take place after the return of Jesus Christ to the earth as it mentions that they were redeemed (verses 3 and 4) and that they are virgins (past tense). This indicates one of two possibilities. The first is the 144,000 were martyred during the seventieth week of Daniel. The second is they were protected from the plagues and they received their resurrected body after the Lord Jesus returned to the earth. We know that the 144,000 were sealed and protected from the demon locusts of the Fifth Trumpet judgment, so if any of them were martyred, it would have to be sometime after the Fifth Trumpet judgment.

Revelation 14:6-8
The Messages of the Angels

> And I saw another angel fly in the midst of heaven, having the everlasting gospel to preach unto them that dwell on the earth, and to every nation, and kindred, and tongue, and people, Saying with a loud voice, Fear God, and give glory to him; for the hour of his judgment is come: and worship him that made heaven, and earth, and the sea, and the fountains of waters. And there followed another angel, saying, Babylon is fallen, is fallen, that great city, because she made all nations drink of the wine of the wrath of her fornication.

The Lord will now send forth His messengers to warn the people of the world that the *thumos* of God is about to begin. One angel is commissioned to preach the everlasting Gospel to all who dwell upon the earth and to warn mankind that the hour of His judgment has come. The message of the everlasting Gospel has not changed. All who believe that Jesus Christ is the Messiah, the Son of God, and believe that God raised Him up from the grave will be saved. Everyone has two paths in front of them. One path is to believe and trust in the Lord Jesus and then to lay down one's life for that belief. The second path is to trust in the beast and worship him and declare that the beast is God. Verse 6 indicates that all races and languages will hear the good news before the mark of the beast is established. Since receiving the mark of the beast will determine a person's eternal destiny, the Lord will dispatch angels to warn all mankind of the consequences that will befall anyone who receives the mark and worships the beast.

The Lord sends a second messenger who announces the hour of God's judgment and that Babylon is fallen. There is a form of Babylon that is a commercial system and then there is a form of Babylon which is a religious system. Both represent Babylon and are judged and punished by the Lord. It is the commercial system that is destroyed by the Lord God Almighty during the final Seventh Bowl or Vial judgment. The judgment of Babylon does not take place here in chapter 14, but is a prophecy of what is to come. In the Book of Jeremiah, the same message is used concerning the fall of Babylon and it refers to a future event when Jeremiah wrote his prophecy. The time is near for Babylon to be judged for her wickedness and rebellion.

Both apostles, John and James, warned and exhorted the true and faithful saints not to love the world or the things that are of the world:

⁴Ye adulterers and adulteresses, know ye not that the friendship of the world is enmity with God? Whosoever therefore will be a friend of the world is the enemy of God. (James 4:4)

¹⁵ Love not the world, neither the things that are in the world. If any man love the world, the love of the Father is not in him. ¹⁶ For all that is in the world, the lust of the flesh, and the lust of the eyes, and the pride of life, is not of the Father, but is of the world. ¹⁷And the world passeth away, and the lust thereof: but he that doeth the will of God abideth for ever. (I John 2:15-17)

There are many prophecies of the ultimate destruction of Babylon, especially in Jeremiah:

³⁹ Therefore the wild beasts of the desert with the wild beasts of the islands shall dwell there, and the owls shall dwell therein: and it shall be no more inhabited for ever; neither shall it be dwelt in from generation to generation. ⁴⁰ As God overthrew Sodom and Gomorrah and the neighbour cities thereof, saith the LORD; so shall no man abide there, neither shall any son of man dwell therein. (Jeremiah 50:39-40)

⁶ Flee out of the midst of Babylon, and deliver every man his soul: be not cut off in her iniquity; for this is the time of the LORD's vengeance; he will render unto her a recompence. ⁷ Babylon hath been a golden cup in the LORD's hand, that made all the earth drunken: the nations have drunken of her wine; therefore the nations are mad. ⁸ Babylon is suddenly fallen and destroyed: howl for her; take balm for her pain, if so be she may be healed. ⁹ We would have healed Babylon, but she is not healed: forsake her, and let us go every one into his own country: for her judgment reacheth unto heaven, and is lifted up even to the skies. (Jeremiah 51:6-9)

²⁵ Behold, I am against thee, O destroying mountain, saith the LORD, which destroyest all the earth: and I will stretch out mine hand upon thee, and roll thee down from the rocks, and will make thee a burnt mountain. ²⁶ And they shall not take of thee a stone for a corner, nor a stone for foundations; but thou shalt be desolate for ever, saith the LORD. (Jeremiah 51:25-26)

All of the prophecies concerning the destruction of Babylon have not been fulfilled yet. Babylon exists today, and there are people living there. Babylon will be destroyed in the Seventh Bowl or Vial judgment as prophesied in Revelation 16:17-19. It is during this time that the prophecies of the destruction of Babylon will be fulfilled.

It is in Revelation 14 that the wrath (*thumos*) of God is first used. *Thumos* refers to a fiery indignation from God, which is fiercer than *orge*. Now the judgments will become more intense as the Lord pours out His vengeance against the kingdom of antichrist.

Revelation 14:9-13
Eternal Punishment

And the third angel followed them, saying with a loud voice, If any man worship the beast and his image, and receive his mark in his forehead, or in his hand, The same shall drink of the wine of the wrath of God, which is poured out without mixture into the cup of his indignation; and he shall be tormented with fire and brimstone in the presence of the holy angels, and in the presence of the Lamb: And the smoke of their torment ascendeth up for ever and ever: and they have no rest day nor night, who worship the beast and his image, and whosoever receiveth the mark of his name. Here is the patience of the saints: here are they that keep the commandments of God, and the faith of Jesus. And I heard a voice from heaven saying unto me, Write, Blessed are the dead which die in the Lord from henceforth: Yea, saith the Spirit, that they may rest from their labours; and their works do follow them.

The third messenger announces the doom on those who will worship the antichrist and his image, and take the mark of the beast. The Lord will not share His glory with another, as Isaiah declares:

⁸ *I am the* LORD: *that is my name: and my glory will I not give to another, neither my praise to graven images.* (Isaiah 42:8)

²⁴ *And they shall go forth, and look upon the carcases of the men that have transgressed against me: for their worm shall not die, neither shall their fire be quenched; and they shall be an abhorring unto all flesh.* (Isaiah 66:24)

The Lord will execute His fierce wrath on those who attribute the character of God to another god or upon themselves. Those who worship the beast and obtain his mark to buy or sell to feed their families will experience the *thumos* of God. Those who keep the commandments of God will not take the mark of the beast. Spending eternity in the lake of fire is a terrifying thought and it should be to those who are considering worshipping the antichrist. In contrast, blessed are they who die in the Lord, as they will be leaving this world and the kingdom of antichrist. They will be present in heaven and experience the kingdom of Jesus Christ with all its glory. The saints of God will experience persecution and even martyrdom when they refuse to take the mark of the beast and refuse to worship him. The Lord promises that those saints who are martyred for their faith will be comforted in heaven.

Despite what some preachers may say, once a person takes the mark of the beast and worships the beast, that person's fate is sealed. There is no going back (Revelation 14:9-11).

Revelation 14:14-20
The Harvest of the Earth

And I looked, and behold a white cloud, and upon the cloud one sat like unto the Son of man, having on his head a golden crown, and in his hand a sharp sickle. And another angel came out of the temple, crying with a loud voice to him that sat on the cloud, Thrust in thy sickle, and reap: for the time is come for thee to reap; for the harvest of the earth is ripe. And he that sat on the cloud thrust in his sickle on the earth; and the earth was reaped. And another angel came out of the temple which is in heaven, he also having a sharp sickle. And another angel came out from the altar, which had power over fire; and cried with a loud cry to him that had the sharp sickle, saying, Thrust in thy sharp sickle, and gather the clusters of the vine of the earth; for her grapes are fully ripe. And the angel thrust in his sickle into the earth,

Revelation

and gathered the vine of the earth, and cast it into the great winepress of the wrath of God. And the winepress was trodden without the city, and blood came out of the winepress, even unto the horse bridles, by the space of a thousand and six hundred furlongs.

The cloud of glory abode at all times in the Tabernacle within the Holy of Holies upon the mercy seat which was the place of atonement (Luke 2:27). It will be a sad day when the Glory of God departs. When the Glory of God does depart, judgment will soon follow. The judgment from the Lord is long overdue, and the Lord has been patient, but now the time has come. The sickle is cast upon or against the earth for judgment. The angelic messenger who calls out to the Lord to complete the judgment is the messenger of God who has authority over the judgment fires of God. The altar not only bore the body of the lamb, but also contained the fire which consumed the lamb. If we do not take Jesus as our Lord and Savior, we must have Him as our judge (Revelation 19:15). The Book of Joel has much to say about this time:

¹For, behold, in those days, and in that time, when I shall bring again the captivity of Judah and Jerusalem, ² I will also gather all nations, and will bring them down into the valley of Jehoshaphat, and will plead with them there for my people and for my heritage Israel, whom they have scattered among the nations, and parted my land. (Joel 3:1-2)

⁹ Proclaim ye this among the Gentiles; Prepare war, wake up the mighty men, let all the men of war draw near; let them come up: ¹⁰ Beat your plowshares into swords and your pruninghooks into spears: let the weak say, I am strong. ¹¹ Assemble yourselves, and come, all ye heathen, and gather yourselves together round about: thither cause thy mighty ones to come down, O LORD. ¹² Let the heathen be wakened, and come up to the valley of Jehoshaphat: for there will I sit to judge all the heathen round about. ¹³ Put ye in the sickle, for the harvest is ripe: come, get you down; for the press is full, the fats overflow; for their wickedness is great. ¹⁴ Multitudes, multitudes in the valley of decision: for the day of the LORD is near in the valley of decision. ¹⁵ The sun and the moon shall be darkened, and the stars shall withdraw their shining. ¹⁶ The LORD also shall roar out of Zion, and utter his voice from Jerusalem; and the heavens and the earth shall shake: but the LORD will be the hope of his people, and the strength of the children of Israel. ¹⁷ So shall ye know that I am the LORD your God dwelling in Zion, my holy mountain: then shall Jerusalem be holy, and there shall no strangers pass through her any more. (Joel 3:9-17).

At this point in the seventieth week of Daniel there are four classes of people alive on the planet earth:

- Those who have taken the mark of the beast and worship the beast;
- The Jews who have not taken the mark of the beast. They recognize that the antichrist, the man they had hailed as their Messiah, is actually a false Messiah. These Jews will flee into the wilderness as recorded in Revelation 12:14;
- The followers of Jesus who do not take the mark and are persecuted by the beast as noted in Revelation 12:17;
- The Gentiles who choose not to take the mark of the beast as they recognize that he is evil. This would be similar to those Germans in World War II that attempted to assassinate Adolf Hitler when they recognized that he was evil and needed to be destroyed. These Gentiles make up the parable of the sheep and goats in Matthew 25:31-46 after Jesus returns to the earth. There are passages in Isaiah where Gentiles who survive the seventieth week of Daniel are commissioned to go throughout the world to bring back the Jews who are in hiding from the kingdom of the antichrist. The Gentiles will search for them and return them back to the land of Israel after the Lord Jesus returns to the earth. However, these Gentiles have not taken the next step to receive the Lord Jesus into their lives as Lord and Savior. In the kingdom age they will have that opportunity as they will realize the prophecies are true and Jesus is reigning as King of Kings and Lord of Lords.

The Gospel of Matthew contains the parable of the wheat and the tares where the tares are prepared for judgment. This parable is essential to understanding the passage in Revelation 14:

24 Another parable put he forth unto them, saying, The kingdom of heaven is likened unto a man which sowed good seed in his field: 25 But while men slept, his enemy came and sowed tares among the wheat, and went his way. 26 But when the blade was sprung up, and brought forth fruit, then appeared the tares also. 27 So the servants of the householder came and said unto him, Sir, didst not thou sow good seed in thy field? from whence then hath it tares? 28 He said unto them, An enemy hath done this. The servants said unto him, Wilt thou then that we go and gather them up? 29 But he said, Nay; lest while ye gather up the tares, ye root up also the wheat with them. 30 Let both grow together until the harvest: and in the time of harvest I will say to the reapers, Gather ye together first the tares, and bind them in bundles to burn them: but gather the wheat into my barn. (Matthew 13:24-30)

36 Then Jesus sent the multitude away, and went into the house: and his disciples came unto him, saying, Declare unto us the parable of the tares of the field. *37* He answered and said unto them, He that soweth the good seed is the Son of man; *38* The field is the world; the good seed are the children of the kingdom; but the tares are the children of the wicked one; *39* The enemy that sowed them is the devil; the harvest is the end of the world; and the reapers are the angels. *40* As therefore the tares are gathered and burned in the fire; so shall it be in the end of this world. *41* The Son of man shall send forth his angels, and they shall gather out of his kingdom all things that offend, and them which do iniquity; *42* and shall cast them into a furnace of fire: there shall be wailing and gnashing of teeth. *43* Then shall the righteous shine forth as the sun in the kingdom of their Father. Who hath ears to hear, let him hear. (Matthew 13:36-43)

The Gospel of Mark also contains a parable similar to the wheat and the tares:

26 And he said, So is the kingdom of God, as if a man should cast seed into the ground; *27* and should sleep, and rise night and day, and the seed should spring and grow up, he knoweth not how. *28* For the earth bringeth forth fruit of herself; first the blade, then the ear, after that the full corn in the ear. *29* But when the fruit is brought forth, immediately he putteth in the sickle, because the harvest is come. *30* And he said, Whereunto shall we liken the kingdom of God? or with what comparison shall we compare it? *31* It is like a grain of mustard seed, which, when it is sown in the earth, is less than all the seeds that be in the earth: *32* But when it is sown, it groweth up, and becometh greater than all herbs, and shooteth out great branches; so that the fowls of the air may lodge under the shadow of it. (Mark 4:26-32)

Before the Seventh Vial or Bowl judgment is poured out, the last believer who has the testimony of the Lord Jesus must leave Babylon the Great (Commercial Babylon). This view is supported by Revelation 16:15 and Revelation 18:4. There are still some saints left on the earth at this late stage in the seventieth week of Daniel (Revelation 7:16-17). The Seventh Bowl or Vial judgment is for the kingdom of antichrist. As the Lord rescued Lot out of Sodom and Gomorrah before judgment came, He will rescue the remaining believers out of Babylon. The final judgments are for the tares. Sometime before this last judgment, the saints who were seen under the altar when the Fifth Seal is opened will have their number complete.

The parable of the wheat and the tares contained in Matthew 13 is essential to understanding End Time Prophecy. Today the churches are full of tares, and the time of judgment is drawing near. The majority of attendees in the churches of Sardis and Laodicea are tares as Jesus indicated that there are only a few names that have remained faithful to Him. Jesus taught a parable about a mustard seed growing into a great tree and the birds of the air find their rest in its branches. This is not normal. The tree is indicative of abnormal growth. Mustard seeds do not grow into great trees. The birds of the air are demons in this parable as they steal away the seed that was sown in order to discourage the listener from giving his life to the Lord Jesus and from following Him. Sadly, Satan and his forces have joined the church and are active in the church leadership today. What Spurgeon predicted has come to pass. When the churches stop feeding the sheep, the clowns will come into the church and will become church leaders and the clowns will entertain the goats.

The final battle described in Revelation 14:20 is the battle of Armageddon. This judgment is for the tares. The battle will cover a great distance of about 200 miles from the valley of Armageddon to the city of Bozrah. Much blood will be shed and many bodies will cover the land.

Chapter 15

Preparation for the Seven Last Plagues

Revelation 15:1-8
The Seven Last Plagues

And I saw another sign in heaven, great and marvellous, seven angels having the seven last plagues; for in them is filled up the wrath of God. And I saw as it were a sea of glass mingled with fire: and them that had gotten the victory over the beast, and over his image, and over his mark, and over the number of his name, stand on the sea of glass, having the harps of God. And they sing the song of Moses the servant of God, and the song of the Lamb, saying, Great and marvellous are thy works, Lord God Almighty; just and true are thy ways, thou King of saints. Who shall not fear thee, O Lord, and glorify thy name? For thou only art holy: for all nations shall come and worship before thee; for thy judgments are made manifest. And after that I looked, and, behold, the temple of the tabernacle of the testimony in heaven was opened: And the seven angels came out of the temple, having the seven plagues, clothed in pure and white linen, and having their breasts girded with golden girdles. And one of the four beasts gave unto the seven angels seven golden vials full of the wrath of God, who liveth for ever and ever. And the temple was filled with smoke from the glory of God, and from his power; and no man was able to enter into the temple, till the seven plagues of the seven angels were fulfilled.

THE THUMOS OF God is about to begin and will be complete after the Seventh Vial or Bowl judgment. The saints call forth worship and praise, despite the suffering that they have endured during the seventieth week of Daniel. For those saints still alive on the earth, they, too, will experience the side effects of some of these great plagues. The number of souls seen under the altar when the Fifth Seal was opened is not yet complete. Their number will be complete before the Seventh Bowl or Vial judgment comes. There are some saints who will be called to endure the entire seventieth week of Daniel. They will be protected by the Lord during the *thumos* of God (Revelation 18:4). The saints are victorious as:

- They had victory over the beast; they overcame him;
- They had victory over his image as they refused to bow down and worship the beast and all he represents;
- They had victory over his mark as they forsook the possessions of this world and chose Almighty God as their chief passion;
- They had victory over the number of his name, which is 666.

The last seven plagues originate from God and from His Temple. The saints in heaven who have been victorious over the beast declare that His judgments are just and true. The messengers delivering these new judgments are clothed in pure and white linen. The *thumos* of God is a judgment that comes forth from a righteous and holy God. Many saints have already been martyred for their faith in the Lord Jesus, and others will be martyred later.

God's ultimate purpose for all nations and all His creation is to worship and praise Him:

10 The four and twenty elders fall down before him that sat on the throne, and worship him that liveth for ever and ever, and cast their crowns before the throne, saying, 11 Thou art worthy, O Lord, to receive glory and honour and power: for thou hast created all things, and for thy pleasure they are and were created. (Revelation 4:10-11)

9 Wherefore God also hath highly exalted him, and given him a name which is above every name: 10 That at the name of Jesus every knee should bow, of things in heaven, and things in earth, and things under the earth; 11 And that every tongue should confess that Jesus Christ is Lord, to the glory of God the Father. (Philippians 2:9-11)

In Philippians 2, the Scriptures declare that one day everyone, believers and unbelievers, shall bow the knee to Him and confess that He is Lord. No one will be exempt from bowing the knee before the Creator of all things.

The Lord desires that everyone be saved and come to believe in the Lord Jesus. He desires everyone to believe that Jesus Christ is the Messiah, the Son of God. He does not want anyone to be lost or spend eternity in the lake of fire. Unfortunately, many will choose not to follow after the Lord.

The Seven Vial or Bowl judgments will complete the *thumos* of God. At the end of the Seventh Bowl or Vial judgment, the Lord Jesus Christ will

Preparation for the Seven Last Plagues

return to the earth. Revelation 15:8 declares that the Temple in heaven was filled with smoke from the glory of God and from His power, and no one was able to enter the Temple until the seven plagues were completed. In the Old Testament, God's presence was often pictured by a cloud or by smoke:

³⁴ Then a cloud covered the tent of the congregation, and the glory of the LORD filled the tabernacle. ³⁵ And Moses was not able to enter into the tent of the congregation, because the cloud abode thereon, and the glory of the LORD filled the tabernacle. (Exodus 40:34-35)

¹ Then Solomon assembled the elders of Israel, and all the heads of the tribes, the chief of the fathers of the children of Israel, unto King Solomon in Jerusalem, that they might bring up the ark of the covenant of the LORD out of the city of David, which is Zion. ² And all the men of Israel assembled themselves unto King Solomon at the feast in the month Ethanim, which is the seventh month. ³ And all the elders of Israel came, and the priests took up the ark. ⁴ And they brought up the ark of the LORD, and the tabernacle of the congregation, and all the holy vessels that were in the tabernacle, even those did the priests and the Levites bring up. ⁵ And King Solomon, and all the congregation of Israel, that were assembled unto him, were with him before the ark, sacrificing sheep and oxen, that could not be told nor numbered for multitude. ⁶ And the priests brought in the ark of the covenant of the LORD unto his place, into the oracle of the house, to the most holy place, even under the wings of the cherubims. ⁷ For the cherubims spread forth their two wings over the place of the ark, and the cherubims covered the ark and the staves thereof above. ⁸ And they drew out the staves, that the ends of the staves were seen out in the holy place before the oracle, and they were not seen without: and there they are unto this day. ⁹ There was nothing in the ark save the two tables of stone, which Moses put there at Horeb, when the LORD made a covenant with the children of Israel, when they came out of the land of Egypt. ¹⁰ And it came to pass, when the priests were come out of the holy place, that the cloud filled the house of the LORD, ¹¹ So that the priests could not stand to minister because of the cloud: for the glory of the LORD had filled the house of the LORD. (I Kings 8:1-11).

Could the temple on the earth that has been defiled by the beast not be accessible at this time also?

Chapter 16
The Vials of Wrath

Revelation 16:1-2
The First Vial Judgment

And I heard a great voice out of the temple saying to the seven angels, Go your ways, and pour out the vials of the wrath of God upon the earth. And the first went, and poured out his vial upon the earth; and there fell a noisome and grievous sore upon the men which had the mark of the beast, and upon them which worshipped his image.

NOW IT IS God speaking from the Temple in heaven. His patience is at an end. A grievous sore upon the inhabitants of earth is the first judgment to be poured out from His vials of wrath, as prophesied in the Book of Deuteronomy:

²⁷ *The LORD will smite thee with the botch of Egypt, and with the emerods, and with the scab, and with the itch, whereof thou canst not be healed.* (Deuteronomy 28:27)

³⁵ *The LORD shall smite thee in the knees, and in the legs, with a sore botch that cannot be healed, from the sole of thy foot unto the top of thy head.* (Deuteronomy 28:35)

This is similar to the judgment placed on the Egyptians during the time of Moses, but this plague is more intense than the plague in Egypt:

⁸ *And the LORD said unto Moses and unto Aaron, Take to you handfuls of ashes of the furnace, and let Moses sprinkle it toward the heaven in the sight of*

Revelation

Pharaoh. ⁹ *And it shall become small dust in all the land of Egypt, and shall be a boil breaking forth with blains upon man, and upon beast, throughout all the land of Egypt.* ¹⁰ *And they took ashes of the furnace, and stood before Pharaoh; and Moses sprinkled it up toward heaven; and it became a boil breaking forth with blains upon man, and upon beast.* ¹¹ *And the magicians could not stand before Moses because of the boils; for the boil was upon the magicians, and upon all the Egyptians.* ¹² *And the LORD hardened the heart of Pharaoh, and he hearkened not unto them; as the LORD had spoken unto Moses.* (Exodus 9:8-12)

The prophecy in Deuteronomy will be fulfilled during this plague. The afflicted are those who worshiped the beast and received his mark. Those who have not received the mark of the beast are not impacted. For a culture that places an emphasis on outward appearance and beauty, this plague presents a tremendous emotional upheaval. Deuteronomy 28 is where the Lord proclaimed blessings if the people obeyed the commandments of the Lord, and curses if they chose to disobey the Lord. The plagues that are mentioned in Deuteronomy 28 are terrible:

⁵⁸ *If thou wilt not observe to do all the words of this law that are written in this book, that thou mayest fear this glorious and fearful name, THE LORD THY GOD;* ⁵⁹ *Then the LORD will make thy plagues wonderful, and the plagues of thy seed, even great plagues, and of long continuance, and sore sicknesses, and of long continuance.* ⁶⁰ *Moreover he will bring upon thee all the diseases of Egypt, which thou wast afraid of; and they shall cleave unto thee.* ⁶¹ *Also every sickness, and every plague, which is not written in the book of this law, them will the LORD bring upon thee, until thou be destroyed.* ⁶² *And ye shall be left few in number, whereas ye were as the stars of heaven for multitude; because thou wouldest not obey the voice of the LORD thy God.* ⁶³ *And it shall come to pass, that as the LORD rejoiced over you to do you good, and to multiply you; so the LORD will rejoice over you to destroy you, and to bring you to nought; and ye shall be plucked from off the land whither thou goest to possess it.* ⁶⁴ *And the LORD shall scatter thee among all people, from the one end of the earth even unto the other; and there thou shalt serve other gods, which neither thou nor thy fathers have known, even wood and stone.* ⁶⁵ *And among these nations shalt thou find no ease, neither shall the sole of thy foot have rest: but the LORD shall give thee there a trembling heart, and failing of eyes, and sorrow of mind:* ⁶⁶ *And thy life shall hang in doubt before thee; and thou shalt fear day and night, and shalt have none assurance of thy life:* ⁶⁷ *In the morning thou shalt say, Would God it were even! And at even thou shalt say, Would God it were morning! For the fear of thine heart wherewith thou shalt fear, and for the sight of thine eyes which thou shalt see.* (Deuteronomy 28:58-67)

The Vials of Wrath

The kingdom of antichrist will experience the horrors of this first plague as the *thumos* of the Father and the Son has commenced. The saints that are alive upon the earth will not experience this plague. The Lord will protect the righteous from the plagues that are being poured out upon the earth:

[12] The word of the LORD came again to me, saying, [13] Son of man, when the land sinneth against me by trespassing grievously, then will I stretch out mine hand upon it, and will break the staff of the bread thereof, and will send famine upon it, and will cut off man and beast from it: [14] Though these three men, Noah, Daniel, and Job, were in it, they should deliver but their own souls by their righteousness, saith the Lord GOD. [15] If I cause noisome beasts to pass through the land, and they spoil it, so that it be desolate, that no man may pass through because of the beasts: [16] Though these three men were in it, as I live, saith the Lord GOD, they shall deliver neither sons nor daughters; they only shall be delivered, but the land shall be desolate. [17] Or if I bring a sword upon that land, and say, Sword, go through the land; so that I cut off man and beast from it: [18] Though these three men were in it, as I live, saith the Lord GOD, they shall deliver neither sons nor daughters, but they only shall be delivered themselves. [19] Or if I send a pestilence into that land, and pour out my fury upon it in blood, to cut off from it man and beast: [20] Though Noah, Daniel, and Job were in it, as I live, saith the Lord GOD, they shall deliver neither son nor daughter; they shall but deliver their own souls by their righteousness. (Ezekiel 14:12-20)

Noah, Daniel and Job are examples of righteous men who the Lord will protect. The Lord knows those who are His.

Revelation 16:3
The Second Vial Judgment

And the second angel poured out his vial upon the sea; and it became as the blood of a dead man: and every living soul died in the sea.

The phrase, "Living soul," is the Greek word *nephesh*, and is referenced 754 times in the Scriptures. And 22 of those 754 times it refers to animals. This plague will destroy the food supply and even the transportation of goods across the seas. The greatest impact will be felt near the ocean front beaches. The death and decay near the beaches will be terrible.

Revelation 16:4-7
The Third Vial judgment

And the third angel poured out his vial upon the rivers and fountains of waters; and they became blood. And I heard the angel of the waters say, Thou art righteous,

Revelation

O Lord, which art, and wast, and shalt be, because thou hast judged thus. For they have shed the blood of saints and prophets, and thou hast given them blood to drink; for they are worthy. And I heard another out of the altar say, Even so, Lord God Almighty, true and righteous are thy judgments.

Fresh water sources are taken away in the third Vial or Bowl judgment. Fresh water will be in high demand when it becomes very hot on the earth. In the Book of Exodus during the time of Moses, God turned the water into blood. The third Vial or Bowl judgment is more devastating than the plague in Egypt (Exodus 7:19-21), because the entire world is impacted:

[19] And the LORD spake unto Moses, Say unto Aaron, Take thy rod, and stretch out thine hand upon the waters of Egypt, upon their streams, upon their rivers, and upon their ponds, and upon all their pools of water, that they may become blood; and that there may be blood throughout all the land of Egypt, both in vessels of wood, and in vessels of stone. [20] And Moses and Aaron did so, as the LORD commanded; and he lifted up the rod, and smote the waters that were in the river, in the sight of Pharaoh, and in the sight of his servants; and all the waters that were in the river were turned to blood. [21] And the fish that was in the river died; and the river stank, and the Egyptians could not drink of the water of the river; and there was blood throughout all the land of Egypt. (Exodus 7:19-21)

With this plague or judgment, the fish from the rivers are impacted. With the last two plagues (the second and third Vial judgments) the food supply upon the earth will be greatly depleted. The plagues are now occurring more frequently and in greater intensity, just like birth pangs as the baby is about to come. The return of Jesus to the earth will be soon.

The saints in heaven are witnessing these events upon the earth:

[9] And when he had opened the fifth seal, I saw under the altar the souls of them that were slain for the word of God, and for the testimony which they held: [10] And they cried with a loud voice, saying, How long, O Lord, holy and true, dost thou not judge and avenge our blood on them that dwell on the earth? [11] And white robes were given unto every one of them; and it was said unto them, that they should rest yet for a little season, until their fellowservants also and their brethren, that should be killed as they were, should be fulfilled. (Revelation 6:9-11)

The one under the altar who is declaring that the Lord's judgments are true and righteous appears to be one of the saints from the Fifth Seal. This verse supports the position that the number of saints under the altar is not yet complete. This is detailed in Revelation 7 and what they endured in verse 16:

9 After this I beheld, and, lo, a great multitude, which no man could number, of all nations, and kindreds, and people, and tongues, stood before the throne, and before the Lamb, clothed with white robes, and palms in their hands; 10 And cried with a loud voice, saying, Salvation to our God which sitteth upon the throne, and unto the Lamb. 11 And all the angels stood round about the throne, and about the elders and the four beasts, and fell before the throne on their faces, and worshipped God, 12 Saying, Amen: Blessing, and glory, and wisdom, and thanksgiving, and honour, and power, and might, be unto our God for ever and ever. Amen. 13 And one of the elders answered, saying unto me, What are these which are arrayed in white robes? And whence came they? 14 And I said unto him, Sir, thou knowest. And he said to me, These are they which came out of great tribulation, and have washed their robes, and made them white in the blood of the Lamb. 15 Therefore are they before the throne of God, and serve him day and night in his temple: and he that sitteth on the throne shall dwell among them. 16 They shall hunger no more, neither thirst any more; neither shall the sun light on them, nor any heat. 17 For the Lamb which is in the midst of the throne shall feed them, and shall lead them unto living fountains of waters: and God shall wipe away all tears from their eyes. (Revelation 7:9-17)

The kingdom of the antichrist is directly targeted with these plagues. The saints under the altar will soon have their number complete.

Revelation 16:8-9
The Fourth Vial Judgment

And the fourth angel poured out his vial upon the sun; and power was given unto him to scorch men with fire. And men were scorched with great heat, and blasphemed the name of God, which hath power over these plagues: and they repented not to give him glory.

The sun was worshipped by Nimrod and his followers in the plains of Shinar. Babylon was the site of the first temple of the sun. These judgments are against the kingdom of the antichrist and Babylon. With the temperature on the planet increasing, fresh water will be in great demand. Few men will be left upon the earth, just as Isaiah prophesied:

4 The earth mourneth and fadeth away, the world languisheth and fadeth away, the haughty people of the earth do languish. 5 The earth also is defiled under the inhabitants thereof; because they have transgressed the laws, changed the ordinance, broken the everlasting covenant. 6 Therefore hath the curse devoured the earth, and they that dwell therein are desolate: therefore the inhabitants of the earth are burned, and few men left. (Isaiah 24:4-6)

Revelation

The wrath of God will be poured out against the kingdom of antichrist in greater intensity than it was against Egypt as the population of the world is dwindling.

There is a passage in Isaiah which reveals that God will make the sun seven times hotter and brighter:

²⁶ *Moreover the light of the moon shall be as the light of the sun, and the light of the sun shall be sevenfold, as the light of seven days, in the day that the* LORD *bindeth up the breach of his people, and healeth the stroke of their wound.* ²⁷ *Behold, the name of the* LORD *cometh from far, burning with his anger, and the burden thereof is heavy: his lips are full of indignation, and his tongue as a devouring fire:* ²⁸ *And his breath, as an overflowing stream, shall reach to the midst of the neck, to sift the nations with the sieve of vanity: and there shall be a bridle in the jaws of the people, causing them to err.* (Isaiah 30:26-28)

Will God move the earth closer to the sun, thereby changing the orbit around the sun as the earth continues to wobble like a drunken man?

Revelation 16:10-11
The Fifth Vial Judgment

And the fifth angel poured out his vial upon the seat of the beast; and his kingdom was full of darkness; and they gnawed their tongues for pain, and blasphemed the God of heaven because of their pains and their sores, and repented not of their deeds.

The good Lord has a sense of humor. First the kingdom of the antichrist is plagued with grievous sores, and now He turns the lights out on the kingdom of the antichrist. The battle is pressed to Satan's citadel. This plague of darkness is a plague that can be felt, and will isolate the people in the capital of the beast. This plague is similar to the plague of darkness in Egypt that occurred during the time of Moses:

²¹ *And the* LORD *said unto Moses, Stretch out thine hand toward heaven, that there may be darkness over the land of Egypt, even darkness which may be felt.* ²² *And Moses stretched forth his hand toward heaven; and there was a thick darkness in all the land of Egypt three days:* ²³ *They saw not one another, neither rose any from his place for three days: but all the children of Israel had light in their dwellings.* (Exodus 10:21-23)

The plague in Egypt was localized. The Fifth Vial or Bowl judgment impacts the kingdom of the antichrist throughout the world. Isaiah also prophesied a plague of darkness that would come upon the earth:

² For, behold, the darkness shall cover the earth, and gross darkness the people: but the LORD shall arise upon thee, and his glory shall be seen upon thee (Isaiah 60:2).

The followers of the antichrist love darkness and refuse to come to the light of the Gospel. Now the Lord gives them a terrible plague of darkness—a darkness that can be felt. This plague, when combined with the previous plagues from the *thumos* of God, will greatly impact the earth and the kingdom of antichrist.

Revelation 16:12-16
The Sixth Vial Judgment

And the sixth angel poured out his vial upon the great river Euphrates; and the water thereof was dried up, that the way of the kings of the east might be prepared. And I saw three unclean spirits like frogs come out of the mouth of the dragon, and out of the mouth of the beast, and out of the mouth of the false prophet. For they are the spirits of devils, working miracles, which go forth unto the kings of the earth and of the whole world, to gather them to the battle of that great day of God Almighty. Behold, I come as a thief. Blessed is he that watcheth, and keepeth his garments, lest he walk naked, and they see his shame. And he gathered them together into a place called in the Hebrew tongue Armageddon.

The four angels who were bound in the great river Euphrates were released during the Sixth Trumpet judgment. Now the Euphrates is dried up, the formidable natural boundary has been removed for the people of Asia and the Far East to move westward. Perhaps the heat of the sun plays a big part in drying up the river, allowing the kings of the east to move westward. In the past there have been battles fought in this region as described below:

²⁰ After all this, when Josiah had prepared the temple, Necho king of Egypt came up to fight against Charchemish by Euphrates: and Josiah went out against him. ²¹ But he sent ambassadors to him, saying, What have I to do with thee, thou king of Judah? I come not against thee this day, but against the house wherewith I have war: for God commanded me to make haste: forbear thee from meddling with God, who is with me, that he destroy thee not. ²² Nevertheless Josiah would not turn his face from him, but disguised himself, that he might fight with him, and hearkened

Revelation

not unto the words of Necho from the mouth of God, and came to fight in the valley of Megiddo. (II Chronicles 35:20-22)

> ⁹ And it shall come to pass in that day, that I will seek to destroy all the nations that come against Jerusalem. ¹⁰ And I will pour upon the house of David, and upon the inhabitants of Jerusalem, the spirit of grace and of supplications: and they shall look upon me whom they have pierced, and they shall mourn for him, as one mourneth for his only son, and shall be in bitterness for him, as one that is in bitterness for his firstborn. ¹¹ In that day shall there be a great mourning in Jerusalem, as the mourning of Hadadrimmon in the valley of Megiddon. (Zechariah 12:9-11)

Megiddo is located in northern Israel, in the Jezreel Valley. There have been great slaughters in Megiddo before: Jabin's hosts with 900 chariots (Judges 4), Gideon over the Midianites (Judges 7), David's slaying of Goliath (I Samuel 17). There is one final battle yet to take place in Megiddo. The great slaughter that will occur during the Seventh Vial or Bowl judgment will surpass them all with the number of bodies over the battlefield. The blood and bodies will cover the battlefield for 200 miles (Revelation 14:20).

Jesus Christ is coming back soon, and the birth pangs are almost over. The Lord Jesus will return to the earth during this battle. It is during the Sixth Vial or Bowl Judgment that the earth is reaped as the last of the martyrs are taken home to heaven to be with Jesus, as noted in Revelation 14:

> ¹² Here is the patience of the saints: here are they that keep the commandments of God, and the faith of Jesus. ¹³ And I heard a voice from heaven saying unto me, Write, Blessed are the dead which die in the Lord from henceforth: Yea, saith the Spirit, that they may rest from their labours; and their works do follow them. ¹⁴ And I looked, and behold a white cloud, and upon the cloud one sat like unto the Son of man, having on his head a golden crown, and in his hand a sharp sickle. ¹⁵ And another angel came out of the temple, crying with a loud voice to him that sat on the cloud, Thrust in thy sickle, and reap: for the time is come for thee to reap; for the harvest of the earth is ripe. ¹⁶ And he that sat on the cloud thrust in his sickle on the earth; and the earth was reaped. (Revelation 14:12-16)

The final Vial or Bowl judgment is for the beast and the kingdom of antichrist. The saints who have the testimony of Jesus and are still on the earth at this time will need to be removed or protected from the Seventh Vial or Bowl judgment. Once the last saint who has the testimony of Jesus is martyred or has left Babylon (Revelation 18:4), the next harvest to take place is the judgment of the tares at the battle of Armageddon:

17 And another angel came out of the temple which is in heaven, he also having a sharp sickle. 18 And another angel came out from the altar, which had power over fire; and cried with a loud cry to him that had the sharp sickle, saying, Thrust in thy sharp sickle, and gather the clusters of the vine of the earth; for her grapes are fully ripe. 19 And the angel thrust in his sickle into the earth, and gathered the vine of the earth, and cast it into the great winepress of the wrath of God. 20 And the winepress was trodden without the city, and blood came out of the winepress, even unto the horse bridles, by the space of a thousand and six hundred furlongs. (Revelation 14:17-20)

The saints who are not appointed to be martyred during the seventieth week of Daniel are called to leave Babylon the Great so they do not participate in her plagues. Just as God waited until Lot departed from Sodom before destroying the wicked, God will remove His people out of Babylon before destroying the wicked:

1And after these things I saw another angel come down from heaven, having great power; and the earth was lightened with his glory. 2 And he cried mightily with a strong voice, saying, Babylon the great is fallen, is fallen, and is become the habitation of devils, and the hold of every foul spirit, and a cage of every unclean and hateful bird. 3 For all nations have drunk of the wine of the wrath of her fornication, and the kings of the earth have committed fornication with her, and the merchants of the earth are waxed rich through the abundance of her delicacies. 4 And I heard another voice from heaven, saying, Come out of her, my people, that ye be not partakers of her sins, and that ye receive not of her plagues. (Revelation 18:1-4)

The saints identified under the altar in the opening of the Fifth Seal (Revelation 6:9-11), will now have their number complete. The last saint appointed to be martyred during the seventieth week of Daniel will be martyred before the Seventh Bowl or Vial judgment. The number of the saints from Revelation 7 is now complete:

9 After this I beheld, and, lo, a great multitude, which no man could number, of all nations, and kindreds, and people, and tongues, stood before the throne, and before the Lamb, clothed with white robes, and palms in their hands; 10 And cried with a loud voice, saying, Salvation to our God which sitteth upon the throne, and unto the Lamb. 11 And all the angels stood round about the throne, and about the elders and the four beasts, and fell before the throne on their faces, and worshipped God, 12 Saying, Amen: Blessing, and glory, and wisdom, and thanksgiving, and honour, and power, and might, be unto our God for ever and ever. Amen. 13 And one of the elders answered, saying unto me, What are these which are arrayed in white robes? And whence came they? 14 And I said unto him, Sir, thou knowest. And he said to me, *These are they which came out of great tribulation, and have washed their robes, and made them white in the blood of the Lamb.* *[15] Therefore are they before the throne of God, and serve him day and night in his temple: and he that sitteth on the throne shall dwell among them.* *[16] They shall hunger no more, neither thirst any more; neither shall the sun light on them, nor any heat.* *[17] For the Lamb which is in the midst of the throne shall feed them, and shall lead them unto living fountains of waters: and God shall wipe away all tears from their eyes.* (Revelation 7:9-17)

The saints in the seventieth week of Daniel have endured a lot. They have endured wars, famine, persecution, lack of water, and the scorching heat of the sun. The final plague is not for the saints who have the testimony of Jesus.

Revelation 16:17-21
The Seventh Vial Judgment

And the seventh angel poured out his vial into the air; and there came a great voice out of the temple of heaven, from the throne, saying, It is done. And there were voices, and thunders, and lightnings; and there was a great earthquake, such as was not since men were upon the earth, so mighty an earthquake, and so great. And the great city was divided into three parts, and the cities of the nations fell: and great Babylon came in remembrance before God, to give unto her the cup of the wine of the fierceness of his wrath. And every island fled away, and the mountains were not found. And there fell upon men a great hail out of heaven, every stone about the weight of a talent: and men blasphemed God because of the plague of the hail; for the plague thereof was exceeding great.

The last Bowl or Vial judgment is poured out with an utterance, "It is done." This plague targets Satan and the kingdom of antichrist. Satan is the prince of the power of the air, as noted in Ephesians 2:2. As prophesied in the Book of Daniel, we see that God's kingdom is about to be set up, and the kingdoms of this world and the kingdom of antichrist are to be overthrown and destroyed:

[44] And in the days of these kings shall the God of heaven set up a kingdom, which shall never be destroyed: and the kingdom shall not be left to other people, but it shall break in pieces and consume all these kingdoms, and it shall stand for ever. *[45] Forasmuch as thou sawest that the stone was cut out of the mountain without hands, and that it brake in pieces the iron, the brass, the clay, the silver, and the gold; the great God hath made known to the king what shall come to pass hereafter: and the dream is certain, and the interpretation thereof sure.* (Daniel 2:44-45)

What was prophesied in the Book of Daniel will come to pass. The future of the earth has been predestined. The Lord Jesus will return to the earth during the reign of the beast, and the age of men ruling over men will be over. Mankind will soon experience the Lord Jesus reigning as King, and righteousness will prevail.

In the Old Testament, blasphemers were put to death by stoning, and here as part of the last Bowl or Vial judgment the blasphemers receive the same punishment. This is similar to the hail in Egypt, but it is more deadly, as the hailstones in this plague weigh 100 pounds:

²² And the LORD said unto Moses, Stretch forth thine hand toward heaven, that there may be hail in all the land of Egypt, upon man, and upon beast, and upon every herb of the field, throughout the land of Egypt. ²³ And Moses stretched forth his rod toward heaven: and the LORD sent thunder and hail, and the fire ran along upon the ground; and the LORD rained hail upon the land of Egypt. ²⁴ So there was hail, and fire mingled with the hail, very grievous, such as there was none like it in all the land of Egypt since it became a nation. ²⁵ And the hail smote throughout all the land of Egypt all that was in the field, both man and beast; and the hail smote every herb of the field, and brake every tree of the field. (Exodus 9:22-25)

The final judgment is truly proceeding from the Throne in heaven and from Him who sits on the Throne. During the final Vial or Bowl judgment, Mystery Babylon (apostate church), Civil Babylon (commercial, city of the antichrist) and Power of the nations (against each other and then against the Lord), will be destroyed and will never rise again.

The judgment on all the nations was prophesied by the prophets of old and in greater detail:

¹Behold, the LORD maketh the earth empty, and maketh it waste, and turneth it upside down, and scattereth abroad the inhabitants thereof. ² And it shall be, as with the people, so with the priest; as with the servant, so with his master; as with the maid, so with her mistress; as with the buyer, so with the seller; as with the lender, so with the borrower; as with the taker of usury, so with the giver of usury to him. ³ The land shall be utterly emptied, and utterly spoiled: for the LORD hath spoken this word. ⁴ The earth mourneth and fadeth away, the world languisheth and fadeth away, the haughty people of the earth do languish. ⁵ The earth also is defiled under the inhabitants thereof; because they have transgressed the laws, changed the ordinance, broken the everlasting covenant. ⁶ Therefore hath the curse devoured the earth, and they that dwell therein are desolate: therefore the inhabitants of the earth are burned, and few men left. (Isaiah 24:1-6)

Revelation

¹⁹ *The earth is utterly broken down, the earth is clean dissolved, the earth is moved exceedingly.* ²⁰ *The earth shall reel to and fro like a drunkard, and shall be removed like a cottage; and the transgression thereof shall be heavy upon it; and it shall fall, and not rise again.* ²¹ *And it shall come to pass in that day, that the LORD shall punish the host of the high ones that are on high, and the kings of the earth upon the earth.* ²² *And they shall be gathered together, as prisoners are gathered in the pit, and shall be shut up in the prison, and after many days shall they be visited.* ²³ *Then the moon shall be confounded, and the sun ashamed, when the LORD of hosts shall reign in mount Zion, and in Jerusalem, and before his ancients gloriously.* (Isaiah 24:19-23)

⁶ *Thou shalt be visited of the LORD of hosts with thunder, and with earthquake, and great noise, with storm and tempest, and the flame of devouring fire.* (Isaiah 29:6).

⁴ *And his feet shall stand in that day upon the mount of Olives, which is before Jerusalem on the east, and the mount of Olives shall cleave in the midst thereof toward the east and toward the west, and there shall be a very great valley; and half of the mountain shall remove toward the north, and half of it toward the south.* ⁵ *And ye shall flee to the valley of the mountains; for the valley of the mountains shall reach unto Azal: yea, ye shall flee, like as ye fled from before the earthquake in the days of Uzziah king of Judah: and the LORD my God shall come, and all the saints with thee.* (Zechariah 14:4-5)

⁶ *For thus saith the LORD of hosts; Yet once, it is a little while, and I will shake the heavens, and the earth, and the sea, and the dry land;* ⁷ *And I will shake all nations, and the desire of all nations shall come: and I will fill this house with glory, saith the LORD of hosts.* (Haggai 2:6-7)

²⁰ *And again the word of the LORD came unto Haggai in the four and twentieth day of the month, saying,* ²¹ *Speak to Zerubbabel, governor of Judah, saying, I will shake the heavens and the earth;* ²² *And I will overthrow the throne of kingdoms, and I will destroy the strength of the kingdoms of the heathen; and I will overthrow the chariots, and those that ride in them; and the horses and their riders shall come down, every one by the sword of his brother.* (Haggai 2:20-22)

The entire earth is impacted by this earthquake, as prophesied in Isaiah 24:1-6, 24:18-20. The earthquake that took place at the Sixth Seal caused the mountains and islands to be moved out of their places, but this one causes them to disappear. The Lord in His mercy does not permit those who have the testimony of Jesus to experience this judgment (Revelation 18:4). These great hailstones are for the blasphemers of the planet and not for those who have the testimony of Jesus. The Lord will have his saints who are left on the earth in a place where the hailstones will not fall.

Chapter 17

The Destruction of Religious Babylon

Revelation 17:1-2
The Great Harlot

And there came one of the seven angels which had the seven vials, and talked with me, saying unto me, Come hither; I will shew unto thee the judgment of the great whore that sitteth upon many waters: With whom the kings of the earth have committed fornication, and the inhabitants of the earth have been made drunk with the wine of her fornication.

THE GREAT GODLESS system in this world is to be judged. All throughout the world, people (rulers and citizens) are made drunk by a counterfeit church or religion. The saints are commanded to be filled with the Holy Spirit, to walk under the anointing of the Holy Spirit, and not to be made drunk by the things of this world. There are churches today that have compromised their faith by allowing the traditions of other religions to infiltrate the church of Jesus Christ. This was the sin of the church of Pergamos, which allowed the traditions of the other religions into the church. The church of Pergamos was exhorted by the Lord Jesus to repent and to remove these pagan practices.

Putting something or someone else in place of God is spiritual harlotry. Here we have the mother of all false religions. The rulers and the common folk are deceived by the godless religious system. Some Bible scholars and church historians believe that the Vatican is the great whore of Revelation 17. The leaders of the Protestant Reformation were certain that the whore represented the Roman Catholic Church in general and the pope in particular. It is the opinion of some scholars that the whore described in Revelation 17 is greater than the Vatican and greater than the Roman Catholic Church. It is thought that the Roman Catholic Church is just a branch out of this counterfeit religion. Yes, one can substitute the Vatican for the woman, and it fits perfectly because the kings and kingdoms of Europe throughout the centuries were controlled by Rome and the Roman Catholic Church. The late Dave Hunt documents the history of the popes that ruled over the kingdoms of the world in his 1994 book, *A Woman Rides the Beast: The Roman Catholic Church and the Last Days*. However, the early church believed that the Roman Empire was the counterfeit religion and that Nero and others could be the antichrist as the Roman Empire shed the blood of many saints in the early years of the church.

God will judge the great harlot for all the blood that has been shed throughout the centuries, much of that blood having been shed by the popes. There are church historians who believe that the church of Thyatira represents the Roman Catholic Church. The church of Thyatira will face judgment and be destroyed with death together with those churches that follow after the teaching of Jezebel, as prophesied in the message to the churches (Revelation 2:23).

In His message to the church of Thyatira, Jesus cites Jezebel as the personification of seduction and false religion (Revelation 2:20). Pagan practices were introduced into the church of Thyatira just as Jezebel introduced Baal worship into the northern tribes of Israel under King Ahab. Pagan practices such as relics, the priesthood, and the selling of indulgences are just a few of the practices that the Lord Jesus holds against the Roman Catholic Church. After the resurrection of Jesus, the priesthood was made obsolete. As the Roman Catholic Church has ruled over the kingdoms of the world throughout the centuries, the churches that represent Pergamos, Thyatira, Sardis and Laodicea will be in bed with the coming antichrist. The wicked seductress will be in league with the antichrist and his political system. It is no coincidence that the great harlot and spiritual seductress labeled "Babylon the Great" is described as the mother of harlots.

False religion did not start and end with Thyatira, but it continued with the church of Sardis. Many church historians identify the church of Sardis with the church age following the Protestant Reformation. The churches of the Protestant Reformation are in a much more sorrowful state, as the church of Sardis had only a few names that remained faithful to the Lord Jesus, whereas the church of Thyatira had a faithful remnant. The churches of the

Protestant Reformation believe they are true and alive unto the Lord, but in reality they are spiritually dead, as the Lord Jesus declared in His message to the church of Sardis (Revelation 3:1).

Revelation 17:3-6
The woman on the Beast

So he carried me away in the spirit into the wilderness: and I saw a woman sit upon a scarlet coloured beast, full of names of blasphemy, having seven heads and ten horns. And the woman was arrayed in purple and scarlet colour, and decked with gold and precious stones and pearls, having a golden cup in her hand full of abominations and filthiness of her fornication: And upon her forehead was a name written, MYSTERY, BABYLON THE GREAT, THE MOTHER OF HARLOTS AND ABOMINATIONS OF THE EARTH. And I saw the woman drunken with the blood of the saints, and with the blood of the martyrs of Jesus: and when I saw her, I wondered with great admiration.

The woman is dressed in scarlet. Scarlet is the symbol of glory of this world. She is in control as she is the rider exercising authority and influence over the beast. The woman represents the culmination of the whole godless religious system. The woman represents the faithless in their moment of final power and control over the world before being destroyed by a civil power, which in turn will be destroyed. The woman rides on the back of the beast with seven heads and ten horns, which is symbolic of the kingdom of antichrist. It is important to realize that the woman sits on the beast that represents past and future world empires.

It is amazing to see a rider on such a ferocious beast. This dreadful beast is described in Daniel 7. It appears that she is in control over the beast, but it is the beast that is using the woman (false religion) to establish his power and authority. At the appropriate time the kingdom of antichrist will destroy the woman, as she will soon be in the way of the ambition of the beast to declare himself God.

The antichrist or the beast is described in Daniel 7:8, 7:20, 7:25, 11:36, Isaiah 14:14, Ezekiel 28:2, 28:6-10, II Thessalonians 2:4 and Revelation 13:1-2. The antichrist, the little horn, comes to power after the ten horns are in power.

[8] I considered the horns, and, behold, there came up among them another little horn, before whom there were three of the first horns plucked up by the roots: and, behold, in this horn were eyes like the eyes of man, and a mouth speaking great things. (Daniel 7:8)

Revelation

²⁰ *And of the ten horns that were in his head, and of the other which came up, and before whom three fell; even of that horn that had eyes, and a mouth that spake very great things, whose look was more stout than his fellows.* (Daniel 7:20).

²⁵ *And he shall speak great words against the most High, and shall wear out the saints of the most High, and think to change times and laws: and they shall be given into his hand until a time and times and the dividing of time.* (Daniel 7:25)

³⁶ *And the king shall do according to his will; and he shall exalt himself, and magnify himself above every god, and shall speak marvellous things against the God of gods, and shall prosper till the indignation be accomplished: for that that is determined shall be done.* (Daniel 11:36)

¹⁴ *I will ascend above the heights of the clouds; I will be like the most High.* (Isaiah 14:14)

² *Son of man, say unto the prince of Tyrus, Thus saith the Lord GOD; Because thine heart is lifted up, and thou hast said, I am a God, I sit in the seat of God, in the midst of the seas; yet thou art a man, and not God, though thou set thine heart as the heart of God.* (Ezekiel 28:2)

⁶ *Therefore thus saith the Lord GOD; Because thou hast set thine heart as the heart of God;* ⁷ *Behold, therefore I will bring strangers upon thee, the terrible of the nations: and they shall draw their swords against the beauty of thy wisdom, and they shall defile thy brightness.* ⁸ *They shall bring thee down to the pit, and thou shalt die the deaths of them that are slain in the midst of the seas.* ⁹ *Wilt thou yet say before him that slayeth thee, I am God? But thou shalt be a man, and no God, in the hand of him that slayeth thee.* ¹⁰ *Thou shalt die the deaths of the uncircumcised by the hand of strangers: for I have spoken it, saith the Lord GOD.* (Ezekiel 28:6-10)

⁴ *Who opposeth and exalteth himself above all that is called God, or that is worshipped; so that he as God sitteth in the temple of God, shewing himself that he is God.* (II Thessalonians 2:4)

¹ *And I stood upon the sand of the sea, and saw a beast rise up out of the sea, having seven heads and ten horns, and upon his horns ten crowns, and upon his heads the name of blasphemy.* ² *And the beast which I saw was like unto a leopard, and his feet were as the feet of a bear, and his mouth as the mouth of a lion: and the dragon gave him his power, and his seat, and great authority.* (Revelation 13:1-2)

The woman riding the beast is dressed in garments of imperial power. This wicked woman has a golden cup in her hand. The golden cup has been associated with Babylon and with the Roman Catholic Church over the

The Destruction of Religious Babylon

centuries. The book, *The Two Babylons, or The Papal Worship Proved to be the Worship of Nimrod and His Wife*, by the late Rev. Alexander Hislop, traces the golden cup of the Roman Catholic Mass to the Babylonian Religion. Babylon has been a golden cup in the Lord's hand as declared in Jeremiah:

⁷ Babylon hath been a golden cup in the LORD's hand, that made all the earth drunken: the nations have drunken of her wine; therefore the nations are mad. (Jeremiah 51:7)

Revelation 18:16 declares that the great city of Commercial Babylon will be adorned with gold, precious stones and pearls. Religion has become a big business. The woman represents that which began with Babylon and has continued throughout history. She is the mother of harlots and the abominations of the earth. To understand the root of Babylon it is necessary to dig into the Scriptures. The Lord in His wisdom has placed clues in the Scriptures to show the root of the Babylonian Religion. Jacob Prasch's message "Roots of Babylon" is a good resource on the origin of the Babylonian Religion.

We know from history that the priests of Babylon migrated to Pergamos after the Medes and Persians had conquered Babylon. We see this also from the Book of Revelation where our Lord exhorts the church of Pergamos to be faithful, as there was a church planted in the city of Pergamos, which was influenced by Babylon and the Babylonian Religion:

¹² And to the angel of the church in Pergamos write; These things saith he which hath the sharp sword with two edges; ¹³ I know thy works, and where thou dwellest, even where Satan's seat is: and thou holdest fast my name, and hast not denied my faith, even in those days wherein Antipas was my faithful martyr, who was slain among you, where Satan dwelleth. (Revelation 2:12-13)

The church was established to be a light to the world. Over time the church was overcome by the wicked influences around it. The pagan practices crept into the church of Pergamos which included the establishing of the priesthood. One of the spiritual blessings that the children of God have today is that every child of God can approach the Father and the Son directly, with confidence and with boldness as revealed in the Book of Hebrews. The child of God does not need to seek a man to be an intercessor between himself and God. Even the lowest and weakest of all the children of God has direct access to the Throne in heaven. The access is open to all the children of God to come.

Revelation

Over time, Rome became influenced by the Babylonian Religion as Pergamos was under the control of the Roman Empire at this time in history. Peter wrote his first epistle from Babylon, but we know from history that Peter went to Rome and not to Iraq where Babylon is located today:

13 The church that is at Babylon, elected together with you, saluteth you; and so doth Marcus my son. (I Peter 5:13)

The Babylonian Religion and its influence had infiltrated Rome from Pergamos. When Babylon was conquered by the Medes and Persians around 538 BC, the 3,000 pagan priests migrated westward to Pergama. By the time of the first century, the pagan religions came via Pergama to the Pantheon in Rome. This is why when Peter wrote his epistle from Rome he writes, "She who is in Babylon greets you." The church at Pergamos which began right has now become corrupted during the latter years of the first century. The church of Pergamos was the third church that the Lord Jesus addressed in the Book of Revelation. In Matthew 13, the third kingdom parable that Jesus taught was about the mustard seed. The third kingdom parable relates to the church of Pergamos (and the fourth kingdom parable relates to the fourth church addressed in the Book of Revelation which was Thyatira). The Lord declared that the mustard seed, an herb, grew into a tree, and that the birds of the air came to lodge in its branches. This is not normal, as mustard seeds do not grow into trees. This signifies a cancerous growth, an abnormal growth. The birds of the air, which are symbolic of demons in the kingdom parables, are seen lodging in the branches of this mustard tree. This signifies that Satan has infiltrated the church of Pergamos. As declared in Matthew 13, we see that birds represent evil. In Matthew 13:3, 13:18, we see the birds coming to snatch away the seed of the sower, lest it bears fruit. Pergamos signifies a mixed marriage church—a church which calls itself a Christian church but is married to the world, which was forbidden, as the apostle Paul wrote in his epistle to the Corinthians (I Corinthians 6:14-16). Therefore, the Roman Empire and even Rome itself was deeply embedded into the Babylonian Religion that originated from the land of Shinar during the time of Nimrod and the Tower of Babel.

There is an unfulfilled prophecy that the Babylonian Religion is to be re-established in the land of Shinar:

5 Then the angel that talked with me went forth, and said unto me, Lift up now thine eyes, and see what is this that goeth forth. 6 And I said, What is it? And he said, This is an ephah that goeth forth. He said moreover, This is their resemblance

The Destruction of Religious Babylon

through all the earth. ⁷ And, behold, there was lifted up a talent of lead: and this is a woman that sitteth in the midst of the ephah. ⁸ And he said, This is wickedness. And he cast it into the midst of the ephah; and he cast the weight of lead upon the mouth thereof. ⁹ Then lifted I up mine eyes, and looked, and, behold, there came out two women, and the wind was in their wings; for they had wings like the wings of a stork: and they lifted up the ephah between the earth and the heaven. ¹⁰ Then said I to the angel that talked with me, Whither do these bear the ephah? ¹¹ And he said unto me, To build it an house in the land of Shinar: and it shall be established, and set there upon her own base. (Zechariah 5:5-11)

We know from the Scriptures that the wicked woman is Jezebel. In Revelation 2, Jezebel was a pagan queen who seduced the people of God by being in league with the political system alongside King Ahab and leading the nation into spiritual harlotry. We know from the kingdom parables that birds are represented as evil, demonic. Not all birds are evil, but in the kingdom parables the birds were represented as stealing away the seed that was sown by the sower. The sower was one who was sowing the Word of God and the birds were devouring the seed to keep it from taking root and bearing fruit. The stork mentioned in the prophecy of Zechariah is a bird. It is a powerful bird. Therefore, the stork represents a powerful demon here in Zechariah 5. The stork with its large wings can carry a heavy payload. Zechariah 5 mentions two women with the wings of a stork carrying a container that has a lead covering. False religion is empowered by powerful demons. The ephah is a container like a big basket. A woman can easily fit inside this basket. On the ephah is a lead plate. Lead is an unholy metal (Ezekiel 22:18). Where is the woman going? She is going to Shinar in Babylon. This is important as now we see that Zechariah 5 climaxes in Revelation 18, the destruction of Babylon the Great. Babylon the Great will be established in the land of Shinar. The religion of Babylon which originated from the land of Shinar will return to the land of Shinar and will be judged there at its original base.

With false religion returning to its original base it is now important to discern the original location of Babylon. This also is given to us in the Scriptures in the Book of Daniel:

¹ In the third year of the reign of Jehoiakim king of Judah came Nebuchadnezzar king of Babylon unto Jerusalem, and besieged it. ² And the Lord gave Jehoiakim king of Judah into his hand, with part of the vessels of the house of God: which he carried into the land of Shinar to the house of his god; and he brought the vessels into the treasure house of his god. (Daniel 1:1-2)

Revelation

During the reign of Nebuchadnezzar, king of Babylon, something very interesting takes place. King Nebuchadnezzar is looking to set up a religion that everyone in his kingdom must adhere to; a religion that will unite his empire. In Daniel 3 the king sets up an image for all to worship:

¹Nebuchadnezzar the king made an image of gold, whose height was threescore cubits, and the breadth thereof six cubits: he set it up in the plain of Dura, in the province of Babylon. ² Then Nebuchadnezzar the king sent to gather together the princes, the governors, and the captains, the judges, the treasurers, the counsellors, the sheriffs, and all the rulers of the provinces, to come to the dedication of the image which Nebuchadnezzar the king had set up. ³ Then the princes, the governors, and captains, the judges, the treasurers, the counsellors, the sheriffs, and all the rulers of the provinces, were gathered together unto the dedication of the image that Nebuchadnezzar the king had set up; and they stood before the image that Nebuchadnezzar had set up. ⁴ Then an herald cried aloud, To you it is commanded, O people, nations, and languages, ⁵ That at what time ye hear the sound of the cornet, flute, harp, sackbut, psaltery, dulcimer, and all kinds of musick, ye fall down and worship the golden image that Nebuchadnezzar the king hath set up: ⁶ And whoso falleth not down and worshippeth shall the same hour be cast into the midst of a burning fiery furnace. (Daniel 3:1-6)

What happened in Daniel 3 will be replayed in the future, as the beast will recreate what the king of Babylon introduced. All mankind will be commanded to worship the image that the beast will set up, and take the number of the beast, or be killed as declared in Revelation 13. The penalty for not worshipping the image was death as noted in Daniel 3, and the penalty for not worshipping the beast or his image will be death. What happened in the past will replay itself again in the future.

We now know where Babylon is located, but in order to find the root of Babylon, we have to dig deeper into the Scriptures. We know that the Babylonian Religion was founded in Shinar, but now we need to look at what transpired in Shinar early in the history of the world.

The Tower of Babel in the land of Shinar was being built as a new world religion was being established, and this is recorded in the Book of Genesis:

¹And the whole earth was of one language, and of one speech. ² And it came to pass, as they journeyed from the east, that they found a plain in the land of Shinar; and they dwelt there. ³ And they said one to another, Go to, let us make brick, and burn them thoroughly. And they had brick for stone, and slime had they for morter. ⁴ And they said, Go to, let us build us a city and a tower, whose top may reach unto heaven; and let us make us a name, lest we be scattered abroad upon the face of the whole earth. ⁵ And the LORD came down to see the city and the tower, which the children of men builded. ⁶ And the LORD said, Behold, the people is one, and they have all one language; and this they begin to do: and now nothing will be restrained from them, which they have imagined to do. ⁷ Go to, let us go down, and there confound their language, that they may not understand one another's speech. ⁸ So the LORD scattered them abroad from thence upon the face of all the earth: and they left off to build the city. ⁹ Therefore is the name of it called Babel; because the LORD did there confound the language of all the earth: and from thence did the LORD scatter them abroad upon the face of all the earth. (Genesis 11:1-9)

The building of the Tower of Babel occurred very early after the flood of Noah. The Lord commanded Noah and his family to go forth throughout the whole earth and replenish it. Instead, men rebelled against the Lord's commandment and dwelt at Shinar where they established a city and built a great tower. This was open rebellion against the God of Noah. It was an attempt by Nimrod to establish his kingdom and throne above the Throne of the God of Noah, as the historical records indicate.

Nimrod, known as the mighty one and a mighty hunter, was against the Lord as he began to build the one-world religion in Shinar as hinted in Genesis:

⁸ And Cush begat Nimrod: he began to be a mighty one in the earth. ⁹ He was a mighty hunter before the LORD: wherefore it is said, Even as Nimrod the mighty hunter before the LORD. ¹⁰ And the beginning of his kingdom was Babel, and Erech, and Accad, and Calneh, in the land of Shinar. (Genesis 10:8-10)

In order to have a kingdom, one must have a king. We see that Nimrod was a king at Babel in the land of Shinar. It was a desire of Nimrod to build a tower to reach unto heaven to protect mankind from any future floods from the God of Noah. Nimrod believed that with the technology of man, he could build a great tower to reach unto the heavens. A tower so large that even the God of Noah would not be able to judge mankind with a flood in the future. It was a desire of Nimrod to exalt himself and set himself above the God of Noah.

The antichrist will persuade mankind to rebel against the God of heaven and against His Son, as this was Satan's ambition to be like the Most High:

¹⁴ I will ascend above the heights of the clouds; I will be like the most High. (Isaiah 14:14)

Revelation

² *Son of man, say unto the prince of Tyrus, Thus saith the Lord* GOD; *Because thine heart is lifted up, and thou hast said, I am a God, I sit in the seat of God, in the midst of the seas; yet thou art a man, and not God, though thou set thine heart as the heart of God.* (Ezekiel 28:2)

⁶ *Therefore thus saith the Lord* GOD; *Because thou hast set thine heart as the heart of God;* ⁷ *Behold, therefore I will bring strangers upon thee, the terrible of the nations: and they shall draw their swords against the beauty of thy wisdom, and they shall defile thy brightness.* ⁸ *They shall bring thee down to the pit, and thou shalt die the deaths of them that are slain in the midst of the seas.* ⁹ *Wilt thou yet say before him that slayeth thee, I am God? But thou shalt be a man, and no God, in the hand of him that slayeth thee.* ¹⁰ *Thou shalt die the deaths of the uncircumcised by the hand of strangers: for I have spoken it, saith the Lord* GOD. (Ezekiel 28:6-10)

In Josephus's, *The antiquities of the Jews*, in Chapter IV, Josephus records the history and rebellion of Nimrod (see appendix B). In the land of Shinar, where the original Babylon Empire was established in the Postdiluvian period, there was the construction of the Tower of Babel with Nimrod and his wife Semiramis. The first Postdiluvian was developed in Shinar as noted in Josephus's, *The antiquities of the Jews*, as well as in portions of the Book of Jasher, and the Epic of Gilgamesh. Here Nimrod marries Semiramis and from this union comes the infant god Tammuz, the demon nemesis with which the Hebrew prophets would later contend. Tammuz was worshipped as an infant held by Madonna, and who eventually came to be imitated by the Roman Catholic Church in a latter expression of Babylon.

The book, *The Two Babylons, or the Papal Worship Proven to be the Worship of Nimrod and His Wife*, by the late Rev. Alexander Hislop, provides evidence that the Papal worship is very similar to the worship of Nimrod and his wife Semiramis. Dave Hunt, in his book mentioned earlier, reveals the character of this woman riding on the beast and her powerful place in the kingdom of antichrist that is to come.

Nimrod and Semiramis

It is thought that Nimrod began his conquests about 1,000 years after the flood. Tradition states that Semiramis was an inn/brothel keeper in the city of Erech, within the land of Shinar. Tradition also states that she was a very beautiful woman. Very little has come down to us through the millennia concerning Semiramis' rise to power, but it is safe to assume that it was initially upon Nimrod's rise to power. Once Nimrod chose Semiramis as his wife it was not fitting to have an ex-harlot sitting as queen upon the throne, so a story was invented that she was a virgin sprung from the sea at Nimrod's landing, and hence a suitable bride for the emperor. The name Semiramis means "sprung from the sea."

Semiramis was the instigator in establishing a false religion aimed at supporting their rule. The religion she invented was based primarily upon a corruption of astrology and astronomy that was passed down after the fall of Adam and Eve in the Garden. The original story depicted by means of the constellations told of Satan's rebellion and the war in the heavens, his subversion of mankind, the fall of Adam and Eve, the promise of One to come who would suffer and die to relieve man from the curse of sin then be installed as Lord of Creation, and the final re-subjugation of the cosmos to God through Him.

These original stories of the constellations were corrupted by Semiramis. She changed the meaning of the constellations where the great dragon (Satan) is depicted as the rightful lord of the universe whose throne has been temporarily usurped by the God of Noah or the Creator of all things. The serpent (Satan) creates man in his present miserable state, but he promises that a child would one day be born of a divine mother—which child would supplant God, become a god himself, and return rulership of the earth to the serpent.

Nimrod allowed Semiramis to retain full control over this religious hierarchy. Sometime later a dispute arose between them over the legitimacy of her son to be born. Nimrod, who having used her to gain power and to establish a new religion and to achieve the position he coveted, turned against her to have her removed as queen and to reveal that she was an inn/brothel keeper and not a virgin drawn from the sea. Semiramis, of course, would not allow this to take place, and devised a plot to overthrow Nimrod and to have him killed.

Following the death of Nimrod, she deceives her subjects into believing that her illegitimate son is a god and his conception was miraculous. Semiramis named her son Tammuz. She continued to rule as Queen of Babylon for 42 more years (another example of the number 42 meaning evil). Tradition declares that when Tammuz came to maturity he demanded that his mother install him as king. She not only refused, but seeing him now as a challenge to her rule, she plotted to murder her son. However, Tammuz became aware of the plot and slew his mother first.

From Babylon, this mystery religion spread to all the surrounding nations. Semiramis was declared to be the mother of god as she gave birth to Tammuz who was declared to be a son of god. Everywhere the symbols were the same. The image of the queen of heaven with the babe in her arms was seen everywhere, though the names might differ as the languages differed.

Semiramis is not directly recorded in the Scriptures, but her son, Tammuz is. The people of Judah had introduced the worship of the queen of heaven (Jeremiah 44:17-19) and the worship of Tammuz in the Temple area that was built by King Solomon (Ezekiel 8:13-14). The Lord referred to this as an abomination. The Lord will not share the Temple with the gods of the Babylonian Religion. In Ezekiel 8:4-5 and Ezekiel 8:23, we can see that the Glory of God begins to leave the Temple and no one seems to notice or care as the worship of Tammuz has filled the hearts and minds of the people.

Among the doctrines of the Babylonian Religion were: the doctrines of purgatorial purification after death; salvation by countless sacraments (such as priestly absolution); sprinkling with holy water; the offering of round cakes to the queen of heaven (as mentioned in Jeremiah 44); dedication of virgins to the gods (which was literally sanctified prostitution); weeping for Tammuz for a period of 40 days prior to the great festival of Istar (who was said to have received her son back from the dead). For it was taught that Tammuz was slain by a wild boar and afterwards brought back to life. To him the egg was sacred as depicting the mystery of his resurrection which was celebrated in the spring.

There are other historical records of the character of Nimrod and his wife. One record is the Gilgamesh religion. The concept of the Gilgamesh religion was that the dragon could prevail against the God of Noah, and that with his technology and control of biology, man could challenge the power of the God of Noah. The concept of the Tower of Babel under the leadership of Nimrod was to immunize the human race from the possibility of another deluge sent as a divine judgment. Nimrod, whose birth is recorded in Genesis 10, became the first type of the antichrist in the Scriptures.

In Revelation 17 we see that once the antichrist no longer has need of the woman, he moves to rid himself of her. As Tammuz removed his mother as she was in the way of him being the king, so the antichrist will remove the church organization and the pope to establish his empire. The beast will now show his true colors and demand that all men worship him as God. All of this is the replay of the first Babylonian Religion in the days of the Tower of Babel, the first harlot religion of Semiramis and the first antichrist Nimrod.

The Destruction of Religious Babylon

This again will be played out by Satan in Revelation 19 when Satan and the antichrist attempt to kill the Lord Jesus as he returns to the earth. During the battle of Armageddon the armies of the world cease fighting one another and turn their weapons on the Lord Jesus as He is returning to the earth, as declared in Psalm 2:

>¹*Why do the heathen rage, and the people imagine a vain thing?* ² *The kings of the earth set themselves, and the rulers take counsel together, against the LORD, and against his anointed, saying,* ³ *Let us break their bands asunder, and cast away their cords from us.* ⁴ *He that sitteth in the heavens shall laugh: the LORD shall have them in derision.* (Psalm 2:1-4)

The ambition of the beast and Satan is to defeat the Lord Jesus and to ensure that the kingdom of antichrist will last forever. Just as Nimrod persuaded men to rebel against the God of Noah and to build a tower so great that the God of Noah would not be able to destroy mankind with another flood, the beast will persuade mankind that united together they can defeat the Lord Jesus with their combined technology. In the end, the beast and his armies will be defeated, as prophesied in Psalm 2. In Revelation 19, the kingdom of antichrist will be defeated when the Lord Jesus returns to the earth in His fierce anger. Proverbs 21:30 declares there is no wisdom, no understanding and no counsel against the Lord.

The sin of Nimrod and the root of Babylon is in establishing one's self above God or in place of God and in establishing a second will in the universe, an alternative to the will of the Creator! This is what Lucifer attempted to do when he persuaded one third of the angels to follow him in his rebellion against the God of heaven. Lucifer must be a very persuasive being in order to convince so many angels to follow him. The beast will also be very persuasive as he deceives many to take his mark and worship him as God. This is the root of the sin of Babylon, the exaltation of oneself to be like the Most High God and to desire to rule in the heavens.

In Revelation 17:6, John saw the woman drunk with the blood of the saints and with the martyrs of Jesus. John was astounded at this event. Just as the Roman Catholic Church in the previous centuries ordered the Jesuits to stomp out the Protestant Reformation, resulting in 900,000 believers being killed, the kingdom of antichrist will also put to death all who oppose it. Much blood was shed by the Church of Rome over the centuries. Nimrod and Semiramis also put to death all who opposed them. The same will take place in the future as the kingdom of antichrist will move against all opposition.

Revelation

The author has chosen Luke 21:36 as the title for this book. The Lord Jesus is commanding His disciples to pray always to escape these things that are coming upon the earth. The plagues will be awful and there will be a great deception from the kingdom of antichrist. The Devil (speaking behind the man of sin, the beast) will be very persuasive in his speeches. If Satan could persuade one third of the angels to rebel against the Creator of all things, the deception that will be present in the seventieth week of Daniel from the mouth of the beast as he brings forth the words from his master, Satan, will be very convincing. The Scriptures reveal that many will follow after the beast and believe his persuasive speeches. He will deceive many into worshipping him and taking his mark. It is wise to heed the warning of the Lord Jesus and to pray always to escape all of these things that are coming upon the earth.

Revelation 17:7-13
The Description of the Beast

And the angel said unto me, Wherefore didst thou marvel? I will tell thee the mystery of the woman, and of the beast that carrieth her, which hath the seven heads and ten horns. The beast that thou sawest was, and is not; and shall ascend out of the bottomless pit, and go into perdition: and they that dwell on the earth shall wonder, whose names were not written in the book of life from the foundation of the world, when they behold the beast that was, and is not, and yet is. And here is the mind which hath wisdom. The seven heads are seven mountains, on which the woman sitteth. And there are seven kings: five are fallen, and one is, and the other is not yet come; and when he cometh, he must continue a short space. And the beast that was, and is not, even he is the eighth, and is of the seven, and goeth into perdition. And the ten horns which thou sawest are ten kings, which have received no kingdom as yet; but receive power as kings one hour with the beast. These have one mind, and shall give their power and strength unto the beast.

Ecclesiasticism has turned into a harlot filled with hatred. A harlot secures favors for herself. She increases her attraction to lure men to her. Rome is called the city of seven hills. Could this be the city where this harlot is sitting? The seven heads of the beast are to be looked upon as seven kings. The seven kings represent political empires or kingdoms as well as individual rulers. The beast is carrying the harlot, so who is ruler over whom? The beast was and is not (existed before but is now in the bottomless pit). The world will wonder about this beast that existed earlier but now comes back from the bottomless pit.

The Destruction of Religious Babylon

The beast is sometimes an empire, and at other times the emperor of an empire. We know from history that Rome is the sixth kingdom, and Rome was the current ruling empire at the time of the apostle John. The fifth empire was the Grecian empire, the fourth was the Medes and Persians, the third was Babylon, the second was Assyria and the first was Egypt. The seventh empire is yet a future empire that will arise and it will be a revived Roman Empire. The eighth and final empire will be the rule of the beast as recorded in the Book of Daniel the prophet:

40 And the fourth kingdom shall be strong as iron: forasmuch as iron breaketh in pieces and subdueth all things: and as iron that breaketh all these, shall it break in pieces and bruise. 41 And whereas thou sawest the feet and toes, part of potters' clay, and part of iron, the kingdom shall be divided; but there shall be in it of the strength of the iron, forasmuch as thou sawest the iron mixed with miry clay. 42 And as the toes of the feet were part of iron, and part of clay, so the kingdom shall be partly strong, and partly broken. 43 And whereas thou sawest iron mixed with miry clay, they shall mingle themselves with the seed of men: but they shall not cleave one to another, even as iron is not mixed with clay. 44 And in the days of these kings shall the God of heaven set up a kingdom, which shall never be destroyed: and the kingdom shall not be left to other people, but it shall break in pieces and consume all these kingdoms, and it shall stand for ever. 45 Forasmuch as thou sawest that the stone was cut out of the mountain without hands, and that it brake in pieces the iron, the brass, the clay, the silver, and the gold; the great God hath made known to the king what shall come to pass hereafter: and the dream is certain, and the interpretation thereof sure. (Daniel 2:40-45)

7 After this I saw in the night visions, and behold a fourth beast, dreadful and terrible, and strong exceedingly; and it had great iron teeth: it devoured and brake in pieces, and stamped the residue with the feet of it: and it was diverse from all the beasts that were before it; and it had ten horns. 8 I considered the horns, and, behold, there came up among them another little horn, before whom there were three of the first horns plucked up by the roots: and, behold, in this horn were eyes like the eyes of man, and a mouth speaking great things. (Daniel 7:7-8)

19 Then I would know the truth of the fourth beast, which was diverse from all the others, exceeding dreadful, whose teeth were of iron, and his nails of brass; which devoured, brake in pieces, and stamped the residue with his feet; 20 And of the ten horns that were in his head, and of the other which came up, and before whom three fell; even of that horn that had eyes, and a mouth that spake very great things, whose look was more stout than his fellows. 21 I beheld, and the same horn made war with the saints, and prevailed against them; 22 Until the Ancient of days came, and judgment was given to the saints of the most High; and the time came that the saints possessed the kingdom. ²³ *Thus he said, The fourth beast shall be the fourth kingdom upon earth, which shall be diverse from all kingdoms, and shall devour the whole earth, and shall tread it down, and break it in pieces.* ²⁴ *And the ten horns out of this kingdom are ten kings that shall arise: and another shall rise after them; and he shall be diverse from the first, and he shall subdue three kings.* ²⁵ *And he shall speak great words against the most High, and shall wear out the saints of the most High, and think to change times and laws: and they shall be given into his hand until a time and times and the dividing of time.* (Daniel 7:19-25)

From the prophet Daniel it appears as if the seventh world empire will be the kingdom of the ten horns that will rise out of the old Roman Empire. This indicates that ten nations or kingdoms from the old Roman Empire will rise again. Once this new empire arises, the beast or antichrist will arise. We are not told the length of time that will occur before the antichrist arises after the kingdom of the ten horns is established. It could be a month, a year, or many years before the man of sin, the son of perdition, arises. It is during the reign of the eighth kingdom that the Lord Jesus will return to earth and will defeat the kingdom of antichrist, and everyone who has taken the mark of beast will be slain by the Lord Jesus.

Revelation 17:14-18
The Death of the Great Whore

These shall make war with the Lamb, and the Lamb shall overcome them: for he is Lord of lords, and King of kings: and they that are with him are called, and chosen, and faithful. And he saith unto me, The waters which thou sawest, where the whore sitteth, are peoples, and multitudes, and nations, and tongues. And the ten horns which thou sawest upon the beast, these shall hate the whore, and shall make her desolate and naked, and shall eat her flesh, and burn her with fire. For God hath put in their hearts to fulfil his will, and to agree, and give their kingdom unto the beast, until the words of God shall be fulfilled. And the woman which thou sawest is that great city, which reigneth over the kings of the earth.

The beast and the kingdoms of this world will make war with the Lamb of God when He returns to the earth, but the Lord Jesus shall overcome them as prophesied in Revelation:

¹⁰ *And I fell at his feet to worship him. And he said unto me, See thou do it not: I am thy fellowservant, and of thy brethren that have the testimony of Jesus: worship God: for the testimony of Jesus is the spirit of prophecy.* ¹¹ *And I saw heaven*

opened, and behold a white horse; and he that sat upon him was called Faithful and True, and in righteousness he doth judge and make war. ^{12} *His eyes were as a flame of fire, and on his head were many crowns; and he had a name written, that no man knew, but he himself.* ^{13} *And he was clothed with a vesture dipped in blood: and his name is called The Word of God.* ^{14} *And the armies which were in heaven followed him upon white horses, clothed in fine linen, white and clean.* ^{15} *And out of his mouth goeth a sharp sword, that with it he should smite the nations: and he shall rule them with a rod of iron: and he treadeth the winepress of the fierceness and wrath of Almighty God.* ^{16} *And he hath on his vesture and on his thigh a name written, KING OF KINGS, AND LORD OF LORDS.* ^{17} *And I saw an angel standing in the sun; and he cried with a loud voice, saying to all the fowls that fly in the midst of heaven, Come and gather yourselves together unto the supper of the great God;* ^{18} *That ye may eat the flesh of kings, and the flesh of captains, and the flesh of mighty men, and the flesh of horses, and of them that sit on them, and the flesh of all men, both free and bond, both small and great.* ^{19} *And I saw the beast, and the kings of the earth, and their armies, gathered together to make war against him that sat on the horse, and against his army.* ^{20} *And the beast was taken, and with him the false prophet that wrought miracles before him, with which he deceived them that had received the mark of the beast, and them that worshipped his image. These both were cast alive into a lake of fire burning with brimstone.* ^{21} *And the remnant were slain with the sword of him that sat upon the horse, which sword proceeded out of his mouth: and all the fowls were filled with their flesh.* (Revelation 19:10-21)

The beast will persuade the nations of the world that they can unite and defeat Jesus when He returns to the earth. This demonic act is also spoken of in Psalm 2. This was the transgression of Nimrod when he persuaded men to follow him in his rebellion against the God of Noah—that in the end, man could prevail against God. Just as Nimrod convinced men that they can build a tower that even God cannot overcome, the beast will convince men that they can prevent the return of Jesus to the earth with their technology and weapons (planes, tanks, missiles, etc.).

Religion (harlot) sits atop the nations of the world, but once the beast has his kingdom confirmed, the beast no longer needs the harlot as she is now in the way. Religion is to be replaced with worshipping the beast. The beast turns against and destroys the harlot, thus fulfilling God's plan with vengeance upon the faithless churches of Pergamos (Revelation 2:16) and Thyatira (Revelation 2:21-23). The Lord is going to avenge the blood that the Roman Catholic Church has shed for hundreds of years, as many church historians have declared.

Revelation

Here is a brief history of the Roman Catholic Church and of some of the popes:

- Pope Innocent III (1198 - 1216) was the most powerful of all the popes. He claimed to be the Vicar of Christ, Vicar of God, Supreme Sovereign over the church and the world. He claimed the right to depose kings and princes and that all things on earth, in heaven and in hell are subject to the Vicar of Christ. Practically all the monarchs of Europe obeyed his will, including the Byzantine Empire. Never in the history of man has any one man exerted more power. He ordered two crusades. He decreed transubstantiation, papal infallibility, forbade the reading of the Bible in the common languages, instituted inquisitions, and ordered the massacre of the Albigenses. More blood was shed under his direction and that of his immediate successors than in any other period in church history, except in the papacy's effort to crush the Reformation in the 16th and 17th centuries.

- Pope Gregory I (590 - 604) was a good man. He established for himself complete control over the churches of Italy, Spain, Gaul, and England. Gregory labored untiringly for the purification of the church. He deposed neglectful or unworthy bishops. In his personal life he was a good man, one of the purest and best of the popes, untiring in his efforts for justice to the oppressed and unbounded in his charities to the poor. The introduction of purgatory was a blemish on his reign.

- With popes Adrian II (867 - 872), John VIII (872 - 882), and Marinus (882 - 884) began the darkest period of the papacy (870 - 1050). Pope Sergius III (904 - 911) was said to have a mistress, named Marozia. She, her mother Theodora, and her sister, filled the papal chair with their paramours and bastard sons. This period in history was called the rule of the harlots (904 - 963). John XII (955 - 963), a grandson of Marozia, was guilty of almost every crime. He violated virgins and widows, lived with his father's mistress, and made the papal palace a brothel. Pope Benedict IX (1033 - 1045) was made pope when he was 12 years old. He surpassed John XII in wickedness by committing murder and adultery in broad daylight. Some called him the worst of all popes.

Here in Revelation 17, the Lord God will avenge the blood of the saints that has been shed for centuries. God has been patient, desiring that all men should repent, and has provided ample time for them to do so. At this point judgment must come, and the wrath of God must be poured out. The church was to be a witness to the world of the love of God. The church was to demonstrate the love of God to the world by its love for one another. Jesus commanded the disciples to love one another. The church was never called to kill one another. This is the great tragedy of the history of the church.

Chapter 18

The Destruction of Commercial Babylon

Revelation 18:1-3
The Prophecy and Fall of Babylon

And after these things I saw another angel come down from heaven, having great power; and the earth was lightened with his glory. And he cried mightily with a strong voice, saying, Babylon the great is fallen, is fallen, and is become the habitation of devils, and the hold of every foul spirit, and a cage of every unclean and hateful bird. For all nations have drunk of the wine of the wrath of her fornication, and the kings of the earth have committed fornication with her, and the merchants of the earth are waxed rich through the abundance of her delicacies.

COMMERCIAL BABYLON IS like Religious Babylon in that they both are under the rule of the antichrist at the same time. They are both ruling as queens and are filled with blasphemy. They both hate the saints and shed their blood. The kings of the earth are polluted by both of them, and Almighty God judges and destroys them both.

Religious Babylon is called Mystery Babylon, while Commercial Babylon is called Babylon the Great. Babylon the Great is a city, not a whore. The city is a port city, not a city on seven hills. Religious Babylon is destroyed by a political power appointed by God (Revelation 17:16-17); Commercial Babylon is destroyed by Almighty God Himself.

Money and commerce have made the nations, kings, and bankers drunk with power. Money and wealth are used to gain influence and power over the rest of mankind. The rich men of the world have their influence

Revelation

upon the rulers of the nations. In many nations, the rich men form the hidden power base, and those in power are mere puppets for the wealthy. Money and commerce are worshipped as even the merchants seek to gain wealth by selling their goods. The commerce and economy of the world are under the direction of Satan and his demons and are used to oppress people and to set up a class system of upper, middle, and lower class people.

Bible scholars have debated over the centuries if Babylon will be rebuilt. Some scholars declared that Babylon was never destroyed by the Persians when Cyrus conquered the city. There are prophecies concerning Babylon that have not yet been fulfilled. Some of the prophecies of the destruction of Babylon were fulfilled when Cyrus conquered the city. There are other prophecies that have a future fulfillment as it appears from the Scriptures that Babylon will be rebuilt:

19 And Babylon, the glory of kingdoms, the beauty of the Chaldees' excellency, shall be as when God overthrew Sodom and Gomorrah. 20 It shall never be inhabited, neither shall it be dwelt in from generation to generation: neither shall the Arabian pitch tent there; neither shall the shepherds make their fold there. 21 But wild beasts of the desert shall lie there; and their houses shall be full of doleful creatures; and owls shall dwell there, and satyrs shall dance there. 22 And the wild beasts of the islands shall cry in their desolate houses, and dragons in their pleasant palaces: and her time is near to come, and her days shall not be prolonged. (Isaiah 13:19-22)

39 Therefore the wild beasts of the desert with the wild beasts of the islands shall dwell there, and the owls shall dwell therein: and it shall be no more inhabited for ever; neither shall it be dwelt in from generation to generation. 40 As God overthrew Sodom and Gomorrah and the neighbour cities thereof, saith the LORD; so shall no man abide there, neither shall any son of man dwell therein. (Jeremiah 50:39-40)

5 Then the angel that talked with me went forth, and said unto me, Lift up now thine eyes, and see what is this that goeth forth. 6 And I said, What is it? And he said, This is an ephah that goeth forth. He said moreover, This is their resemblance through all the earth. 7 And, behold, there was lifted up a talent of lead: and this is a woman that sitteth in the midst of the ephah. 8 And he said, This is wickedness. And he cast it into the midst of the ephah; and he cast the weight of lead upon the mouth thereof. 9 Then lifted I up mine eyes, and looked, and, behold, there came out two women, and the wind was in their wings; for they had wings like the wings of a stork: and they lifted up the ephah between the earth and the heaven. 10 Then said I to the angel that talked with me, Whither do these bear the ephah? 11 And he said unto me, To build it an house in the land of Shinar: and it shall be established, and set there upon her own base. (Zechariah 5:5-11)

The Destruction of Commercial Babylon

There are Scriptures in Isaiah, Jeremiah, and Zechariah that have not been fulfilled concerning the utter destruction of Babylon. Today there are people living in Babylon which is located in Iraq. Just like there are prophecies concerning the first and second coming of the Lord Jesus, there are prophecies of the destruction of Babylon that are yet to come.

The Commercial city of Babylon will be rebuilt and the most likely location will be in the land of Shinar where the Tower of Babel was established, as prophesied by Zechariah. The future of Babylon will be the home of demons, a prison for every foul spirit and a cage for every unclean and hated bird (demons). Babylon is to be a perpetual desolation and a memorial for everyone to remember its death as prophesied by the prophet Isaiah (Isaiah 34:9-17).

The timing of the destruction of Babylon will occur during the Seventh Vial or Bowl judgment as recorded in Revelation:

17 And the seventh angel poured out his vial into the air; and there came a great voice out of the temple of heaven, from the throne, saying, It is done. 18 And there were voices, and thunders, and lightnings; and there was a great earthquake, such as was not since men were upon the earth, so mighty an earthquake, and so great. 19 And the great city was divided into three parts, and the cities of the nations fell: and great Babylon came in remembrance before God, to give unto her the cup of the wine of the fierceness of his wrath. (Revelation 16:17-19)

Revelation 18:4-5
The Plea to God's People

And I heard another voice from heaven, saying, Come out of her, my people, that ye be not partakers of her sins, and that ye receive not of her plagues. For her sins have reached unto heaven, and God hath remembered her iniquities.

This is a plea for God's people not to lust after this world or the things that are of the world, because this world is passing away and the lusts thereof. Christians are called to be separated from this world; to be in the world but not of the world. In today's society money is needed to buy and sell. However, money is also used to separate people into upper, middle, and lower classes. When the Lord Jesus returns and sets up His kingdom that will last for 1,000 years, commerce as we know it will be very different; all things may be purchased without money. All men will be equal as there will be no class system. There will be no more earthly kings and kingdoms that will enslave other men or start wars to take for themselves the wealth of other nations

Revelation

and people. The Lord Jesus will be the King and all things may be purchased without money.

God warns His people to leave Commercial Babylon before the Seventh Vial is poured out upon the earth. The Lord will not pour out His wrath until His people have left Babylon:

15 Behold, I come as a thief. Blessed is he that watcheth, and keepeth his garments, lest he walk naked, and they see his shame. 16 And he gathered them together into a place called in the Hebrew tongue Armageddon. 17 And the seventh angel poured out his vial into the air; and there came a great voice out of the temple of heaven, from the throne, saying, It is done. 18 And there were voices, and thunders, and lightnings; and there was a great earthquake, such as was not since men were upon the earth, so mighty an earthquake, and so great. 19 And the great city was divided into three parts, and the cities of the nations fell: and great Babylon came in remembrance before God, to give unto her the cup of the wine of the fierceness of his wrath. (Revelation 16:15-19)

God's people are to leave Babylon just as Lot left Sodom and Gomorrah before the cities were destroyed. We see a physical departure of God's saints before the final plague is poured out upon the earth. There will be a place on the earth that will be protected from the final judgment that is to come. Once the last saint has departed from Babylon, the last plague will soon commence. It is not God's plan to destroy His people when He pours out His *thumos* and judges Babylon. The Lord will not destroy the righteous with the wicked:

20 Go ye forth of Babylon, flee ye from the Chaldeans, with a voice of singing declare ye, tell this, utter it even to the end of the earth; say ye, The LORD hath redeemed his servant Jacob. (Isaiah 48:20)

11 Depart ye, depart ye, go ye out from thence, touch no unclean thing; go ye out of the midst of her; be ye clean, that bear the vessels of the LORD. (Isaiah 52:11)

8 Remove out of the midst of Babylon, and go forth out of the land of the Chaldeans, and be as the he goats before the flocks. 9 For, lo, I will raise and cause to come up against Babylon an assembly of great nations from the north country: and they shall set themselves in array against her; from thence she shall be taken: their arrows shall be as of a mighty expert man; none shall return in vain. 10 And Chaldea shall be a spoil: all that spoil her shall be satisfied, saith the LORD. (Jeremiah 50:8-10)

6 Flee out of the midst of Babylon, and deliver every man his soul: be not cut off in her iniquity; for this is the time of the LORD's vengeance; he will render unto

The Destruction of Commercial Babylon

her a recompence. ⁷ Babylon hath been a golden cup in the LORD's hand, that made all the earth drunken: the nations have drunken of her wine; therefore the nations are mad. ⁸ Babylon is suddenly fallen and destroyed: howl for her; take balm for her pain, if so be she may be healed. ⁹ We would have healed Babylon, but she is not healed: forsake her, and let us go every one into his own country: for her judgment reacheth unto heaven, and is lifted up even to the skies. (Jeremiah 51:6-9)

⁶ Ho, ho, come forth, and flee from the land of the north, saith the LORD: for I have spread you abroad as the four winds of the heaven, saith the LORD. ⁷ Deliver thyself, O Zion, that dwellest with the daughter of Babylon. (Zechariah 2:6-7)

¹⁷ Wherefore come out from among them, and be ye separate, saith the Lord, and touch not the unclean thing; and I will receive you. ¹⁸ And will be a Father unto you, and ye shall be my sons and daughters, saith the Lord Almighty. (II Corinthians 6:17-18)

¹Go to now, ye rich men, weep and howl for your miseries that shall come upon you. ² Your riches are corrupted, and your garments are motheaten. ³ Your gold and silver is cankered; and the rust of them shall be a witness against you, and shall eat your flesh as it were fire. Ye have heaped treasure together for the last days. ⁴ Behold, the hire of the labourers who have reaped down your fields, which is of you kept back by fraud, crieth: and the cries of them which have reaped are entered into the ears of the Lord of Sabbath. ⁵ Ye have lived in pleasure on the earth, and been wanton; ye have nourished your hearts, as in a day of slaughter. ⁶ Ye have condemned and killed the just; and he doth not resist you. (James 5:1-6)

It is amazing how true believers can continue their affiliations and relationships with apostate organizations. As recorded in James, the wealth of this world is going to vanish away and become a snare to those possessed by their possessions. What is lacking today in the churches is discernment. With so little truth being proclaimed from the pulpits of the churches today, the individual saint must study the Scriptures on their own if they are to know the Word of God. As truth will be hidden in this terrible great tribulation period, the Lord God Almighty will be warning men of what is coming upon the earth.

Revelation 18:6-8
The Payment Babylon Will Receive

Reward her even as she rewarded you, and double unto her double according to her works: in the cup which she hath filled fill to her double. How much she hath glorified herself, and lived deliciously, so much torment and sorrow give her: for she

Revelation

saith in her heart, I sit a queen, and am no widow, and shall see no sorrow. Therefore shall her plagues come in one day, death, and mourning, and famine; and she shall be utterly burned with fire: for strong is the Lord God who judgeth her.

The saint is called to do unto Commercial Babylon as Commercial Babylon has done unto the saints, even double. This reveals the character of God toward Babylon and all it represents. This kind of severe judgment is recorded elsewhere in the Scriptures:

[4] If the theft be certainly found in his hand alive, whether it be ox, or ass, or sheep; he shall restore double. [5] If a man shall cause a field or vineyard to be eaten, and shall put in his beast, and shall feed in another man's field; of the best of his own field, and of the best of his own vineyard, shall he make restitution. [6] If fire break out, and catch in thorns, so that the stacks of corn, or the standing corn, or the field, be consumed therewith; he that kindled the fire shall surely make restitution. [7] If a man shall deliver unto his neighbour money or stuff to keep, and it be stolen out of the man's house; if the thief be found, let him pay double. [8] If the thief be not found, then the master of the house shall be brought unto the judges, to see whether he have put his hand unto his neighbour's goods. [9] For all manner of trespass, whether it be for ox, for ass, for sheep, for raiment, or for any manner of lost thing which another challengeth to be his, the cause of both parties shall come before the judges; and whom the judges shall condemn, he shall pay double unto his neighbour. (Exodus 22:4-9)

[2] Speak ye comfortably to Jerusalem, and cry unto her, that her warfare is accomplished, that her iniquity is pardoned: for she hath received of the LORD's hand double for all her sins. (Isaiah 40:2)

[18] And first I will recompense their iniquity and their sin double; because they have defiled my land, they have filled mine inheritance with the carcases of their detestable and abominable things. (Jeremiah 16:18)

[18] Let them be confounded that persecute me, but let not me be confounded: let them be dismayed, but let not me be dismayed: bring upon them the day of evil, and destroy them with double destruction. (Jeremiah 17:18)

Before the conclusion of World War II, as the American army was liberating the concentration camps, there were instances where the Jews turned on the Germans who imprisoned them. This is one of the most recent examples of a race of people turning on their captors when the opportunity arises. The commercial system of this world has been cruel and oppressive to Christians and Jews.

The Destruction of Commercial Babylon

Babylon the Great is fallen, is fallen. There is a double announcement that emphasizes the speed and finality with which judgment is coming. Babylon the Great has become demonic with sensuous pleasures—a sinful city. The Scriptures declare that the wages of sin is death. Those who delight in the pleasures of sin must be ready to receive the payment that is due, which is death, spiritual death. These people lusted after the things of this world, including the bodies and souls of men. When judgment comes against this commercial system, it will be swift and complete.

There are other passages of Scripture that reveal why Almighty God will utterly destroy Babylon in a single day:

5 Sit thou silent, and get thee into darkness, O daughter of the Chaldeans: for thou shalt no more be called, The lady of kingdoms. 6 I was wroth with my people, I have polluted mine inheritance, and given them into thine hand: thou didst shew them no mercy; upon the ancient hast thou very heavily laid thy yoke. 7 And thou saidst, I shall be a lady for ever: so that thou didst not lay these things to thy heart, neither didst remember the latter end of it. 8 Therefore hear now this, thou that art given to pleasures, that dwellest carelessly, that sayest in thine heart, I am, and none else beside me; I shall not sit as a widow, neither shall I know the loss of children: 9 But these two things shall come to thee in a moment in one day, the loss of children, and widowhood: they shall come upon thee in their perfection for the multitude of thy sorceries, and for the great abundance of thine enchantments. 10 For thou hast trusted in thy wickedness: thou hast said, None seeth me. Thy wisdom and thy knowledge, it hath perverted thee; and thou hast said in thine heart, I am, and none else beside me. 11 Therefore shall evil come upon thee; thou shalt not know from whence it riseth: and mischief shall fall upon thee; thou shalt not be able to put it off: and desolation shall come upon thee suddenly, which thou shalt not know. 12 Stand now with thine enchantments, and with the multitude of thy sorceries, wherein thou hast laboured from thy youth; if so be thou shalt be able to profit, if so be thou mayest prevail. 13 Thou art wearied in the multitude of thy counsels. Let now the astrologers, the stargazers, the monthly prognosticators, stand up, and save thee from these things that shall come upon thee. (Isaiah 47:5-13)

In one day mighty Babylon will become a widow and will see much sorrow. The mighty economic system of the world shall come tumbling down suddenly, and all those who have lost their wealth will be weeping over their lost riches.

Isaiah also declares that the Lord God Almighty will punish the inhabitants of the earth because of the bloodshed that has taken place, and will take place in the future:

Revelation

²⁰ *Come, my people, enter thou into thy chambers, and shut thy doors about thee: hide thyself as it were for a little moment, until the indignation be overpast.* ²¹ *For, behold, the* LORD *cometh out of his place to punish the inhabitants of the earth for their iniquity: the earth also shall disclose her blood, and shall no more cover her slain. (Isaiah 26:20-21)*

Babylon shall be destroyed suddenly like Tyrus of old. The city of Tyrus was believed to be a city that could not be conquered. The people of Tyrus trusted in the safety of their island and believed that no invader could possibly destroy their city. This is a warning to Babylon. When judgment comes it will be thorough and complete:

¹⁵ *Thus saith the Lord* GOD *to Tyrus; Shall not the isles shake at the sound of thy fall, when the wounded cry, when the slaughter is made in the midst of thee?* ¹⁶ *Then all the princes of the sea shall come down from their thrones, and lay away their robes, and put off their broidered garments: they shall clothe themselves with trembling; they shall sit upon the ground, and shall tremble at every moment, and be astonished at thee.* ¹⁷ *And they shall take up a lamentation for thee, and say to thee, How art thou destroyed, that wast inhabited of seafaring men, the renowned city, which wast strong in the sea, she and her inhabitants, which cause their terror to be on all that haunt it!* ¹⁸ *Now shall the isles tremble in the day of thy fall; yea, the isles that are in the sea shall be troubled at thy departure.* ¹⁹ *For thus saith the Lord* GOD; *When I shall make thee a desolate city, like the cities that are not inhabited; when I shall bring up the deep upon thee, and great waters shall cover thee;* ²⁰ *When I shall bring thee down with them that descend into the pit, with the people of old time, and shall set thee in the low parts of the earth, in places desolate of old, with them that go down to the pit, that thou be not inhabited; and I shall set glory in the land of the living;* ²¹ *I will make thee a terror, and thou shalt be no more: though thou be sought for, yet shalt thou never be found again, saith the Lord* GOD. *(Ezekiel 26:15-21)*

The prophet Ezekiel also declares that Commercial Babylon will be magnificent in its prime upon the earth:

¹*The word of the* LORD *came again unto me, saying,* ² *Now, thou son of man, take up a lamentation for Tyrus;* ³ *And say unto Tyrus, O thou that art situate at the entry of the sea, which art a merchant of the people for many isles, Thus saith the Lord* GOD; *O Tyrus, thou hast said, I am of perfect beauty.* ⁴ *Thy borders are in the midst of the seas, thy builders have perfected thy beauty.* ⁵ *They have made all thy ship boards of fir trees of Senir: they have taken cedars from Lebanon to make masts for thee.* ⁶ *Of the oaks of Bashan have they made thine oars; the company of the Ashurites have made thy benches of ivory, brought out of the isles of Chittim.*

The Destruction of Commercial Babylon

7 Fine linen with broidered work from Egypt was that which thou spreadest forth to be thy sail; blue and purple from the isles of Elishah was that which covered thee. 8 The inhabitants of Zidon and Arvad were thy mariners: thy wise men, O Tyrus, that were in thee, were thy pilots. 9 The ancients of Gebal and the wise men thereof were in thee thy calkers: all the ships of the sea with their mariners were in thee to occupy thy merchandise. 10 They of Persia and of Lud and of Phut were in thine army, thy men of war: they hanged the shield and helmet in thee; they set forth thy comeliness. 11 The men of Arvad with thine army were upon thy walls round about, and the Gammadims were in thy towers: they hanged their shields upon thy walls round about; they have made thy beauty perfect. 12 Tarshish was thy merchant by reason of the multitude of all kind of riches; with silver, iron, tin, and lead, they traded in thy fairs. 13 Javan, Tubal, and Meshech, they were thy merchants: they traded the persons of men and vessels of brass in thy market. 14 They of the house of Togarmah traded in thy fairs with horses and horsemen and mules. 15 The men of Dedan were thy merchants; many isles were the merchandise of thine hand: they brought thee for a present horns of ivory and ebony. 16 Syria was thy merchant by reason of the multitude of the wares of thy making: they occupied in thy fairs with emeralds, purple, and broidered work, and fine linen, and coral, and agate. 17 Judah, and the land of Israel, they were thy merchants: they traded in thy market wheat of Minnith, and Pannag, and honey, and oil, and balm. 18 Damascus was thy merchant in the multitude of the wares of thy making, for the multitude of all riches; in the wine of Helbon, and white wool. 19 Dan also and Javan going to and fro occupied in thy fairs: bright iron, cassia, and calamus, were in thy market. 20 Dedan was thy merchant in precious clothes for chariots. 21 Arabia, and all the princes of Kedar, they occupied with thee in lambs, and rams, and goats: in these were they thy merchants. 22 The merchants of Sheba and Raamah, they were thy merchants: they occupied in thy fairs with chief of all spices, and with all precious stones, and gold. 23 Haran, and Canneh, and Eden, the merchants of Sheba, Asshur, and Chilmad, were thy merchants. 24 These were thy merchants in all sorts of things, in blue clothes, and broidered work, and in chests of rich apparel, bound with cords, and made of cedar, among thy merchandise. 25 The ships of Tarshish did sing of thee in thy market: and thou wast replenished, and made very glorious in the midst of the seas. (Ezekiel 27:1-25)

Ezekiel 27:26-36 describes how the people of the earth will mourn and lament at the sudden destruction of Commercial Babylon. The fulfillment of this prophecy will be when Almighty God pours out His wrath upon this city as part of the Seventh Vial or Bowl judgment:

26 Thy rowers have brought thee into great waters: the east wind hath broken thee in the midst of the seas. 27 Thy riches, and thy fairs, thy merchandise, thy

Revelation

mariners, and thy pilots, thy calkers, and the occupiers of thy merchandise, and all thy men of war, that are in thee, and in all thy company which is in the midst of thee, shall fall into the midst of the seas in the day of thy ruin. [28] The suburbs shall shake at the sound of the cry of thy pilots. [29] And all that handle the oar, the mariners, and all the pilots of the sea, shall come down from their ships, they shall stand upon the land; [30] And shall cause their voice to be heard against thee, and shall cry bitterly, and shall cast up dust upon their heads, they shall wallow themselves in the ashes: [31] And they shall make themselves utterly bald for thee, and gird them with sackcloth, and they shall weep for thee with bitterness of heart and bitter wailing. [32] And in their wailing they shall take up a lamentation for thee, and lament over thee, saying, What city is like Tyrus, like the destroyed in the midst of the sea? [33] When thy wares went forth out of the seas, thou filledst many people; thou didst enrich the kings of the earth with the multitude of thy riches and of thy merchandise. [34] In the time when thou shalt be broken by the seas in the depths of the waters thy merchandise and all thy company in the midst of thee shall fall. [35] All the inhabitants of the isles shall be astonished at thee, and their kings shall be sore afraid, they shall be troubled in their countenance. [36] The merchants among the people shall hiss at thee; thou shalt be a terror, and never shalt be any more. (Ezekiel 27:26-36)

This devastating destruction is also continued in Revelation 18:9-19.

Revelation 18:9-19
The People Affected by the Fall of Babylon

And the kings of the earth, who have committed fornication and lived deliciously with her, shall bewail her, and lament for her, when they shall see the smoke of her burning, standing afar off for the fear of her torment, saying, Alas, alas that great city Babylon, that mighty city! For in one hour is thy judgment come. And the merchants of the earth shall weep and mourn over her; for no man buyeth their merchandise any more: The merchandise of gold, and silver, and precious stones, and of pearls, and fine linen, and purple, and silk, and scarlet, and all thyine wood, and all manner vessels of ivory, and all manner vessels of most precious wood, and of brass, and iron, and marble, And cinnamon, and odours, and ointments, and frankincense, and wine, and oil, and fine flour, and wheat, and beasts, and sheep, and horses, and chariots, and slaves, and souls of men. And the fruits that thy soul lusted after are departed from thee, and all things which were dainty and goodly are departed from thee, and thou shalt find them no more at all. The merchants of these things, which were made rich by her, shall stand afar off for the fear of her torment, weeping and wailing, and saying, Alas, alas that great city, that was clothed in fine linen, and purple, and scarlet, and decked with gold, and precious stones, and pearls!

The Destruction of Commercial Babylon

For in one hour so great riches is come to nought. And every shipmaster, and all the company in ships, and sailors, and as many as trade by sea, stood afar off, And cried when they saw the smoke of her burning, saying, What city is like unto this great city! And they cast dust on their heads, and cried, weeping and wailing, saying, Alas, alas that great city, wherein were made rich all that had ships in the sea by reason of her costliness! For in one hour is she made desolate.

The prophecy of the fall of Babylon the Great in Revelation 14:8 and Revelation 16:17-19 will be fulfilled in Revelation 18.

17 And the seventh angel poured out his vial into the air; and there came a great voice out of the temple of heaven, from the throne, saying, It is done. 18 And there were voices, and thunders, and lightnings; and there was a great earthquake, such as was not since men were upon the earth, so mighty an earthquake, and so great. 19 And the great city was divided into three parts, and the cities of the nations fell: and great Babylon came in remembrance before God, to give unto her the cup of the wine of the fierceness of his wrath. (Revelation 16:17-19)

Today the city of Babylon is located in Iraq, and the city is not currently near the sea. The land of Shinar is not near a seaport city today. However, after the Sixth Seal judgment the geography of the earth will change as recorded in Revelation 6:14:

14 And the heaven departed as a scroll when it is rolled together; and every mountain and island were moved out of their places. (Revelation 6:14)

Today there are Bible scholars who believe that cities such as New York or even Hollywood represent Babylon the Great because they are seaport cities. The problem with this view is that Nimrod most likely did not travel to America to set up his kingdom. The prophecy in Zechariah 5 clearly reveals that the land of Shinar is to be the location of Commercial Babylon. The problem with the land of Shinar not being a seaport area could easily be remedied during the plague of the Sixth Seal judgment. The Sixth Seal judgment speaks of islands that will disappear and mountain ranges that will no longer be great mountains. As part of the Sixth Seal judgment the earth will not look like it does today. Those land masses south of Shinar today will be under water and the land of Shinar will become a seaport city. The Sixth Seal judgment appears to involve more than cosmic disturbances as the geography of the earth will be changed. The *orge* of God will appear to commence with the Sixth Seal. It will be a time of great fear as men are in dread of what is coming upon the earth.

Now the merchants of the earth will observe and experience that their great wealth and desires are destroyed and burned. The sad part is that there is no repentance that follows this destruction, only sorrow that their wealth is burned as prophesied by Jeremiah:

46 At the noise of the taking of Babylon the earth is moved, and the cry is heard among the nations. (Jeremiah 50:46)

Today commerce and the economy are controlled by the wealthy who seek to keep others enslaved. One example is the credit card companies that are behind the credit card debt as they seek to increase their wealth at the expense of others. People are encouraged to live above their means and purchase goods and services that they are not able to afford. They are encouraged to use credit cards and pay only the minimum monthly balance. There is nothing wrong with a credit card if it is used wisely and the balance is paid by the end of the month. The tragedy comes when people cannot afford to pay off the balance at the end of the month and they get into debt on their credit cards by paying only the minimum monthly balance that includes a high interest. The buyer ends up being a slave to the seller.

In just one hour all the wealth of the merchants comes to nothing. The real estate of the wealthy will be destroyed by the 100 pound hailstones that are part of the final judgment upon the earth (Revelation 16:17-21).

Revelation 18:20-24
The Pronouncement of the Fall of Babylon

Rejoice over her, thou heaven, and ye holy apostles and prophets; for God hath avenged you on her. And a mighty angel took up a stone like a great millstone, and cast it into the sea, saying, Thus with violence shall that great city Babylon be thrown down, and shall be found no more at all. And the voice of harpers, and musicians, and of pipers, and trumpeters, shall be heard no more at all in thee; and no craftsman, of whatsoever craft he be, shall be found any more in thee; and the sound of a millstone shall be heard no more at all in thee; And the light of a candle shall shine no more at all in thee; and the voice of the bridegroom and of the bride shall be heard no more at all in thee: for thy merchants were the great men of the earth; for by thy sorceries were all nations deceived. And in her was found the blood of prophets, and of saints, and of all that were slain upon the earth.

The apostles and prophets are called to rejoice over the destruction of Babylon and all it represents. A city that was full of life will in one hour become lifeless. Babylon will be destroyed and it will never rise again as prophesied in the Book of Jeremiah:

> ⁵⁹ *The word which Jeremiah the prophet commanded Seraiah the son of Neriah, the son of Maaseiah, when he went with Zedekiah the king of Judah into Babylon in the fourth year of his reign. And this Seraiah was a quiet prince.* ⁶⁰ *So Jeremiah wrote in a book all the evil that should come upon Babylon, even all these words that are written against Babylon.* ⁶¹ *And Jeremiah said to Seraiah, When thou comest to Babylon, and shalt see, and shalt read all these words;* ⁶² *Then shalt thou say, O LORD, thou hast spoken against this place, to cut it off, that none shall remain in it, neither man nor beast, but that it shall be desolate for ever.* ⁶³ *And it shall be, when thou hast made an end of reading this book, that thou shalt bind a stone to it, and cast it into the midst of Euphrates:* ⁶⁴ *And thou shalt say, Thus shall Babylon sink, and shall not rise from the evil that I will bring upon her: and they shall be weary. Thus far are the words of Jeremiah.* (Jeremiah 51:59-64)

Babylon will be destroyed by the Lord. The location of the city is in the land of the Chaldeans, which was where the Babylonian empire was first established in the land of Shinar:

> ²⁵ *The LORD hath opened his armoury, and hath brought forth the weapons of his indignation: for this is the work of the Lord GOD of hosts in the land of the Chaldeans.* (Jeremiah 50:25)

When the Lord Jesus returns to the earth to establish His kingdom a new economic system will be set up where all goods and services will be purchased without money. The Lord Jesus will rule over the nations with a rod of iron.

Chapter 19

The Return of Jesus Christ

Revelation 19:1-4
Great Rejoicing in Heaven

And after these things I heard a great voice of much people in heaven, saying, Alleluia; Salvation, and glory, and honour, and power, unto the Lord our God: For true and righteous are his judgments: for he hath judged the great whore, which did corrupt the earth with her fornication, and hath avenged the blood of his servants at her hand. And again they said, Alleluia and her smoke rose up for ever and ever. And the four and twenty elders and the four beasts fell down and worshipped God that sat on the throne, saying, Amen; Alleluia.

THE PHRASE "AFTER these things" refers to the Seventh Vial or Bowl judgment as Babylon is destroyed during this plague. "Hallelujah" was used for the first time in the Scriptures when the Ark of the Covenant was installed at Mount Zion during the reign of King David. Now Babylon is destroyed (Religious and Commercial) and the Lord Jesus is getting ready to return, hallelujah!

There is much rejoicing when the wicked are overthrown. Everyone in heaven sings before God: the angels, the twenty four elders, and the cherubim. All rejoice with praise and worship. God's judgments are true and righteous. God's saints have been redeemed from the penalty and power of sin. Now the Lord Jesus Christ is about to enjoy fellowship with His saints at a great feast.

Revelation

Revelation 19:5-10
The Marriage Supper of the Lamb

And a voice came out of the throne, saying, Praise our God, all ye his servants, and ye that fear him, both small and great. And I heard as it were the voice of a great multitude, and as the voice of many waters, and as the voice of mighty thunderings, saying, Alleluia: for the Lord God omnipotent reigneth. Let us be glad and rejoice, and give honour to him: for the marriage of the Lamb is come, and his wife hath made herself ready. And to her was granted that she should be arrayed in fine linen, clean and white: for the fine linen is the righteousness of saints. And he saith unto me, Write, Blessed are they which are called unto the marriage supper of the Lamb. And he saith unto me, These are the true sayings of God. And I fell at his feet to worship him. And he said unto me, See thou do it not: I am thy fellowservant, and of thy brethren that have the testimony of Jesus: worship God: for the testimony of Jesus is the spirit of prophecy.

God the Father joins in the praise celebration. All of the servants of God break out in praise and rejoicing as there is a great marriage feast in heaven. The marriage feast is described in the Gospels of Luke and Matthew:

15 And when one of them that sat at meat with him heard these things, he said unto him, Blessed is he that shall eat bread in the kingdom of God. 16 Then said he unto him, A certain man made a great supper, and bade many: 17 and sent his servant at supper time to say to them that were bidden, Come; for all things are now ready. 18 And they all with one consent began to make excuse. The first said unto him, I have bought a piece of ground, and I must needs go and see it: I pray thee have me excused. 19 And another said, I have bought five yoke of oxen, and I go to prove them: I pray thee have me excused. 20 And another said, I have married a wife, and therefore I cannot come. 21 So that servant came, and shewed his lord these things. Then the master of the house being angry said to his servant, Go out quickly into the streets and lanes of the city, and bring in hither the poor, and the maimed, and the halt, and the blind. 22 And the servant said, Lord, it is done as thou hast commanded, and yet there is room. 23 And the lord said unto the servant, Go out into the highways and hedges, and compel them to come in, that my house may be filled. 24 For I say unto you, That none of those men which were bidden shall taste of my supper. (Luke 14:15-24)

1 And Jesus answered and spake unto them again by parables, and said, 2 The kingdom of heaven is like unto a certain king, which made a marriage for his son, 3 And sent forth his servants to call them that were bidden to the wedding: and they would not come. 4 Again, he sent forth other servants, saying, Tell them which are bidden, Behold, I have prepared my dinner: my oxen and my fatlings are killed, and all things are ready: come unto the marriage. ⁵ But they made light of it, and went their ways, one to his farm, another to his merchandise: ⁶ and the remnant took his servants, and entreated them spitefully, and slew them. ⁷ But when the king heard thereof, he was wroth: and he sent forth his armies, and destroyed those murderers, and burned up their city. ⁸ Then saith he to his servants, The wedding is ready, but they which were bidden were not worthy. ⁹ Go ye therefore into the highways, and as many as ye shall find, bid to the marriage. ¹⁰ So those servants went out into the highways, and gathered together all as many as they found, both bad and good: and the wedding was furnished with guests. ¹¹ And when the king came in to see the guests, he saw there a man which had not on a wedding garment: ¹² and he saith unto him, Friend, how camest thou in hither not having a wedding garment? And he was speechless. ¹³ Then said the king to the servants, Bind him hand and foot, and take him away, and cast him into outer darkness, there shall be weeping and gnashing of teeth. ¹⁴ For many are called, but few are chosen. (Matthew 22:1-14)

It is truly amazing that so many people are not excited concerning the marriage feast in heaven. They are distracted and caught up with the material possessions and concerns of this world. The commerce and economy of this world has snared many. Even in the Epistles of Paul, the marriage feast is found:

² For I am jealous over you with godly jealousy: for I have espoused you to one husband, that I may present you as a chaste virgin to Christ. (II Corinthians 11:2)

²² Wives, submit yourselves unto your own husbands, as unto the Lord. ²³ For the husband is the head of the wife, even as Christ is the head of the church: and he is the saviour of the body. ²⁴ Therefore as the church is subject unto Christ, so let the wives be to their own husbands in every thing. ²⁵ Husbands, love your wives, even as Christ also loved the church, and gave himself for it; ²⁶ That he might sanctify and cleanse it with the washing of water by the word, ²⁷ That he might present it to himself a glorious church, not having spot, or wrinkle, or any such thing; but that it should be holy and without blemish. (Ephesians 5:22-27)

The marriage feast is open to everyone. What a glorious day that will be. There is even the suggestion that there will be a double marriage in heaven: the Father and Israel, and Christ and the church as hinted at in the Scriptures:

⁴ Thou shalt no more be termed Forsaken; neither shall thy land any more be termed Desolate: but thou shalt be called Hephzibah, and thy land Beulah: for the LORD delighteth in thee, and thy land shall be married. ⁵ For as a young man marrieth a virgin, so shall thy sons marry thee: and as the bridegroom rejoiceth over the bride, so shall thy God rejoice over thee. (Isaiah 62:4-5)

Almighty God will rejoice over His people, Israel. A glorious future is coming for the nation of Israel. The marriage feast is just one event where the Father and Son will be worshipped and honored. They have created all things and by them all things exist. The author is also anticipating that glorious day, and being in heaven and joining in the praise and worship of the One who created all things.

The testimony of Jesus is the spirit of prophecy. Prophecy is intended to glorify Jesus. The Lord Jesus is the central feature of prophecy, and any teaching of prophecy that takes away our minds and hearts from Him is a teaching that is not properly being communicated. Everyone preaching from the pulpit must have this verse in memory every time they stand up and proclaim the Gospel message to their congregations (Revelation 19:10). The Lord Jesus needs to be the center of every sermon from every pulpit. It is all about Jesus and not man. The author has heard too many sermons from the pulpits where the preacher talks about himself and his family for most of the message. Every sermon should be under the anointing and the power of the Holy Spirit, and contain the message of the Lord Jesus.

Revelation 19:11-16
The Spectacular Description of the Coming Glory

And I saw heaven opened, and behold a white horse; and he that sat upon him was called Faithful and True, and in righteousness he doth judge and make war. His eyes were as a flame of fire, and on his head were many crowns; and he had a name written, that no man knew, but he himself. And he was clothed with a vesture dipped in blood: and his name is called The Word of God. And the armies which were in heaven followed him upon white horses, clothed in fine linen, white and clean. And out of his mouth goeth a sharp sword, that with it he should smite the nations: and he shall rule them with a rod of iron: and he treadeth the winepress of the fierceness and wrath of Almighty God. And he hath on his vesture and on his thigh a name written, KING OF KINGS, AND LORD OF LORDS.

Now from the opened heavens comes forth the Lord Jesus Christ in all glory and majesty that has been ascribed to Him throughout the Scriptures. He is returning to judge and make war in righteousness. He tramples the nations in the great winepress of God's wrath as the kingdom of antichrist makes war with the Lord Jesus when He returns to the earth:

The Return of Jesus Christ

> 27 Behold, the name of the LORD cometh from far, burning with his anger, and the burden thereof is heavy: his lips are full of indignation, and his tongue as a devouring fire: 28 And his breath, as an overflowing stream, shall reach to the midst of the neck, to sift the nations with the sieve of vanity: and there shall be a bridle in the jaws of the people, causing them to err. 29 Ye shall have a song, as in the night when a holy solemnity is kept; and gladness of heart, as when one goeth with a pipe to come into the mountain of the LORD, to the mighty One of Israel. 30 And the LORD shall cause his glorious voice to be heard, and shall shew the lighting down of his arm, with the indignation of his anger, and with the flame of a devouring fire, with scattering, and tempest, and hailstones. 31 For through the voice of the LORD shall the Assyrian be beaten down, which smote with a rod. 32 And in every place where the grounded staff shall pass, which the LORD shall lay upon him, it shall be with tabrets and harps: and in battles of shaking will he fight with it. 33 For Tophet is ordained of old; yea, for the king it is prepared; he hath made it deep and large: the pile thereof is fire and much wood; the breath of the LORD, like a stream of brimstone, doth kindle it. (Isaiah 30:27-33)

Isaiah 30:33 declares the future home of the wicked where the first inhabitants will be the antichrist and the false prophet. The Lord Jesus is returning to the earth and His anger is directed at the nations of the world because they have worshipped the beast as God and have followed after the beast, and have trusted in the beast and his kingdom. The kingdom of antichrist will make war with the Lord Jesus but it will be a very short one. The nations of this world will fight a battle that they cannot win. The antichrist deceived the nations of the world just as Nimrod deceived the people on the earth after the great flood. The sword of the Lord is bathed in blood as He makes war against the kingdom of antichrist. The bodies of the armies of the beast will extend for 200 miles (Revelation 14:20).

There are many other Scriptures in the Old Testament that refer to the great coming of Jesus Christ to the earth as KING OF KINGS AND LORD OF LORDS and of His great wrath against the nations:

> ¹Come near, ye nations, to hear; and hearken, ye people: let the earth hear, and all that is therein; the world, and all things that come forth of it. ² For the indignation of the LORD is upon all nations, and his fury upon all their armies: he hath utterly destroyed them, he hath delivered them to the slaughter. ³ Their slain also shall be cast out, and their stink shall come up out of their carcases, and the mountains shall be melted with their blood. ⁴ And all the host of heaven shall be dissolved, and the heavens shall be rolled together as a scroll: and all their host shall fall down, as the leaf falleth off from the vine, and as a falling fig from the fig tree. ⁵ For my sword

shall be bathed in heaven: behold, it shall come down upon Idumea, and upon the people of my curse, to judgment. ⁶ The sword of the LORD is filled with blood, it is made fat with fatness, and with the blood of lambs and goats, with the fat of the kidneys of rams: for the LORD hath a sacrifice in Bozrah, and a great slaughter in the land of Idumea. ⁷ And the unicorns shall come down with them, and the bullocks with the bulls; and their land shall be soaked with blood, and their dust made fat with fatness. ⁸ For it is the day of the LORD's vengeance, and the year of recompences for the controversy of Zion. (Isaiah 34:1-8)

¹³ The LORD shall go forth as a mighty man, he shall stir up jealousy like a man of war: he shall cry, yea, roar; he shall prevail against his enemies. ¹⁴ I have long time holden my peace; I have been still, and refrained myself: now will I cry like a travailing woman; I will destroy and devour at once. ¹⁵ I will make waste mountains and hills, and dry up all their herbs; and I will make the rivers islands, and I will dry up the pools. (Isaiah 42:13-15)

¹Who is this that cometh from Edom, with dyed garments from Bozrah? This that is glorious in his apparel, travelling in the greatness of his strength? I that speak in righteousness, mighty to save. ² Wherefore art thou red in thine apparel, and thy garments like him that treadeth in the winefat? ³ I have trodden the winepress alone; and of the people there was none with me: for I will tread them in mine anger, and trample them in my fury; and their blood shall be sprinkled upon my garments, and I will stain all my raiment. ⁴ For the day of vengeance is in mine heart, and the year of my redeemed is come. ⁵ And I looked, and there was none to help; and I wondered that there was none to uphold: therefore mine own arm brought salvation unto me; and my fury, it upheld me. ⁶ And I will tread down the people in mine anger, and make them drunk in my fury, and I will bring down their strength to the earth. (Isaiah 63:1-6)

¹⁵ For, behold, the LORD will come with fire, and with his chariots like a whirlwind, to render his anger with fury, and his rebuke with flames of fire. ¹⁶ For by fire and by his sword will the LORD plead with all flesh: and the slain of the LORD shall be many. (Isaiah 66:15-16)

²⁷ Therefore thou shalt say unto them, Thus saith the LORD of hosts, the God of Israel; Drink ye, and be drunken, and spue, and fall, and rise no more, because of the sword which I will send among you. ²⁸ And it shall be, if they refuse to take the cup at thine hand to drink, then shalt thou say unto them, Thus saith the LORD of hosts; Ye shall certainly drink. ²⁹ For, lo, I begin to bring evil on the city which is called by my name, and should ye be utterly unpunished? Ye shall not be unpunished: for I will call for a sword upon all the inhabitants of the earth, saith the LORD of

hosts. ³⁰ *Therefore prophesy thou against them all these words, and say unto them, The LORD shall roar from on high, and utter his voice from his holy habitation; he shall mightily roar upon his habitation; he shall give a shout, as they that tread the grapes, against all the inhabitants of the earth. ³¹ A noise shall come even to the ends of the earth; for the LORD hath a controversy with the nations, he will plead with all flesh; he will give them that are wicked to the sword, saith the LORD. ³² Thus saith the LORD of hosts, Behold, evil shall go forth from nation to nation, and a great whirlwind shall be raised up from the coasts of the earth. ³³ And the slain of the LORD shall be at that day from one end of the earth even unto the other end of the earth: they shall not be lamented, neither gathered, nor buried; they shall be dung upon the ground.* (Jeremiah 25:27-33)

⁹ Proclaim ye this among the Gentiles; Prepare war, wake up the mighty men, let all the men of war draw near; let them come up: ¹⁰ Beat your plowshares into swords and your pruninghooks into spears: let the weak say, I am strong. ¹¹ Assemble yourselves, and come, all ye heathen, and gather yourselves together round about: thither cause thy mighty ones to come down, O LORD. ¹² Let the heathen be wakened, and come up to the valley of Jehoshaphat: for there will I sit to judge all the heathen round about. ¹³ Put ye in the sickle, for the harvest is ripe: come, get you down; for the press is full, the fats overflow; for their wickedness is great. ¹⁴ Multitudes, multitudes in the valley of decision: for the day of the LORD is near in the valley of decision. ¹⁵ The sun and the moon shall be darkened, and the stars shall withdraw their shining. ¹⁶ The LORD also shall roar out of Zion, and utter his voice from Jerusalem; and the heavens and the earth shall shake: but the LORD will be the hope of his people, and the strength of the children of Israel. ¹⁷ So shall ye know that I am the LORD your God dwelling in Zion, my holy mountain: then shall Jerusalem be holy, and there shall no strangers pass through her any more. (Joel 3:9-17)

⁷ Hold thy peace at the presence of the Lord GOD: for the day of the LORD is at hand: for the LORD hath prepared a sacrifice, he hath bid his guests. ⁸ And it shall come to pass in the day of the LORD's sacrifice, that I will punish the princes, and the king's children, and all such as are clothed with strange apparel. ⁹ In the same day also will I punish all those that leap on the threshold, which fill their masters' houses with violence and deceit. ¹⁰ And it shall come to pass in that day, saith the LORD, that there shall be the noise of a cry from the fish gate, and an howling from the second, and a great crashing from the hills. ¹¹ Howl, ye inhabitants of Maktesh, for all the merchant people are cut down; all they that bear silver are cut off. (Zephaniah 1:7-11)

Revelation

³ Then shall the LORD go forth, and fight against those nations, as when he fought in the day of battle. ⁴ And his feet shall stand in that day upon the mount of Olives, which is before Jerusalem on the east, and the mount of Olives shall cleave in the midst thereof toward the east and toward the west, and there shall be a very great valley; and half of the mountain shall remove toward the north, and half of it toward the south. ⁵ And ye shall flee to the valley of the mountains; for the valley of the mountains shall reach unto Azal: yea, ye shall flee, like as ye fled from before the earthquake in the days of Uzziah king of Judah: and the LORD my God shall come, and all the saints with thee (Zechariah 14:3-5).

⁸ And it shall be in that day, that living waters shall go out from Jerusalem; half of them toward the former sea, and half of them toward the hinder sea: in summer and in winter shall it be. ⁹ And the LORD shall be king over all the earth: in that day shall there be one LORD, and his name one. ¹⁰ All the land shall be turned as a plain from Geba to Rimmon south of Jerusalem: and it shall be lifted up, and inhabited in her place, from Benjamin's gate unto the place of the first gate, unto the corner gate, and from the tower of Hananeel unto the king's winepresses. ¹¹ And men shall dwell in it, and there shall be no more utter destruction; but Jerusalem shall be safely inhabited. ¹² And this shall be the plague wherewith the LORD will smite all the people that have fought against Jerusalem; their flesh shall consume away while they stand upon their feet, and their eyes shall consume away in their holes, and their tongue shall consume away in their mouth. ¹³ And it shall come to pass in that day, that a great tumult from the LORD shall be among them; and they shall lay hold every one on the hand of his neighbour, and his hand shall rise up against the hand of his neighbour. ¹⁴ And Judah also shall fight at Jerusalem; and the wealth of all the heathen round about shall be gathered together, gold, and silver, and apparel, in great abundance. ¹⁵ And so shall be the plague of the horse, of the mule, of the camel, and of the ass, and of all the beasts that shall be in these tents, as this plague. (Zechariah 14:8-15)

It is tragic that so much death and destruction follows when the wicked rule the earth. One wicked ruler along with the propaganda of his false prophet will lead to much destruction and death.

When the Lord Jesus returns to the earth the Jews will then recognize that He was the Messiah all along:

⁹ And it shall come to pass in that day, that I will seek to destroy all the nations that come against Jerusalem. ¹⁰ And I will pour upon the house of David, and upon the inhabitants of Jerusalem, the spirit of grace and of supplications: and they shall look upon me whom they have pierced, and they shall mourn for him, as one mourneth

for his only son, and shall be in bitterness for him, as one that is in bitterness for his firstborn. ¹¹ *In that day shall there be a great mourning in Jerusalem, as the mourning of Hadadrimmon in the valley of Megiddon.* ¹² *And the land shall mourn, every family apart; the family of the house of David apart, and their wives apart; the family of the house of Nathan apart, and their wives apart;* ¹³ *The family of the house of Levi apart, and their wives apart; the family of Shimei apart, and their wives apart;* ¹⁴ *All the families that remain, every family apart, and their wives apart.* (Zechariah 12:9-14).

⁶ *And one shall say unto him, What are these wounds in thine hands? Then he shall answer, Those with which I was wounded in the house of my friends.* (Zechariah 13:6).

The prophecies in the Book of Zechariah declare the mourning of the Jews when they recognize that Jesus was indeed their Messiah. For centuries many Jews believed the message from their rabbis that Jesus was not the Messiah. Now the day has come that the Jews will recognize that the Lord Jesus was and is the Messiah, the hope of Israel.

The final battle is also described in Revelation 14 after the wheat and the tares have been separated:

¹⁴ *And I looked, and behold a white cloud, and upon the cloud one sat like unto the Son of man, having on his head a golden crown, and in his hand a sharp sickle.* ¹⁵ *And another angel came out of the temple, crying with a loud voice to him that sat on the cloud, Thrust in thy sickle, and reap: for the time is come for thee to reap; for the harvest of the earth is ripe.* ¹⁶ *And he that sat on the cloud thrust in his sickle on the earth; and the earth was reaped.* ¹⁷ *And another angel came out of the temple which is in heaven, he also having a sharp sickle.* ¹⁸ *And another angel came out from the altar, which had power over fire; and cried with a loud cry to him that had the sharp sickle, saying, Thrust in thy sharp sickle, and gather the clusters of the vine of the earth; for her grapes are fully ripe.* ¹⁹ *And the angel thrust in his sickle into the earth, and gathered the vine of the earth, and cast it into the great winepress of the wrath of God.* ²⁰ *And the winepress was trodden without the city, and blood came out of the winepress, even unto the horse bridles, by the space of a thousand and six hundred furlongs.* (Revelation 14:14-20)

All things are naked and open to the eyes of Him to whom we must give an account. This is a terrible judgment as the Lord defeats the kingdom of antichrist and many are slain in battle. It is recorded in Isaiah that the Lord declares why men must be punished:

Revelation

¹Behold, the LORD maketh the earth empty, and maketh it waste, and turneth it upside down, and scattereth abroad the inhabitants thereof. ² And it shall be, as with the people, so with the priest; as with the servant, so with his master; as with the maid, so with her mistress; as with the buyer, so with the seller; as with the lender, so with the borrower; as with the taker of usury, so with the giver of usury to him. ³ The land shall be utterly emptied, and utterly spoiled: for the LORD hath spoken this word. ⁴ The earth mourneth and fadeth away, the world languisheth and fadeth away, the haughty people of the earth do languish. ⁵ The earth also is defiled under the inhabitants thereof; because they have transgressed the laws, changed the ordinance, broken the everlasting covenant. ⁶ Therefore hath the curse devoured the earth, and they that dwell therein are desolate: therefore the inhabitants of the earth are burned, and few men left. (Isaiah 24:1-6)

The Lord reveals why He is pouring out His wrath upon men: man has transgressed the laws of God, changed the ordinance and broken the everlasting covenant. To transgress the laws of God, one must know what the laws are and then deliberately choose to break them. Changing the ordinance indicates that men choose to rewrite those laws that God provided for them to live by. To break the everlasting covenant that God has provided for men shows the contempt that wicked men have toward a holy God.

Revelation 19:17-21
The Terrible Destruction to Come

And I saw an angel standing in the sun; and he cried with a loud voice, saying to all the fowls that fly in the midst of heaven, Come and gather yourselves together unto the supper of the great God; That ye may eat the flesh of kings, and the flesh of captains, and the flesh of mighty men, and the flesh of horses, and of them that sit on them, and the flesh of all men, both free and bond, both small and great. And I saw the beast, and the kings of the earth, and their armies, gathered together to make war against him that sat on the horse, and against his army. And the beast was taken, and with him the false prophet that wrought miracles before him, with which he deceived them that had received the mark of the beast, and them that worshipped his image. These both were cast alive into a lake of fire burning with brimstone. And the remnant were slain with the sword of him that sat upon the horse, which sword proceeded out of his mouth: and all the fowls were filled with their flesh.

All men and women have a choice that they must make: to attend the wedding supper banquet dressed in white linen or to go to the banquet and have one's flesh picked clean by birds. We have a Midrash here where the enemies of Jesus (Herod and Pilate) put aside their differences and unite against Jesus. Now the kings of the earth stop fighting each other and unite to fight against the Lord Jesus Christ as prophesied by Isaiah:

¹The burden of Babylon, which Isaiah the son of Amoz did see. ² Lift ye up a banner upon the high mountain, exalt the voice unto them, shake the hand, that they may go into the gates of the nobles. ³ I have commanded my sanctified ones, I have also called my mighty ones for mine anger, even them that rejoice in my highness. ⁴ The noise of a multitude in the mountains, like as of a great people; a tumultuous noise of the kingdoms of nations gathered together: the LORD of hosts mustereth the host of the battle. ⁵ They come from a far country, from the end of heaven, even the LORD, and the weapons of his indignation, to destroy the whole land (Isaiah 13:1-5).

A great multitude from many nations will take part in this final battle. This great multitude will be destroyed when the Lord Jesus returns, and the bodies will cover the land for 200 miles.

The beast and the false prophet are captured by the Lord Jesus and are immediately judged for their sins and transgressions. They are to be the first inhabitants of the lake of fire. They will be joined by the Devil and his angels after the 1,000-year reign of Jesus Christ is over. The Devil and his angels have another judgment that awaits them as described in Revelation 20.

Chapter 20

The Kingdom Age and the Final Judgment

Revelation 20:1-3
Satan and His Angels are Bound for a Thousand Years

And I saw an angel come down from heaven, having the key of the bottomless pit and a great chain in his hand. And he laid hold on the dragon, that old serpent, which is the Devil, and Satan, and bound him a thousand years, And cast him into the bottomless pit, and shut him up, and set a seal upon him, that he should deceive the nations no more, till the thousand years should be fulfilled: and after that he must be loosed a little season.

SATAN HAS ALWAYS desired to rule, but his millenia of striving against God prove futile. His final reward? He ends up getting dust as declared in Isaiah and Ezekiel:

12 How art thou fallen from heaven, O Lucifer, son of the morning! How art thou cut down to the ground, which didst weaken the nations! 13 For thou hast said in thine heart, I will ascend into heaven, I will exalt my throne above the stars of God: I will sit also upon the mount of the congregation, in the sides of the north: 14 I will ascend above the heights of the clouds; I will be like the most High. 15 Yet thou shalt be brought down to hell, to the sides of the pit. (Isaiah 14:12-15)

12 Son of man, take up a lamentation upon the king of Tyrus, and say unto him, Thus saith the Lord GOD; Thou sealest up the sum, full of wisdom, and perfect in beauty. 13 Thou hast been in Eden the garden of God; every precious stone was thy covering, the sardius, topaz, and the diamond, the beryl, the onyx, and the jasper, the sapphire, the emerald, and the carbuncle, and gold: the workmanship of thy tabrets and of thy pipes was prepared in thee in the day that thou wast created. *14 Thou art the anointed cherub that covereth; and I have set thee so: thou wast upon the holy mountain of God; thou hast walked up and down in the midst of the stones of fire. 15 Thou wast perfect in thy ways from the day that thou wast created, till iniquity was found in thee. 16 By the multitude of thy merchandise they have filled the midst of thee with violence, and thou hast sinned: therefore I will cast thee as profane out of the mountain of God: and I will destroy thee, O covering cherub, from the midst of the stones of fire. 17 Thine heart was lifted up because of thy beauty, thou hast corrupted thy wisdom by reason of thy brightness: I will cast thee to the ground, I will lay thee before kings, that they may behold thee.* (Ezekiel 28:12-17)

Satan is called the dragon, the unclean and foul monster, old serpent, devil, slanderer, false accuser, and the adversary. The Devil and his angels will be locked up for the 1,000-year reign of the Lord Jesus Christ. They will not be permitted to deceive or entice anyone to sin for 1,000 years. There is a chain that can bind spiritual beings! The pit is described in Revelation 9, from where the demon locusts were released once the pit was opened as part of the Fifth Trumpet judgment. There are demons so terrible that the Lord keeps them locked up in the pit, not to be released until the Fifth Trumpet judgment. The demons that were loosed will also be bound up with Satan for 1,000 years. The Lord has the key to the bottomless pit and no creature can open the pit without His permission.

Those who believe that Satan is presently bound in the bottomless pit and that the 1,000-year reign of Jesus Christ represents the current church age are hard pressed to prove their point with all the evil in existence in the world since the first century. The kingdom age also declares that men will live for 1,000 years. Today there are few who live one hundred years on the earth (Isaiah 65:20). Truly the kingdom reign of the Lord Jesus Christ has not occurred. There are passages in the Old Testament that declare this coming event where the evil spirits will be chained up:

21 And it shall come to pass in that day, that the LORD shall punish the host of the high ones that are on high, and the kings of the earth upon the earth. 22 And they shall be gathered together, as prisoners are gathered in the pit, and shall be shut up in the prison, and after many days shall they be visited. (Isaiah 24:21-22)

2 And it shall come to pass in that day, saith the LORD of hosts, that I will cut off the names of the idols out of the land, and they shall no more be remembered: and also I will cause the prophets and the unclean spirit to pass out of the land. (Zechariah 13:2)

Other passages such as II Peter 2:4 and Jude 6 speak of angels who have sinned and have been delivered into chains of darkness to be reserved for judgment:

⁴ *For if God spared not the angels that sinned, but cast them down to hell, and delivered them into chains of darkness, to be reserved unto judgment.* (II Peter 2:4)

⁶ *And the angels which kept not their first estate, but left their own habitation, he hath reserved in everlasting chains under darkness unto the judgment of the great day.* (Jude 6)

These passages reveal that there are some demons that are so terrible that the Lord keeps them locked up.

Revelation 20:4-6
The First Resurrection

And I saw thrones, and they sat upon them, and judgment was given unto them: and I saw the souls of them that were beheaded for the witness of Jesus, and for the word of God, and which had not worshipped the beast, neither his image, neither had received his mark upon their foreheads, or in their hands; and they lived and reigned with Christ a thousand years. But the rest of the dead lived not again until the thousand years were finished. This is the first resurrection. Blessed and holy is he that hath part in the first resurrection: on such the second death hath no power, but they shall be priests of God and of Christ, and shall reign with him a thousand years.

This prophecy or event is also recorded in the Book of Daniel, as Daniel saw the thrones that are to be set up when the Lord Jesus will judge the nations at His return:

⁹ *I beheld till the thrones were cast down, and the Ancient of days did sit, whose garment was white as snow, and the hair of his head like the pure wool: his throne was like the fiery flame, and his wheels as burning fire.* ¹⁰ *A fiery stream issued and came forth from before him: thousand thousands ministered unto him, and ten thousand times ten thousand stood before him: the judgment was set, and the books were opened.* ¹¹ *I beheld then because of the voice of the great words which the horn spake: I beheld even till the beast was slain, and his body destroyed, and given to the burning flame.* ¹² *As concerning the rest of the beasts, they had their dominion taken away: yet their lives were prolonged for a season and time.* ¹³ *I saw in the night visions, and, behold, one like the Son of man came with the clouds of heaven, and came to the Ancient of days, and they brought him near before him.* ¹⁴ *And there was given him dominion, and glory, and a kingdom, that all people, nations, and languages,*

Revelation

should serve him: his dominion is an everlasting dominion, which shall not pass away, and his kingdom that which shall not be destroyed. (Daniel 7:9-14)

In Revelation 20, John sees the true believers of the Old and New Testament ages sitting on thrones. Now the tribulation saints—those who endured the persecution from the kingdom of antichrist—are united with the Lord Jesus to live and reign for 1,000 years. This is the first resurrection.

When people died before Jesus Christ was crucified on the cross, they were sent to Hades. Hades was divided into two compartments. One section was for the saved or righteous and was referred to as Abraham's Bosom. The other section was for the lost or wicked people:

[22] And it came to pass, that the beggar died, and was carried by the angels into Abraham's bosom: the rich man also died, and was buried; [23] And in hell he lift up his eyes, being in torments, and seeth Abraham afar off, and Lazarus in his bosom. [24] And he cried and said, Father Abraham, have mercy on me, and send Lazarus, that he may dip the tip of his finger in water, and cool my tongue; for I am tormented in this flame. [25] But Abraham said, Son, remember that thou in thy lifetime receivedst thy good things, and likewise Lazarus evil things: but now he is comforted, and thou art tormented. [26] And beside all this, between us and you there is a great gulf fixed: so that they which would pass from hence to you cannot; neither can they pass to us, that would come from thence. (Luke 16:22-26)

In the story of the rich man and the beggar Lazarus, Lazarus upon his death was carried to the section of Hades that was reserved for the righteous. The rich man died and was sent to the section of Hades where the wicked are being held. The thief on the cross who was dying alongside the Lord Jesus was promised that upon death he was to be carried to the section where the righteous were located before the resurrection of the Lord Jesus:

[43] And Jesus said unto him, Verily I say unto thee, Today shalt thou be with me in paradise. (Luke 23:43)

In the Book of Acts, Peter witnessed to the people declaring that when Jesus rose from the grave He emptied the section of Hades where the righteous were kept (Abraham's Bosom):

[25] For David speaketh concerning him, I foresaw the Lord always before my face, for he is on my right hand, that I should not be moved: [26] Therefore did my heart rejoice, and my tongue was glad; moreover also my flesh shall rest in hope: [27] Because thou wilt not leave my soul in hell, neither wilt thou suffer thine Holy One to see corruption. [28] Thou hast made known to me the ways of life; thou shalt make me full

The Kingdom Age and the Final Judgment

of joy with thy countenance. ²⁹ Men and brethren, let me freely speak unto you of the patriarch David, that he is both dead and buried, and his sepulchre is with us unto this day. ³⁰ Therefore being a prophet, and knowing that God had sworn with an oath to him, that of the fruit of his loins, according to the flesh, he would raise up Christ to sit on his throne; ³¹ He seeing this before spake of the resurrection of Christ, that his soul was not left in hell, neither his flesh did see corruption. (Acts 2:25-31)

When the Lord Jesus arose from the dead, all the saints of the Old Testament arose with Him as revealed in Matthew's Gospel:

⁵² And the graves were opened; and many bodies of the saints which slept arose, ⁵³ and came out of the graves after his resurrection, and went into the holy city, and appeared unto many. (Matthew 27:52-53)

The resurrection of the Lord Jesus was the start of the first resurrection:

²² For as in Adam all die, even so in Christ shall all be made alive. ²³ But every man in his own order: Christ the firstfruits; afterward they that are Christ's at his coming. ²⁴ Then cometh the end, when he shall have delivered up the kingdom to God, even the Father; when he shall have put down all rule and all authority and power. ²⁵ For he must reign, till he hath put all enemies under his feet. ²⁶ The last enemy that shall be destroyed is death. (I Corinthians 15:22-26)

I Corinthians 15 reveals the beginning of the first resurrection. It began with Christ ascending to heaven and concludes here in Revelation 20. When a saint dies today, he ascends directly to heaven to be with the Lord Jesus. The death of the believer in the Lord Jesus Christ today will be included in the first resurrection which began 2,000 years ago. The first resurrection concludes here in Revelation 20.

In Revelation 20 we see that the bride of Christ will reign with Jesus Christ as kings and priests during the kingdom age. This is also prophesied elsewhere in the Scriptures:

¹² If we suffer, we shall also reign with him: if we deny him, he also will deny us. (II Timothy 2:12)

⁶ And hath made us kings and priests unto God and his Father; to him be glory and dominion for ever and ever. Amen. (Revelation 1:6)

⁹ And they sung a new song, saying, Thou art worthy to take the book, and to open the seals thereof: for thou wast slain, and hast redeemed us to God by thy blood out of every kindred, and tongue, and people, and nation; ¹⁰ And hast made us unto our God kings and priests: and we shall reign on the earth. (Revelation 5:9-10)

Revelation

A Temple will be built as prophesied by the prophet Ezekiel in chapters 40 through 48. The Scriptures also speak of religious festivals during the 1,000-year reign of Jesus Christ:

16 And it shall come to pass, that every one that is left of all the nations which came against Jerusalem shall even go up from year to year to worship the King, the LORD of hosts, and to keep the feast of tabernacles. 17 And it shall be, that whoso will not come up of all the families of the earth unto Jerusalem to worship the King, the LORD of hosts, even upon them shall be no rain. 18 And if the family of Egypt go not up, and come not, that have no rain; there shall be the plague, wherewith the LORD will smite the heathen that come not up to keep the feast of tabernacles. 19 This shall be the punishment of Egypt, and the punishment of all nations that come not up to keep the feast of tabernacles. 20 In that day shall there be upon the bells of the horses, HOLINESS UNTO THE LORD; and the pots in the LORD's house shall be like the bowls before the altar. 21 Yea, every pot in Jerusalem and in Judah shall be holiness unto the LORD of hosts: and all they that sacrifice shall come and take of them, and seethe therein: and in that day there shall be no more the Canaanite in the house of the LORD of hosts. (Zechariah 14:16-21)

In addition to the religious festivals, there are many Scriptures that speak of the glorious events that will take place in the kingdom age. Men and women will live for 1,000 years (Isaiah 65:20). There will be no sickness and no sorrow. Everything can be purchased without money during this period. It will be a glorious time. The kingdom age along with the many blessings have been foretold by the prophet Isaiah and many other prophets:

23 In that day shall there be a highway out of Egypt to Assyria, and the Assyrian shall come into Egypt, and the Egyptian into Assyria, and the Egyptians shall serve with the Assyrians. 24 In that day shall Israel be the third with Egypt and with Assyria, even a blessing in the midst of the land: 25 Whom the LORD of hosts shall bless, saying, Blessed be Egypt my people, and Assyria the work of my hands, and Israel mine inheritance. (Isaiah 19:23-25)

1 Ho, every one that thirsteth, come ye to the waters, and he that hath no money; come ye, buy, and eat; yea, come, buy wine and milk without money and without price. 2 Wherefore do ye spend money for that which is not bread? And your labour for that which satisfieth not? Hearken diligently unto me, and eat ye that which is good, and let your soul delight itself in fatness. (Isaiah 55:1-2)

1 Arise, shine; for thy light is come, and the glory of the LORD is risen upon thee. 2 For, behold, the darkness shall cover the earth, and gross darkness the people: but the LORD shall arise upon thee, and his glory shall be seen upon thee. 3 And the

The Kingdom Age and the Final Judgment

Gentiles shall come to thy light, and kings to the brightness of thy rising. ⁴ Lift up thine eyes round about, and see: all they gather themselves together, they come to thee: thy sons shall come from far, and thy daughters shall be nursed at thy side. ⁵ Then thou shalt see, and flow together, and thine heart shall fear, and be enlarged; because the abundance of the sea shall be converted unto thee, the forces of the Gentiles shall come unto thee. ⁶ The multitude of camels shall cover thee, the dromedaries of Midian and Ephah; all they from Sheba shall come: they shall bring gold and incense; and they shall shew forth the praises of the LORD. ⁷ All the flocks of Kedar shall be gathered together unto thee, the rams of Nebaioth shall minister unto thee: they shall come up with acceptance on mine altar, and I will glorify the house of my glory. ⁸ Who are these that fly as a cloud, and as the doves to their windows? ⁹ Surely the isles shall wait for me, and the ships of Tarshish first, to bring thy sons from far, their silver and their gold with them, unto the name of the LORD thy God, and to the Holy One of Israel, because he hath glorified thee. ¹⁰ And the sons of strangers shall build up thy walls, and their kings shall minister unto thee: for in my wrath I smote thee, but in my favour have I had mercy on thee. ¹¹ Therefore thy gates shall be open continually; they shall not be shut day nor night; that men may bring unto thee the forces of the Gentiles, and that their kings may be brought. ¹² For the nation and kingdom that will not serve thee shall perish; yea, those nations shall be utterly wasted. ¹³ The glory of Lebanon shall come unto thee, the fir tree, the pine tree, and the box together, to beautify the place of my sanctuary; and I will make the place of my feet glorious. ¹⁴ The sons also of them that afflicted thee shall come bending unto thee; and all they that despised thee shall bow themselves down at the soles of thy feet; and they shall call thee; The city of the LORD, The Zion of the Holy One of Israel. ¹⁵ Whereas thou has been forsaken and hated, so that no man went through thee, I will make thee an eternal excellency, a joy of many generations. ¹⁶ Thou shalt also suck the milk of the Gentiles, and shalt suck the breast of kings: and thou shalt know that I the LORD am thy Saviour and thy Redeemer, the mighty One of Jacob. ¹⁷ For brass I will bring gold, and for iron I will bring silver, and for wood brass, and for stones iron: I will also make thy officers peace, and thine exactors righteousness. (Isaiah 60:1-17)

¹For Zion's sake will I not hold my peace, and for Jerusalem's sake I will not rest, until the righteousness thereof go forth as brightness, and the salvation thereof as a lamp that burneth. ² And the Gentiles shall see thy righteousness, and all kings thy glory: and thou shalt be called by a new name, which the mouth of the LORD shall name. ³ Thou shalt also be a crown of glory in the hand of the LORD, and a royal diadem in the hand of thy God. ⁴ Thou shalt no more be termed Forsaken; neither shall thy land any more be termed Desolate: but thou shalt be called Hephzibah, and thy land Beulah: for the LORD delighteth in thee, and thy land shall

be married. ⁵ For as a young man marrieth a virgin, so shall thy sons marry thee: and as the bridegroom rejoiceth over the bride, so shall thy God rejoice over thee. (Isaiah 62:1-5)

²⁰ There shall be no more thence an infant of days, nor an old man that hath not filled his days: for the child shall die an hundred years old; but the sinner being an hundred years old shall be accursed. ²¹ And they shall build houses, and inhabit them; and they shall plant vineyards, and eat the fruit of them. ²² They shall not build, and another inhabit; they shall not plant, and another eat: for as the days of a tree are the days of my people, and mine elect shall long enjoy the work of their hands. ²³ They shall not labour in vain, nor bring forth for trouble; for they are the seed of the blessed of the LORD, and their offspring with them. ²⁴ And it shall come to pass, that before they call, I will answer; and while they are yet speaking, I will hear. ²⁵ The wolf and the lamb shall feed together, and the lion shall eat straw like the bullock: and dust shall be the serpent's meat. They shall not hurt nor destroy in all my holy mountain, saith the LORD. (Isaiah 65:20-25)

¹At the same time, saith the LORD, will I be the God of all the families of Israel, and they shall be my people. ² Thus saith the LORD, The people which were left of the sword found grace in the wilderness; even Israel, when I went to cause him to rest. ³ The LORD hath appeared of old unto me, saying, Yea, I have loved thee with an everlasting love: therefore with lovingkindness have I drawn thee. ⁴ Again I will build thee, and thou shalt be built, O virgin of Israel: thou shalt again be adorned with thy tabrets, and shalt go forth in the dances of them that make merry. ⁵ Thou shalt yet plant vines upon the mountains of Samaria: the planters shall plant, and shall eat them as common things. ⁶ For there shall be a day, that the watchmen upon the mount Ephraim shall cry, Arise ye, and let us go up to Zion unto the LORD our God. ⁷ For thus saith the LORD; Sing with gladness for Jacob, and shout among the chief of the nations: publish ye, praise ye, and say, O LORD, save thy people, the remnant of Israel. ⁸ Behold, I will bring them from the north country, and gather them from the coasts of the earth, and with them the blind and the lame, the woman with child and her that travaileth with child together: a great company shall return thither. ⁹ They shall come with weeping, and with supplications will I lead them: I will cause them to walk by the rivers of waters in a straight way, wherein they shall not stumble: for I am a father to Israel, and Ephraim is my firstborn. ¹⁰ Hear the word of the LORD, O ye nations, and declare it in the isles afar off, and say, He that scattered Israel will gather him, and keep him, as a shepherd doth his flock. ¹¹ For the LORD hath redeemed Jacob, and ransomed him from the hand of him that was stronger than he. ¹² Therefore they shall come and sing in the height of Zion, and shall flow together to the goodness of the LORD, for wheat, and for wine, and for oil, and for

the young of the flock and of the herd: and their soul shall be as a watered garden; and they shall not sorrow any more at all. ¹³ Then shall the virgin rejoice in the dance, both young men and old together: for I will turn their mourning into joy, and will comfort them, and make them rejoice from their sorrow. ¹⁴ And I will satiate the soul of the priests with fatness, and my people shall be satisfied with my goodness, saith the LORD. (Jeremiah 31:1-14)

¹Moreover the word of the LORD came unto Jeremiah the second time, while he was yet shut up in the court of the prison, saying, ² Thus saith the LORD the maker thereof, the LORD that formed it, to establish it; the LORD is his name; ³ Call unto me, and I will answer thee, and show thee great and mighty things, which thou knowest not. ⁴ For thus saith the LORD, the God of Israel, concerning the houses of this city, and concerning the houses of the kings of Judah, which are thrown down by the mounts, and by the sword; ⁵ They come to fight with the Chaldeans, but it is to fill them with the dead bodies of men, whom I have slain in mine anger and in my fury, and for all whose wickedness I have hid my face from this city. ⁶ Behold, I will bring it health and cure, and I will cure them, and will reveal unto them the abundance of peace and truth. ⁷ And I will cause the captivity of Judah and the captivity of Israel to return, and will build them, as at the first. ⁸ And I will cleanse them from all their iniquity, whereby they have sinned against me; and I will pardon all their iniquities, whereby they have sinned, and whereby they have transgressed against me. ⁹ And it shall be to me a name of joy, a praise and an honour before all the nations of the earth, which shall hear all the good that I do unto them: and they shall fear and tremble for all the goodness and for all the prosperity that I procure unto it. ¹⁰ Thus saith the LORD; Again there shall be heard in this place, which ye say shall be desolate without man and without beast, even in the cities of Judah, and in the streets of Jerusalem, that are desolate, without man, and without inhabitant, and without beast, ¹¹ The voice of joy, and the voice of gladness, the voice of the bridegroom, and the voice of the bride, the voice of them that shall say, Praise the LORD of hosts: for the LORD is good; for his mercy endureth for ever: and of them that shall bring the sacrifice of praise into the house of the LORD. For I will cause to return the captivity of the land, as at the first, saith the LORD. ¹² Thus saith the LORD of hosts; Again in this place, which is desolate without man and without beast, and in all the cities thereof, shall be an habitation of shepherds causing their flocks to lie down. ¹³ In the cities of the mountains, in the cities of the vale, and in the cities of the south, and in the land of Benjamin, and in the places about Jerusalem, and in the cities of Judah, shall the flocks pass again under the hands of him that telleth them, saith the LORD. ¹⁴ Behold, the days come, saith the LORD, that I will perform that good thing which I have promised unto the house of Israel and to the house of

Revelation

Judah. ¹⁵ In those days, and at that time, will I cause the Branch of righteousness to grow up unto David; and he shall execute judgment and righteousness in the land. ¹⁶ In those days shall Judah be saved, and Jerusalem shall dwell safely: and this is the name wherewith she shall be called, The LORD our righteousness. ¹⁷ For thus saith the LORD; David shall never want a man to sit upon the throne of the house of Israel; ¹⁸ Neither shall the priests the Levites want a man before me to offer burnt offerings, and to kindle meat offerings, and to do sacrifice continually. ¹⁹ And the word of the LORD came unto Jeremiah, saying, ²⁰ Thus saith the LORD; If ye can break my covenant of the day, and my covenant of the night, and that there should not be day and night in their season; ²¹ Then may also my covenant be broken with David my servant, that he should not have a son to reign upon his throne; and with the Levites the priests, my ministers. ²² As the host of heaven cannot be numbered, neither the sand of the sea measured: so will I multiply the seed of David my servant, and the Levites that minister unto me. (Jeremiah 33:1-22)

¹¹ For thus saith the Lord GOD; Behold, I, even I, will both search my sheep, and seek them out. ¹² As a shepherd seeketh out his flock in the day that he is among his sheep that are scattered; so will I seek out my sheep, and will deliver them out of all places where they have been scattered in the cloudy and dark day. ¹³ And I will bring them out from the people, and gather them from the countries, and will bring them to their own land, and feed them upon the mountains of Israel by the rivers, and in all the inhabited places of the country. ¹⁴ I will feed them in a good pasture, and upon the high mountains of Israel shall their fold be: there shall they lie in a good fold, and in a fat pasture shall they feed upon the mountains of Israel. ¹⁵ I will feed my flock, and I will cause them to lie down, saith the Lord GOD. ¹⁶ I will seek that which was lost, and bring again that which was driven away, and will bind up that which was broken, and will strengthen that which was sick: but I will destroy the fat and the strong; I will feed them with judgment. ¹⁷ And as for you, O my flock, thus saith the Lord GOD; Behold, I judge between cattle and cattle, between the rams and the he goats. ¹⁸ Seemeth it a small thing unto you to have eaten up the good pasture, but ye must tread down with your feet the residue of your pastures? And to have drunk of the deep waters, but ye must foul the residue with your feet? ¹⁹ And as for my flock, they eat that which ye have trodden with your feet; and they drink that which ye have fouled with your feet. ²⁰ Therefore thus saith the Lord GOD unto them; Behold, I, even I, will judge between the fat cattle and between the lean cattle. ²¹ Because ye have thrust with side and with shoulder, and pushed all the diseased with your horns, till ye have scattered them abroad; ²² Therefore will I save my flock, and they shall no more be a prey; and I will judge between cattle and cattle. ²³ And I will set up one shepherd over them, and he shall feed them, even my servant David;

The Kingdom Age and the Final Judgment

he shall feed them, and he shall be their shepherd. ²⁴ And I the LORD will be their God, and my servant David a prince among them; I the LORD have spoken it. ²⁵ And I will make with them a covenant of peace, and will cause the evil beasts to cease out of the land: and they shall dwell safely in the wilderness, and sleep in the woods. ²⁶ And I will make them and the places round about my hill a blessing; and I will cause the shower to come down in his season; there shall be showers of blessing. ²⁷ And the tree of the field shall yield her fruit, and the earth shall yield her increase, and they shall be safe in their land, and shall know that I am the LORD, when I have broken the bands of their yoke, and delivered them out of the hand of those that served themselves of them. ²⁸ And they shall no more be a prey to the heathen, neither shall the beast of the land devour them; but they shall dwell safely, and none shall make them afraid. ²⁹ And I will raise up for them a plant of renown, and they shall be no more consumed with hunger in the land, neither bear the shame of the heathen any more. ³⁰ Thus shall they know that I the LORD their God am with them, and that they, even the house of Israel, are my people, saith the Lord GOD. ³¹ And ye my flock, the flock of my pasture, are men, and I am your God, saith the Lord GOD. (Ezekiel 34:11-31)

¹⁵ The word of the LORD came again unto me, saying, ¹⁶ Moreover, thou son of man, take thee one stick, and write upon it, For Judah, and for the children of Israel his companions: then take another stick, and write upon it, For Joseph, the stick of Ephraim and for all the house of Israel his companions: ¹⁷ And join them one to another into one stick; and they shall become one in thine hand. ¹⁸ And when the children of thy people shall speak unto thee, saying, Wilt thou not shew us what thou meanest by these? ¹⁹ Say unto them, Thus saith the Lord GOD; Behold, I will take the stick of Joseph, which is in the hand of Ephraim, and the tribes of Israel his fellows, and will put them with him, even with the stick of Judah, and make them one stick, and they shall be one in mine hand. ²⁰ And the sticks whereon thou writest shall be in thine hand before their eyes. ²¹ And say unto them, Thus saith the Lord GOD; Behold, I will take the children of Israel from among the heathen, whither they be gone, and will gather them on every side, and bring them into their own land: ²² And I will make them one nation in the land upon the mountains of Israel; and one king shall be king to them all: and they shall be no more two nations, neither shall they be divided into two kingdoms any more at all. ²³ Neither shall they defile themselves any more with their idols, nor with their detestable things, nor with any of their transgressions: but I will save them out of all their dwellingplaces, wherein they have sinned, and will cleanse them: so shall they be my people, and I will be their God. ²⁴ And David my servant shall be king over them; and they all shall have one shepherd: they shall also walk in my judgments, and observe my statutes, and do them. ²⁵ And they shall dwell in the

land that I have given unto Jacob my servant, wherein your fathers have dwelt; and they shall dwell therein, even they, and their children, and their children's children for ever: and my servant David shall be their prince for ever. 26 Moreover I will make a covenant of peace with them; it shall be an everlasting covenant with them: and I will place them, and multiply them, and will set my sanctuary in the midst of them for evermore. 27 My tabernacle also shall be with them: yea, I will be their God, and they shall be my people. 28 And the heathen shall know that I the LORD do sanctify Israel, when my sanctuary shall be in the midst of them for evermore. (Ezekiel 37:15-28)

¹But in the last days it shall come to pass, that the mountain of the house of the LORD shall be established in the top of the mountains, and it shall be exalted above the hills; and people shall flow unto it. ² And many nations shall come, and say, Come, and let us go up to the mountain of the LORD, and to the house of the God of Jacob; and he will teach us of his ways, and we will walk in his paths: for the law shall go forth of Zion, and the word of the LORD from Jerusalem. ³ And he shall judge among many people, and rebuke strong nations afar off; and they shall beat their swords into plowshares, and their spears into pruninghooks: nation shall not lift up a sword against nation, neither shall they learn war any more. ⁴ But they shall sit every man under his vine and under his fig tree; and none shall make them afraid: for the mouth of the LORD of hosts hath spoken it. (Micah 4:1-4)

¹⁴ Sing, O daughter of Zion; shout, O Israel; be glad and rejoice with all the heart, O daughter of Jerusalem. ¹⁵ The LORD hath taken away thy judgments, he hath cast out thine enemy: the king of Israel, even the LORD, is in the midst of thee: thou shalt not see evil any more. ¹⁶ In that day it shall be said to Jerusalem, Fear thou not: and to Zion, Let not thine hands be slack. ¹⁷ The LORD thy God in the midst of thee is mighty; he will save, he will rejoice over thee with joy; he will rest in his love, he will joy over thee with singing. ¹⁸ I will gather them that are sorrowful for the solemn assembly, who are of thee, to whom the reproach of it was a burden. ¹⁹ Behold, at that time I will undo all that afflict thee: and I will save her that halteth, and gather her that was driven out; and I will get them praise and fame in every land where they have been put to shame. ²⁰ At that time will I bring you again, even in the time that I gather you: for I will make you a name and a praise among all people of the earth, when I turn back your captivity before your eyes, saith the LORD. (Zephaniah 3:14-20)

The Scriptures proclaim the glorious reign of the Lord Jesus Christ over the whole earth as King of Kings and Lord of Lords. There will be peace on the earth during the reign of the Lord Jesus.

Revelation 20:7-10
Satan and His Angels are Released Upon the Earth

And when the thousand years are expired, Satan shall be loosed out of his prison, and shall go out to deceive the nations which are in the four quarters of the earth, Gog, and Magog, to gather them together to battle: the number of whom is as the sand of the sea. And they went up on the breadth of the earth, and compassed the camp of the saints about, and the beloved city: and fire came down from God out of heaven, and devoured them. And the devil that deceived them was cast into the lake of fire and brimstone, where the beast and the false prophet are, and shall be tormented day and night for ever and ever.

Upon his release from the bottomless pit after the 1,000-year period has expired, the Devil will once again deceive the nations of the world. He will look for a man who the nations of the world will admire and follow, similar to Nimrod. This man, under Satan's influence, will deceive and persuade the nations of the world to rebel against the Lord Jesus. His message may contain the promise that he can lead the nations of the world into a better future.

The mention of Gog and Magog is contained in the Book of Ezekiel chapters 38 and 39. The prophecy in Ezekiel will have its complete fulfillment when the enemies of God come against Mount Zion and are destroyed. This is another example of Midrash as the Lord destroys those who are in rebellion in their attempt to overthrow Jesus. Some Bible scholars believe the prophecy within Ezekiel 38 and 39 will be partially fulfilled before the seventieth week of Daniel, but the final fulfillment of Ezekiel 38 and 39 will be at the end of the kingdom age as revealed here in chapter 20.

Revelation 20:11-15
The Great White Throne Judgment

And I saw a great white throne, and him that sat on it, from whose face the earth and the heaven fled away; and there was found no place for them. And I saw the dead, small and great, stand before God; and the books were opened: and another book was opened, which is the book of life: and the dead were judged out of those things which were written in the books, according to their works. And the sea gave up the dead which were in it; and death and hell delivered up the dead which were in them: and they were judged every man according to their works. And death and hell were cast into the lake of fire. This is the second death. And whosoever was not found written in the book of life was cast into the lake of fire.

Revelation

The first thing John sees is the Great White Throne. This is the seat of authority for the next events that will take place. Then John sees the One who is seated on the Throne of Authority where the judgments are to be pronounced. There is no further appeal. The books will be opened and everyone at the Great White Throne judgment will be granted a fair trial and judgment. All truth will be revealed. The final judgment is for those who are spiritually dead as prophesied in Isaiah 65:17. The word dead is used repeatedly throughout chapter 20.

There is more than one set of books in heaven. There are at least two records concerning the believers. There is the roll of the elect chosen in Christ before the foundation of the world (Ephesians 1:3-6). Another book concerning the believers is the record of all their thoughts and meditations concerning their Lord:

[20] *Notwithstanding in this rejoice not, that the spirits are subject unto you; but rather rejoice, because your names are written in heaven.* (Luke 10:20)

[16] *Then they that feared the LORD spake often one to another: and the LORD hearkened, and heard it, and a book of remembrance was written before him for them that feared the LORD, and that thought upon his name.* (Malachi 3:16)

The Book of Life records the names of those who are saved. Those whose names are not found written in the Book of Life will be cast into the lake of fire. Mark in his Gospel warns of this awful place which will be the final destination of the wicked:

[42] *And whosoever shall offend one of these little ones that believe in me, it is better for him that a millstone were hanged about his neck, and he were cast into the sea.* [43] *And if thy hand offend thee, cut it off: it is better for thee to enter into life maimed, than having two hands to go into hell, into the fire that never shall be quenched:* [44] *Where their worm dieth not, and the fire is not quenched.* [45] *And if thy foot offend thee, cut it off: it is better for thee to enter halt into life, than having two feet to be cast into hell, into the fire that never shall be quenched:* [46] *Where their worm dieth not, and the fire is not quenched.* [47] *And if thine eye offend thee, pluck it out: it is better for thee to enter into the kingdom of God with one eye, than having two eyes to be cast into hell fire:* [48] *Where their worm dieth not, and the fire is not quenched.* (Mark 9:42-48)

Spiritual death is the separation of physically-alive people from a relationship with God because of sin. The wages of sin is death, spiritual death. After they die, these men and women will be spiritually dead in the lake of fire. Sin separates man from the Holy God as declared in the Scriptures:

The Kingdom Age and the Final Judgment

¹Behold, the LORD's hand is not shortened, that it cannot save; neither his ear heavy, that it cannot hear: ² But your iniquities have separated between you and your God, and your sins have hid his face from you, that he will not hear. (Isaiah 59:1-2)

¹And you hath he quickened, who were dead in trespasses and sins. (Ephesians 2:1)

God removes the old creation followed by the final judgment before He creates all things new. The old heaven and earth are coming to a close, a New Heaven and Earth are about to begin:

¹⁷ For, behold, I create new heavens and a new earth: and the former shall not be remembered, nor come into mind. (Isaiah 65:17)

²⁸ Marvel not at this: for the hour is coming, in the which all that are in the graves shall hear his voice, ²⁹ And shall come forth; they that have done good, unto the resurrection of life; and they that have done evil, unto the resurrection of damnation. (John 5:28-29)

¹⁰ But the day of the Lord will come as a thief in the night; in the which the heavens shall pass away with a great noise, and the elements shall melt with fervent heat, the earth also and the works that are therein shall be burned up. ¹¹ Seeing then that all these things shall be dissolved, what manner of persons ought ye to be in all holy conversation and godliness, ¹² Looking for and hasting unto the coming of the day of God, wherein the heavens being on fire shall be dissolved, and the elements shall melt with fervent heat? ¹³ Nevertheless we, according to his promise, look for new heavens and a new earth, wherein dwelleth righteousness. (II Peter 3:10-13)

³⁵ Heaven and earth shall pass away, but my words shall not pass away. (Matthew 24:35)

The glorious new future is described in the next chapters.

Chapter 21

The New Heaven and New Earth

Revelation 21:1-8
Introduction to the New Jerusalem

And I saw a new heaven and a new earth: for the first heaven and the first earth were passed away; and there was no more sea. And I John saw the holy city, New Jerusalem, coming down from God out of heaven, prepared as a bride adorned for her husband. And I heard a great voice out of heaven saying, Behold, the tabernacle of God is with men, and he will dwell with them, and they shall be his people, and God himself shall be with them, and be their God. And God shall wipe away all tears from their eyes; and there shall be no more death, neither sorrow, nor crying, neither shall there be any more pain: for the former things are passed away. And he that sat upon the throne said, Behold, I make all things new. And he said unto me, Write: for these words are true and faithful. And he said unto me, It is done. I am Alpha and Omega, the beginning and the end. I will give unto him that is athirst of the fountain of the water of life freely. He that overcometh shall inherit all things; and I will be his God, and he shall be my son. But the fearful, and unbelieving, and the abominable, and murderers, and whoremongers, and sorcerers, and idolaters, and all liars, shall have their part in the lake which burneth with fire and brimstone: which is the second death.

THE WORD OF God does not leave us in darkness as to His plan for the future. The history of time is finished, and the history of eternity is about to begin. God's day has come, and evil has been cleansed from the earth as foretold by Peter:

Revelation

¹⁰ *But the day of the Lord will come as a thief in the night; in the which the heavens shall pass away with a great noise, and the elements shall melt with fervent heat, the earth also and the works that are therein shall be burned up.* ¹¹ *Seeing then that all these things shall be dissolved, what manner of persons ought ye to be in all holy conversation and godliness,* ¹² *looking for and hasting unto the coming of the day of God, wherein the heavens being on fire shall be dissolved, and the elements shall melt with fervent heat?* ¹³ *Nevertheless we, according to his promise, look for new heavens and a new earth, wherein dwelleth righteousness.* (II Peter 3:10-13)

God is going to make all things new. In the New Heaven and the New Earth, God is going to dwell with men. The saints will experience oneness and communion with God (I John 1:3-4). Sin, which hinders oneness and communion with God, will be removed. Death, sorrow and pain will cease to exist. These things will surely come to pass as God declares that these words are true and faithful.

The list of those who are to be excluded from the New Heaven and the New Earth is revealed. The fearful (timid or without faith) lead the list. In Acts 17:22, Paul refers to the people of Athens as superstitious or very religious. The Greek word for superstitious is *deimidaimonestcros*. The Greek word for fearful in Revelation 21:8 is *deilos*. *Deilos* usually means timid, without faith. However, *deimidaimonestcros* is a base of the word *deilos* and in this context it could refer to those who are very religious, but not in a Christian sense, as Christianity is a relationship and not a religion. Those who reject God's way and instead develop their own religion are those who are very religious. Usually it is the cults where people develop their own religious beliefs. These people lead the list of those who are thrown into the lake of fire.

Those who continue in sinful practices without repentance are manifesting that they have never been born again as Paul the apostle declares in his epistle to the Galatians and the Ephesians:

¹⁹ *Now the works of the flesh are manifest, which are these; Adultery, fornication, uncleanness, lasciviousness,* ²⁰ *Idolatry, witchcraft, hatred, variance, emulations, wrath, strife, seditions, heresies,* ²¹ *Envyings, murders, drunkenness, revellings, and such like: of the which I tell you before, as I have also told you in time past, that they which do such things shall not inherit the kingdom of God.* (Galatians 5:19-21)

⁵ *For this ye know, that no whoremonger, nor unclean person, nor covetous man, who is an idolater, hath any inheritance in the kingdom of Christ and of God.* ⁶ *Let*

The New Heaven and New Earth

no man deceive you with vain words: for because of these things cometh the wrath of God upon the children of disobedience. (Ephesians 5:5-6)

Paul's desire is that all men be saved, but he warns the members of the church to avoid those sinful practices that will keep a person from partaking in the New Heaven and the New Earth. Those who prefer to live a sinful life that Paul warns against will not inherit the glorious future that God Himself will create. These words from God are true and faithful. All men are faced with a choice as to where they want to spend eternity.

Revelation 21:9-21
God's Glorious City

And there came unto me one of the seven angels which had the seven vials full of the seven last plagues, and talked with me, saying, Come hither, I will shew thee the bride, the Lamb's wife. And he carried me away in the spirit to a great and high mountain, and shewed me that great city, the holy Jerusalem, descending out of heaven from God, Having the glory of God: and her light was like unto a stone most precious, even like a jasper stone, clear as crystal; And had a wall great and high, and had twelve gates, and at the gates twelve angels, and names written thereon, which are the names of the twelve tribes of the children of Israel: On the east three gates; on the north three gates; on the south three gates; and on the west three gates. And the wall of the city had twelve foundations, and in them the names of the twelve apostles of the Lamb. And he that talked with me had a golden reed to measure the city, and the gates thereof, and the wall thereof. And the city lieth foursquare, and the length is as large as the breadth: and he measured the city with the reed, twelve thousand furlongs. The length and the breadth and the height of it are equal. And he measured the wall thereof, an hundred and forty and four cubits, according to the measure of a man, that is, of the angel. And the building of the wall of it was of jasper: and the city was pure gold, like unto clear glass. And the foundations of the wall of the city were garnished with all manner of precious stones. The first foundation was jasper; the second, sapphire; the third, a chalcedony; the fourth, an emerald; The fifth, sardonyx; the sixth, sardius; the seventh, chrysolyte; the eighth, beryl; the ninth, a topaz; the tenth, a chrysoprasus; the eleventh, a jacinth; the twelfth, an amethyst. And the twelve gates were twelve pearls: every several gate was of one pearl: and the street of the city was pure gold, as it were transparent glass.

One of the angels who delivered the seven final plagues is presented with the privilege to reveal to John the news of the glorious new city. How wonderful it is to declare glorious events that are to come. The city is

Revelation

amazing. It is shaped like a cube, 1,500 miles square. The city contains 12 precious stones, and the names of the 12 tribes of the children of Israel. It is interesting to note that the breastplate of the high priest was foursquare and had the same precious stones as the city. The breastplate also had the names of the tribes of children of Israel as described in Exodus:

15 And thou shalt make the breastplate of judgment with cunning work; after the work of the ephod thou shalt make it; of gold, of blue, and of purple, and of scarlet, and of fine twined linen, shalt thou make it. 16 Foursquare it shall be being doubled; a span shall be the length thereof, and a span shall be the breadth thereof. 17 And thou shalt set in it settings of stones, even four rows of stones: the first row shall be a sardius, a topaz, and a carbuncle: this shall be the first row. 18 And the second row shall be an emerald, a sapphire, and a diamond. 19 And the third row a ligure, an agate, and an amethyst. 20 And the fourth row a beryl, and an onyx, and a jasper: they shall be set in gold in their inclosings. 21 And the stones shall be with the names of the children of Israel, twelve, according to their names, like the engravings of a signet; every one with his name shall they be according to the twelve tribes. 22 And thou shalt make upon the breastplate chains at the ends of wreathen work of pure gold. 23 And thou shalt make upon the breastplate two rings of gold, and shalt put the two rings on the two ends of the breastplate. 24 And thou shalt put the two wreathen chains of gold in the two rings which are on the ends of the breastplate. 25 And the other two ends of the two wreathen chains thou shalt fasten in the two ouches, and put them on the shoulderpieces of the ephod before it. 26 And thou shalt make two rings of gold, and thou shalt put them upon the two ends of the breastplate in the border thereof, which is in the side of the ephod inward. 27 And two other rings of gold thou shalt make, and shalt put them on the two sides of the ephod underneath, toward the forepart thereof, over against the other coupling thereof, above the curious girdle of the ephod. 28 And they shall bind the breastplate by the rings thereof unto the rings of the ephod with a lace of blue, that it may be above the curious girdle of the ephod, and that the breastplate be not loosed from the ephod. 29 And Aaron shall bear the names of the children of Israel in the breastplate of judgment upon his heart, when he goeth in unto the holy place, for a memorial before the LORD continually. (Exodus 28:15-29)

Revelation 21:22-27
No Need for a Temple

And I saw no temple therein: for the Lord God Almighty and the Lamb are the temple of it. And the city had no need of the sun, neither of the moon, to shine in it: for the glory of God did lighten it, and the Lamb is the light thereof. And the nations

The New Heaven and New Earth

of them which are saved shall walk in the light of it: and the kings of the earth do bring their glory and honour into it. And the gates of it shall not be shut at all by day: for there shall be no night there. And they shall bring the glory and honour of the nations into it. And there shall in no wise enter into it any thing that defileth, neither whatsoever worketh abomination, or maketh a lie: but they which are written in the Lamb's book of life.

There is neither sun nor moon in the New Heaven and the New Earth. The creation of the New Heaven and the New Earth has been declared in the Book of Isaiah:

17 *For, behold, I create new heavens and a new earth: and the former shall not be remembered, nor come into mind.* 18 *But be ye glad and rejoice for ever in that which I create: for, behold, I create Jerusalem a rejoicing, and her people a joy.* 19 *And I will rejoice in Jerusalem, and joy in my people: and the voice of weeping shall be no more heard in her, nor the voice of crying.* (Isaiah 65:17-19)

The glory of God illuminates the city, and the Lamb is its light:

18 *Violence shall no more be heard in thy land, wasting nor destruction within thy borders; but thou shalt call thy walls Salvation, and thy gates Praise.* 19 *The sun shall be no more thy light by day; neither for brightness shall the moon give light unto thee: but the LORD shall be unto thee an everlasting light, and thy God thy glory.* 20 *Thy sun shall no more go down; neither shall thy moon withdraw itself: for the LORD shall be thine everlasting light, and the days of thy mourning shall be ended.* 21 *Thy people also shall be all righteous: they shall inherit the land for ever, the branch of my planting, the work of my hands, that I may be glorified.* 22 *A little one shall become a thousand, and a small one a strong nation: I the LORD will hasten it in his time.* (Isaiah 60:18-22)

What a glorious future! The Lord will hasten the creation of the New Heaven and the New Earth at the appropriate time.

Revelation 21:21-24 speaks of the nations of those who are saved. Will the Lord create a new race of men as part of the New Heaven and the New Earth? This is a question that God will answer when the time is appropriate. We do know that it is the Lord's plan that all nations worship Him:

22 *For as the new heavens and the new earth, which I will make, shall remain before me, saith the LORD, so shall your seed and your name remain.* (Isaiah 66:22)

4 *All the earth shall worship thee, and shall sing unto thee; they shall sing to thy name. Selah.* (Psalm 66:4)

Revelation

⁹ *But ye are a chosen generation, a royal priesthood, an holy nation, a peculiar people; that ye should shew forth the praises of him who hath called you out of darkness into his marvellous light.* (I Peter 2:9)

God has made each of us uniquely different. He loves you; He values you, and has invited you to be a part of His eternal family. It is the wish of the author that every reader of this book decides to follow the Lord Jesus, and to make the Lord Jesus the Lord over their life. It would be the joy of the author if even one soul decides to follow the Lord Jesus after reading this book. One day we will all see Him who loved us and we will be like Him:

² *Beloved, now are we the sons of God, and it doth not yet appear what we shall be: but we know that, when he shall appear, we shall be like him; for we shall see him as he is.* (I John 3:2)

Chapter 22
He Is Coming Quickly

Revelation 22:1-5
The River of Life and the Tree of Life

And he shewed me a pure river of water of life, clear as crystal, proceeding out of the throne of God and of the Lamb. In the midst of the street of it, and on either side of the river, was there the tree of life, which bare twelve manner of fruits, and yielded her fruit every month: and the leaves of the tree were for the healing of the nations. And there shall be no more curse: but the throne of God and of the Lamb shall be in it; and his servants shall serve him: and they shall see his face; and his name shall be in their foreheads. And there shall be no night there; and they need no candle, neither light of the sun; for the Lord God giveth them light: and they shall reign for ever and ever.

The tree of life which was first introduced in the Book of Genesis is visible again on the New Earth on both sides of the river of life:

22 And the LORD God said, Behold, the man is become as one of us, to know good and evil: and now, lest he put forth his hand, and take also of the tree of life, and eat, and live for ever: 23 Therefore the LORD God sent him forth from the garden of Eden, to till the ground from whence he was taken. 24 So he drove out the man; and he placed at the east of the garden of Eden Cherubims, and a flaming sword which turned every way, to keep the way of the tree of life. (Genesis 3:22-24)

The angel showed John a river of pure water that was crystal clear originating from the Throne of God. In the midst of the river and on both

Revelation

sides was the tree of life, whose fruit enables one to live forever. John also tells us that we shall see God face to face, and His name shall be in our foreheads. There is a mention of the nations that will inhabit the New Earth and the leaves of the tree of life will be for their healing. On the New Earth there will be no more death, sin, rebellion, pain, and sorrow. It will be a glorious time. Today people choose not to come to the tree of life (Jesus); instead they choose the tree of death.

Revelation 22:6-15
He Comes Quickly

And he said unto me, These sayings are faithful and true: and the Lord God of the holy prophets sent his angel to shew unto his servants the things which must shortly be done. Behold, I come quickly: blessed is he that keepeth the sayings of the prophecy of this book. And I John saw these things, and heard them. And when I had heard and seen, I fell down to worship before the feet of the angel which shewed me these things. Then saith he unto me, See thou do it not: for I am thy fellowservant, and of thy brethren the prophets, and of them which keep the sayings of this book: worship God. And he saith unto me, Seal not the sayings of the prophecy of this book: for the time is at hand. He that is unjust, let him be unjust still: and he which is filthy, let him be filthy still: and he that is righteous, let him be righteous still: and he that is holy, let him be holy still. And, behold, I come quickly; and my reward is with me, to give every man according as his work shall be. I am Alpha and Omega, the beginning and the end, the first and the last. Blessed are they that do his commandments, that they may have right to the tree of life, and may enter in through the gates into the city. For without are dogs, and sorcerers, and whoremongers, and murderers, and idolaters, and whosoever loveth and maketh a lie.

The prophetic visions of John are complete. He is brought back to the present, and through him our Lord gives His last invitation to all men so that they may be prepared to enter the heavenly Holy City and partake of His blessings. The promises of God are faithful and true, they will come to pass. Three times in chapter 22 Jesus makes mention of His return, indicating that He is coming quickly. When the Lord declares something more than once it is best to take heed to the declaration. When Jesus comes quickly, it will be in a moment, in a twinkling of an eye. The Lord Jesus in Luke 21 exhorted His disciples to watch and to pray always that they may be accounted worthy to escape all of the things that shall come to pass and to stand before the Son of Man. It is His desire that we watch and pray, especially as we see the signs of His coming are near. The world is becoming more evil every day and the kingdom of antichrist may be soon approaching.

Jesus, the living Word of God, pays great honor to the written Word of God. The child of God should have the same reverence for the Holy Scriptures. The Psalms declare that the Lord has magnified His word above His name:

2 I will worship toward thy holy temple, and praise thy name for thy lovingkindness and for thy truth: for thou hast magnified thy word above all thy name. (Psalm 138:2)

We are not to only recite the word; we are to keep the word. It is the desire of the Lord that we obey His commandments. It is important to know and to read His commandments, but the Lord places the emphasis on obeying His commandments. Disciples are trained by obeying the commandments of the Lord.

The main intent of prophecy is to cause us to obey what God has declared and to apply what we have learned. Prophecy was never intended for us to gain knowledge of the future for the sake of knowledge alone, but prophecy is to have an effect on how we live. Prophecy should motivate the child of God to live a holy life, as John declared in his first epistle:

2 Beloved, now are we the sons of God, and it doth not yet appear what we shall be: but we know that, when he shall appear, we shall be like him; for we shall see him as he is. 3 And every man that hath this hope in him purifieth himself, even as he is pure. (I John 3:2-3)

Outside the city are dogs, sorcerers, the sexually immoral, the murders, idolaters, and those who love and practice lies. The Greek word for dogs is *kuon*. It is the same word that is used in Matthew and Philippians:

6 Give not that which is holy unto the dogs, neither cast ye your pearls before swine, lest they trample them under their feet, and turn again and rend you. (Matthew 7:6)

2 Beware of dogs, beware of evil workers, beware of the concision. (Philippians 3:2)

The word "dogs" refers to those who do not want to come to God in the pre-described gift of salvation that God has supplied through Jesus Christ. An example would be those who believe that God does not have a Son or those who believe that one cannot approach God directly. As children of God, we can come to the Throne of God with confidence and in boldness. We have oneness and communion with the Father and with the Son as John declared in his first epistle:

Revelation

³ *That which we have seen and heard declare we unto you, that ye also may have fellowship with us: and truly our fellowship is with the Father, and with his Son Jesus Christ.* ⁴ *And these things write we unto you, that your joy may be full.* (I John 1:3-4)

John was exhorted not to worship anyone but Jesus. Jesus is the way, the truth and the life, and no one can approach the Father unless they believe that Jesus Christ is the Messiah, the Son of God. The dogs attempt to create their own way of coming to God.

Revelation 22:16-21
Salvation is a Free Gift and We Are Not to Alter the Book

I Jesus have sent mine angel to testify unto you these things in the churches. I am the root and the offspring of David, and the bright and morning star. And the Spirit and the bride say, Come. And let him that heareth say, Come. And let him that is athirst come. And whosoever will, let him take the water of life freely. For I testify unto every man that heareth the words of the prophecy of this book, If any man shall add unto these things, God shall add unto him the plagues that are written in this book: And if any man shall take away from the words of the book of this prophecy, God shall take away his part out of the book of life, and out of the holy city, and from the things which are written in this book. He which testifieth these things saith, Surely I come quickly. Amen. Even so, come, Lord Jesus. The grace of our Lord Jesus Christ be with you all. Amen.

Our Lord will return speedily once the prophecies of the Book of Revelation begin to come to pass. Now is the time to know and understand what the future holds. This book is not to be sealed as the Book of Daniel was to be sealed:

⁴ *But thou, O Daniel, shut up the words, and seal the book, even to the time of the end: many shall run to and fro, and knowledge shall be increased.* (Daniel 12:4)

⁹ *And he said, Go thy way, Daniel: for the words are closed up and sealed till the time of the end.* ¹⁰ *Many shall be purified, and made white, and tried; but the wicked shall do wickedly: and none of the wicked shall understand; but the wise shall understand.* (Daniel 12:9-10)

¹*This second epistle, beloved, I now write unto you; in both which I stir up your pure minds by way of remembrance:* ² *That ye may be mindful of the words which were spoken before by the holy prophets, and of the commandment of us the apostles of the Lord and Saviour:* ³ *Knowing this first, that there shall come in the last days scoffers, walking after their own lusts,* ⁴ *And saying, Where is the promise of his*

coming? For since the fathers fell asleep, all things continue as they were from the beginning of the creation. (II Peter 3:1-4)

The Book of Daniel was to be closed until the last days. Today the Book of Daniel has been opened, studied and understood. This is a strong indication that these are indeed the last days and that the Lord Jesus is coming quickly.

We are commanded not to alter the Scriptures in any way. We are not to add to or subtract from the Word of God. The Lord declared that He magnifies His word above His name (Psalm 138:2). A fearful warning has been given to anyone who does alter the words of the Holy God. We are exhorted and encouraged to come to the Lord and to open our hearts and lives to Him. Let us be watching and praying for His glorious appearing. Even so, come quickly Lord Jesus.

Final Thoughts
The Great Multitude

BIBLE SCHOLARS ARE divided as to the identity of the saints under the altar when the Fifth Seal is opened (Revelation 6:9-11), and the identity of the great multitude that endured the Great Tribulation (Revelation 7:9-17). Some believe that the identity of this multitude is the saints who came to faith in Jesus Christ after the harpazo. Others hold to the belief that this multitude represents the church as the harpazo will occur later in the seventieth week of Daniel.

Those scholars who follow the harpazo Before the First Seal is opened or the Pre-Tribulation view believe that this multitude represents the saints who came to faith in Jesus Christ after Jesus comes for His church. A great spiritual awakening or revival is the only explanation for a multitude this great to believe in the Lord Jesus in such a short period of time. There is some internal evidence to support this view:

- The apostle John did not recognize this multitude. If the multitude represented the church, the apostle John would have recognized them (Revelation 7:13-14).
- The multitude appears to have experienced the plagues that were reserved for the *thumos* of God (Revelation 7:16; Revelation 16:4-8). If the church is not destined to experience the *orge* or *thumos* of God, how can this multitude represent the church?

Revelation

Scholars who believe that the harpazo occurs later in the seventieth week of Daniel and that this vast multitude is representative of the church also have some internal evidence for their support:

- This multitude must be the church as how could a great multitude of people from the backslidden churches of Pergamos, Thyatira, Sardis and Laodicea come to faith in Jesus Christ when they have no discernment and cannot recognize truth from error. If the members from these churches cannot recognize truth from error before the antichrist appears, how will they recognize the deception of the antichrist and his false prophet? The members of these churches are not willing to live for Jesus today, and it is difficult to comprehend that they would choose to die for Jesus during the Great Tribulation period.

- The restrainer will no longer be holding back the forces of evil and this allows the antichrist to rise to power (I Thessalonians 2:3-8). The restrainer is believed to be the Holy Spirit and if the Holy Spirit is no longer restraining evil, where will the conviction of sin originate from to bring forth a great revival.

There are arguments on both sides as to the identity of this great multitude. The identity of the multitude has a direct correlation with the timing of the harpazo. The list of arguments on both sides should not be considered exhaustive. Knowledge will increase in the Last Days. The church should not be divided over the timing of the harpazo.

Summary of the Views of the Harpazo that Were Covered in the Book

The following three events relate to the harpazo:

- The apostasy must take place first (II Thessalonians 2:3);
- The antichrist must be revealed before the harpazo (II Thessalonians 2:3);
- The harpazo must occur before the *orge* of God commences (I Thessalonians 1:10; I Thessalonians 5:9; Revelation 6:12-17).

Pre-Tribulation View – the belief that Jesus Christ will come for His church before the seven-year tribulation period or before the seventieth week of Daniel (Daniel 9:24-27).

The scholars who support this view believe that the church is in heaven before the start of the seventieth week of Daniel (Revelation 1:19; Revelation 4:1). They recognize that the Lord Jesus is not seated on His throne as a

Final Thoughts

mediator between God and man, but has transitioned from the Lamb of God to the Lion of the tribe of Judah (Revelation 5:5-7; Hebrews 1:3; Hebrews 7:22-27). This signifies that the Lord Jesus has left His Throne to call His church home to heaven. The church is complete in heaven and in their glorified bodies, which is supported by the King James Version as translated from the Received Text (Revelation 5:9-10).

The weakness of this view is that there are no Scriptures to support that the antichrist will be revealed to the faithful church before the seventieth week of Daniel commences. Also, the prophet Elijah would need to appear before the seventieth week of Daniel and this is not possible as the ministry of the two witnesses covers only 1,260 days. The two witnesses are martyred during the Great Tribulation period; therefore it is not possible that their ministry begins before the seventieth week of Daniel. Since the prophet Elijah must appear before The Day of the Lord, the Day of the Lord would need to start before the seventieth week of Daniel, and there are no Scriptures to support this view (Malachi 4:5).

There are scholars who believe that the church is not complete in heaven, which is supported by the modern English versions translated from the Alexandrian manuscripts (Revelation 5:9-10).

Before the First Seal is Opened View – the belief that the church will see the beginning of the seventieth week of Daniel (Daniel 9:24-27) and the revealing of the antichrist when he makes a covenant with the Jews before Jesus comes for His church, which would be Before the First Seal is opened.

The scholars who support this view believe that the church is in heaven Before the First Seal is opened as the antichrist has been revealed to the faithful church (Revelation 1:19; Revelation 4:1; Daniel 9:24-27). The Lord Jesus is not seated on His throne as a mediator between God and man, but has transitioned from the Lamb of God to the Lion of the tribe of Judah (Revelation 5:5-7; Hebrews 1:3; Hebrews 7:22-27). This signifies that the Lord Jesus has left His Throne to call His church home to heaven. The church is complete in heaven and in their glorified bodies which is supported by the King James Version which is translated from the Received Text (Revelation 5:9-10). The Day of the Lord begins when the Lord Jesus receives the Scroll from the Father.

The Lord will send the prophet Elijah (one of the two witnesses) to the earth before the Day of the Lord (Malachi 4:5). The ministry of the two witnesses covers 1,260 days and the two witnesses are martyred after the start of the Sixth Trumpet which is in the second half of the three-and-a-half years

Revelation

of the seventieth week of Daniel. The starting point of the ministry of the two witnesses will be at least five months (most likely more) after the start of the seventieth week of Daniel. Since the Day of the Lord follows the harpazo, there must be a time period of at least five months from the starting point of the seventieth week of Daniel to the opening of the First Seal.

There are scholars who believe that the church is not complete in heaven, which is supported by the modern English versions translated from the Alexandrian manuscripts (Revelation 5:9-10).

Mid-Tribulational View – the belief that Jesus will return for the church-age believers in the middle of the seven-year tribulation. This would be the Mid-Point of the seventieth week of Daniel (Daniel 9:24-27) and at the start of the Great Tribulation when the abomination of desolation is set up in the rebuilt Temple.

The scholars who support this view believe that the faithful church will need to identify the antichrist before the harpazo (II Thessalonians 2:1-4). They believe that he will be identified once he sets up his image in the rebuilt Jewish Temple and declares himself God.

One of the weaknesses of this view is that the timing of the harpazo is rigid and does not take into account the *orge* of God (I Thessalonians 1:10; I Thessalonians 5:9; Revelation 6:12-17). The other weakness is that the day of the harpazo can be calculated by adding 1,260 days to the day that the antichrist signs a covenant with the nation of Israel. This would contradict the Scriptures because no man knows the day or hour of His coming for His church (Matthew 24:36).

The Sixth Seal View – the belief that the coming of Christ for His church coincides with the announcement of the Sixth Seal.

The scholars who support this view believe the antichrist will be revealed to the faithful church when his image is established in the Temple (II Thessalonians 2:1-4) which coincides with the announcement of the Sixth Seal. The harpazo commences when the Sixth Seal is opened as the wording in Matthew, Mark, and Revelation are identical (Matthew 24:29-31; Mark 13:24-27; Revelation 6:12-17). At this time the church will be complete in heaven and in their glorified bodies. The church will not experience the Great Tribulation, except for the unfaithful church of Thyatira. The *orge* of God and the Day of the Lord commence immediately after the harpazo (Isaiah 13:6-13; Isaiah 24:1-20; Joel 2:31; I Thessalonians 1:10; I Thessalonians 5:9), as the sun shall be turned into darkness and the moon into blood before the great and terrible Day of the Lord comes.

Final Thoughts

The Intra-Seal View – the belief that the coming of Christ for His church will be after the announcement of the Sixth Seal but before the Seventh Seal is opened. There is a pause after the announcement of the Sixth Seal and before the plagues of the Sixth Seal are unleashed upon the earth. Before the pause is over, Christ comes for His church and the awful plagues of the Sixth Seal are unleashed.

The scholars who support this view believe the antichrist will be revealed to the faithful church when his image is set up in the Temple (II Thessalonians 2:1-4) and he establishes the mark that all men must have in order to buy or sell (Revelation 13:11-18). The plagues of the Sixth Seal will begin after the harpazo which signifies the start of the *orge* of God (Matthew 24:29-31; Mark 13:24-27; Revelation 6:12-17; I Thessalonians 1:10; I Thessalonians 5:9). At this time the church will be complete in heaven and in their glorified bodies. The Day of the Lord commences immediately after the harpazo (Isaiah 13:6-13; Isaiah 24:1-20; Joel 2:31), as the sun shall be turned into darkness and the moon into blood before the great and terrible Day of the Lord comes. Ezekiel 9:1-11 is used to reveal that the Glory of the Lord is departing, which is symbolic of the harpazo and then the marking of His people (which is symbolic of the 144,000 Israelites being sealed) before judgment begins and then the wrath of God is poured out.

Pre-Wrath View – the view that the rapture of the church will occur when the Seventh Seal is opened. The wrath of God will begin with the Trumpet judgments.

The scholars who support this view believe the antichrist will be revealed to the faithful church when his image is set up in the Temple (II Thessalonians 2:1-4) and he establishes the mark that all men must have in order to buy or sell (Revelation 13:11-18). The church will experience the Great Tribulation except for the true and faithful believers as they will be protected from its horrors. These scholars believe the Great Tribulation begins at the Fifth Seal and concludes before the Seventh Seal is opened. The *orge* of God does not start until the opening of the Seventh Seal (I Thessalonians 1:10; I Thessalonians 5:9) as the Sixth Seal represents only cosmic disturbances. The harpazo will commence after the opening of the Seventh Seal and at this time the church will be complete in heaven and in their glorified bodies. The Day of the Lord commences immediately after the harpazo (Isaiah 13:6-13; Isaiah 24:1-20; Joel 2:31) as the sun shall be turned into darkness and the moon into blood before the great and terrible Day of the Lord comes.

Revelation

One weakness in the Pre-Wrath view relates to the marking of the 144,000 Israelites. The example in Ezekiel 9 reveals that the glory of God departs (symbolic of the harpazo) before the marking of the righteous (symbolic of the 144,000 Israelites) commences. According to the Scriptures, the marking of the 144,000 Israelites occurs before the Seventh Seal is opened (Revelation 7:1-8).

Post-Tribulation View but Earlier – the view that the rapture of the church will occur before the Bowl Judgments.

The scholars who support this view believe that the harpazo will occur at the last trump (I Corinthians 15:52) which is the last Trumpet judgment (Revelation 11:15-19). The church will experience the *orge* of God but not the *thumos* of God. The *thumos* of God is introduced after the Seventh Trumpet is announced.

The weakness in this view relates to what the apostle Paul declared in his epistle to the Thessalonians, that the church is not appointed to the *orge* of God (I Thessalonians 1:10; I Thessalonians 5:9). The harpazo cannot occur after the Sixth Seal as this would contradict the Scriptures (Revelation 6:12-17). Any view of the harpazo indicating that it will take place after the *orge* of God has commenced would contradict what the apostle Paul and the apostle John declared.

Post-Tribulational View – the view that the rapture and second coming of Jesus Christ are the same event. This would be at the conclusion of the seventieth week of Daniel (Daniel 9:24-27).

The scholars who support this view believe that the church will not be excluded from the *orge* and *thumos* of God. The church will be persecuted during the seventieth week of Daniel as it is today.

The weakness in this view relates to what the apostle Paul declared in his epistle to the Thessalonians that the church is not appointed to the *orge* of God (I Thessalonians 1:10; I Thessalonians 5:9). The harpazo cannot occur after the Sixth Seal as this would contradict the Scriptures (Revelation 6:12-17). Any view of the harpazo indicating that it will take place after the *orge* of God has commenced would contradict what the apostle Paul and the apostle John declared.

Partial Rapture View – only the spirit filled believers will be raptured. The carnal believers and the unsaved will go through the entire seven year tribulation (seventieth week of Daniel). This would represent the parable of the ten virgins as recorded in Matthew (Matthew 25:1-13).

Final Thoughts

The message to the churches of Thyatira and Sardis is a proof text that there are members from these churches that will be left behind, and only a faithful remnant from Thyatira and a few members from the church of Sardis will be taken up when the Lord Jesus appears. In Luke 21:36 the Lord Jesus commanded His disciples to pray always that they may be worthy to escape all of these things that will be coming upon the earth.

There are some scholars who believe that once a person believes that Jesus Christ is the Son of God and has risen from the dead, they are eternally secure (Romans 10:9-10). Meanwhile, other Scriptures that exhort a believer to live a righteous life are ignored (Hebrews 10:26-27).

A-Tribulational View – there is no literal period of time in the future known as the tribulation period. This view denies that there is to be a rapture of the church.

There are some scholars who believe that there is no event (harpazo) in which Jesus will appear and take His church home to heaven.

The Scripture verses in I Corinthians 15:51-52 and I Thessalonians 4:15-17 prove that there is a future event during which the Lord Jesus will remove the true and faithful saints to heaven.

Conclusion

If one is expecting the harpazo to occur before or shortly after the start of the seventieth week of Daniel, one should not be discouraged if the harpazo has not occurred. The Lord Jesus in the Gospel of Matthew exhorted His disciples to continue to watch and be ready for His coming:

45 Who then is a faithful and wise servant, whom his lord hath made ruler over his household, to give them meat in due season? 46 Blessed is that servant, whom his lord when he cometh shall find so doing. 47 Verily I say unto you, That he shall make him ruler over all his goods. 48 But and if that evil servant shall say in his heart, My lord delayeth his coming; 49 And shall begin to smite his fellowservants, and to eat and drink with the drunken; 50 The lord of that servant shall come in a day when he looketh not for him, and in an hour that he is not aware of, 51 And shall cut him asunder, and appoint him his portion with the hypocrites: there shall be weeping and gnashing of teeth. (Matthew 24:45-51)

The church is to adhere to the words of the Lord Jesus regarding the Last Days. The Lord Jesus commanded His disciples to watch and pray always that we may be accounted worthy to escape all these things that will come upon the earth.

Appendix A
Sir Robert Anderson – The Coming Prince

SIR ROBERT ANDERSON, in his book, *The Coming Prince*, has provided detailed calculations to prove mathematically that Jesus of Nazareth was the Messiah that the Jews were looking for. He also proves that no other man could be considered the Messiah other than Jesus of Nazareth.

The seventy weeks prophesied in Daniel 9:24-27 represent seventy-times-seven prophetic years of 360 days, according to the Babylonian calendar, to be reckoned from the issuing of an edict for the rebuilding of the city— the street and walls of Jerusalem. Artaxerxes Longimanus, in the twentieth year of his reign, authorized Nehemiah to rebuild the fortification of Jerusalem. His reign began in 465 BC.

Our Lord's public ministry began in the 15th year of Tiberius Caesar. The date that Jesus began His ministry was between August, AD 28 and April, AD 29. Jesus was crucified in AD 32. The decree to rebuild the city was the 1st of Nissan, 445 BC. The 1st of Nissan was on March 14, in the year 445 BC. The triumphal entry is recorded in Luke 19:29-42. The 10th of Nissan in AD 32 was on April 6. Therefore, the interval of time is from March 14, 445 BC – April 6, AD 32. Jesus now permits Himself to be proclaimed as the Coming King, the son of David. Before this event, He never allowed the crowds to proclaim Him as king until His triumphant entry into Jerusalem which was 173,880 days (483 years) after the decree was given to rebuild and restore the city of Jerusalem.

However, there is a problem as the period in question appears to cover 476 years and 24 days, instead of 483 years (as 445 BC – AD 32 is only 476

Revelation

years). To solve this problem we need to use the calendar that we use today, which contains 365 days along with its leap years. We need to use the Julian calendar because we no longer use the 360-day Babylonian calendar. The new calculation is:

$476 \times 365 = 173{,}740$ days
Add (March 14 to April 6) = 24 days
Add for leap years = 116 days
173,880 days
69 weeks of years of 360 days is: $69 \times 7 \times 360 = 173{,}880$ days

Appendix B

Taken from *Josephus: The Complete Works*

Copyright ©1981 by William Whiston. Published by Kregel Publications, Grand Rapids, MI. Used by permission of the publisher. All rights reserved.

Josephus, Antiquities of the Jews: Concerning the Tower of Babylon, and the Confusion of Tongues.

1. Now the sons of Noah were three, Shem and Japhet, and Ham, born one hundred years before the deluge.[2] These first of all descended from the mountains into the plains, and fixed their habitation there; and persuaded others, who were greatly afraid of the lower grounds on account of the flood, and so were very loth to come down from the higher places, to venture to follow their examples. Now the plain, in which they first dwelt, was called *Shinar*. God also commanded them to send colonies abroad, for the through peopling of the earth; that they might not raise seditions among themselves, but might cultivate a great part of the earth, and enjoy its fruits after a plentiful manner. But they were so ill instructed, they did not obey God. For which reason they fell into calamities, and were made sensible by experience of what sin they had been guilty of. For when they flourished with a numerous youth, God admonished them again to send out colonies. But they imagining the prosperity they enjoyed was not derived from the favor of God, but supposing that their own power was the proper cause of the plentiful condition they were in, did not obey him. Nay they added to this their disobedience to the divine will, the suspicion that they were

therefore ordered to send out separate colonies, that, being divided asunder, they might the more easily be oppressed.

2. Now it was Nimrod who excited them to such an affront and contempt of God. He was the grand-son of Ham, the son of Noah: a bold man, and of great strength of hand. He persuaded them not to ascribe it to God, as if it was through his means that they were happy; but to believe that it was their own courage which procured that happiness. He also gradually changed the government into tyranny; seeing no other way of turning men from the fear of God, but to bring them into a constant dependence on his own power. He also said, "He would be revenged on God, if he should have a mind to drown the world again: for that he would build a Tower too high for the waters to be able to reach; and that he would avenge himself on God for destroying their fore-fathers."

3. [About An. 2520] Now the multitude were very ready to follow the determination of Nimrod, and to esteem it a piece of cowardice to submit to God: and they built a Tower; neither sparing any pains, nor being in any degree negligent about the work. And, by reason of the multitude of hands employed in it, it grew very high, sooner than anyone could expect. But the thickness of it was so great, and it was so strongly built, that thereby its great height seemed, upon the view, to be less than it really was. It was built of burnt brick, cemented together with morter, made of *bitumen*; that it might not be liable to admit water. When God saw that they acted so madly, he did not resolve to destroy them utterly; since they were not grown wiser by the destruction of the former sinners: but he caused a tumult among them, by producing in them diverse languages; and causing, that through the multitude of those languages, they should not be able to understand one another. The place wherein they built the Tower is now called *Babylon*: because of the confusion of that language which they readily understood before: for the Hebrews mean by the word *Babel, Confusion*. The *Sibyll* also makes mention of this tower, (21) and of the confusion of the language when she says thus: "When all men were of one language, some of them built a high tower, as if they would thereby ascend up to heaven. But the Gods sent storms of wind, and overthrew the tower, and gave every one his peculiar language. And for this reason it was that the city was called *Babylon*." But as to the plan of Shinar, in the country of Babylonia, Hestiæus mentions it, when he says thus, "Such of the Priests as were saved took the sacred vessels of Jupiter Enyalius, and came to Shinar of Babylonia."

Appendix C
Seven Years

THERE IS AN interesting word search through the Scriptures for the phrase, "seven years." There are Scriptures that suggest the Lord may send a time of prosperity before the horrible days that are described in the Book of Revelation. In the Book of Genesis during the time of Joseph, there was to be a period of seven years of plenty and seven years of famine. It is possible from Genesis 41:26-54, that the Lord will send a time of prosperity upon the earth before the seventieth week of Daniel begins, which will be the last seven years on planet earth where human government rules.

Ezekiel 39:9 declares that Israel will be burning weapons for seven years. Could this verse be one of the events that describes the seven years of prosperity before the seventieth week of Daniel?

In the first year of King Hezekiah there was a revival followed by a time of prosperity as Hezekiah sought the Lord. In the fourteenth year of Hezekiah's reign, the Assyrian King invaded Judah and sought to capture Jerusalem as recorded in Isaiah 36:1. The king of Assyria (type of the antichrist) sent Rabshakeh (type of the false prophet) to Jerusalem requesting their surrender, and making great boasts against the Lord as the antichrist will do when he breaks his covenant with the nation of Israel. Genesis 10:8-11 declares that the kingdom of Assyria came out of Babel which is in the land of Shinar. The Assyrian is a type of the antichrist as declared in Isaiah 52:4. In Isaiah 37:36-37, the Lord sent one angel who destroyed the Assyrian army in one night. This is a type, an illustration, as Jesus will return and defeat the armies of the antichrist when he marches to Jerusalem.

Bibliography

Aland, Kurt: "The Greek New Testament: Its Present and Future Editions," *Journal of Biblical Literature*, LXXXVII / June 1968.
Amazon Nation: *Semiramis, Queen of Assyria*.
Anderson, Sir Robert: *The Coming Prince*, 1986.
Barnhouse, Donald Grey: *Revelation*, eleventh printing, 1971.
Carson, D.A.: *The King James Version Debate, A Plea for Realism*, second printing, 1980.
Dager, Albert James: *The Day of Yahweh: A Biblical Eschatology With a Study on the Book of Revelation*, 2012.
Forbush, William Byron: *Fox's Book of Martyrs, A History of the Lives, Sufferings and Deaths of the Early Christians and Protestant Martyrs*, seventeenth printing, 1980.
Forvan, George F.: *SEMIRAMIS: Legendary Mysterious Great Queen of Assyria*.
Fuller, David Otis D.D.: *Which Bible?*, fifth edition, 1980.
Fuller, David Otis D.D.: *True or False?*, third printing, 1978.
Fuller, David Otis D.D.: *Counterfeit or Genuine Mark 16? John 8?*, Second edition, 1978.
Halley, Dr. Henry H.: *Halley's Bible Handbook*, New Revised Edition, twenty-fourth edition, 1965.
Hawkins, Yisrayl: *The Original Goddess: Semiramis of Babylon*, House of Yahweh.
Hislop, Rev. Alexander: *The Two Babylons or the Papal Worship*, second edition, 1959.
Hocking, David: *The Coming World Leader*, 2000.
Hunt, Dave: *The Roman Catholic Church and the Last Days – A Woman Rides the Beast*, 1994.

Revelation

Ironside, Harry A: *Babylonian Religion.* Prasch, James Jacob: *Harpazo, the Intra-Seal Rapture of the Church,* 2014.

Prasch, James Jacob: *Shadows of the Beast, How the Identity of the Coming Antichrist Will be Revealed to the Faithful Church,* 2011.

Prasch, James Jacob: *The Dilemma of Laodicea,* 2010.

Prasch, James Jacob: *Roots of Babylon,* Moriel Ministries, moriel.org.

Rosenthal, Marvin: *The Pre-Wrath Rapture of the Church,* 1990.

Self, Bryce: *Semiramis, Queen of Babylon,* http://ldolphin.org/semir.html, 1984.

Stokes, G.T.: *Acts of the Apostles, Vol. II.*

Smith, Chuck with David Wimbish: *The Last Days, The Middle East and the Book of Revelation,* 1991.

Whiston, William: *Josephus, the Antiquities of the Jews,* 1981, Complete Works, page 30.

Wilson, Robert Dick: "A Scientific Investigation of the Old Testament," (Philadelphia: *The Sunday School Times* CO., 1926)

https://www.biblegateway.com/ All Scripture references are from Bible Gateway with their kind permission.

http://www.revival-library.org/index.php/catalogues-menu/revival-miscellanies/revival-prayer/prayer-and-revival Prayer and Revival, J. Edwin Orr.

Index

Abomination of desolation, 11, 14, 56, 76, 122, 130, 133, 143, 147, 154, 164, 268
Abraham, 36, 54, 119, 164, 240
Abyss, 119-120
Adrian II, 208
Ahab, 136, 192, 197
Alexander the Great, 151
Alexandrian manuscripts, 7, 8, 66, 68, 70-71, 267, 268
Altar, 31, 67, 79-82, 85, 101, 103-105, 107, 121, 123, 129, 130, 169, 170, 172, 176, 182-183, 187, 233, 242, 243, 265
Ammon, 75, 148
Apostasy, 52, 56, 109, 129, 266
Armageddon, 89, 109, 115, 173, 185, 186, 203, 214
Asklepios, 31
Assyria, 153, 156, 157, 159, 162, 164, 205, 242, 277, 279
Asteroid, 110, 115, 116
Athena, 31
A-Tribulation, 14, 45, 271
Baal, 39, 192
Babel, 35, 154, 196, 198-200, 202, 213, 276, 277
Babylon, 5, 11, 34, 36, 89, 109-111, 116, 151, 153, 156, 158-161, 163, 166-168, 172, 183, 186-189, 191-198, 200, 201, 203, 205, 211-223, 225, 235, 275, 276, 279, 280
Balak, 30-33
Before the First Seal, 6, 13, 19, 20, 53-57, 64-66, 85-87, 90, 137, 265, 267
Book of Life, 41, 43, 142, 149, 204, 249, 250, 257, 262
Bottomless Pit, 117-121, 134, 137, 142, 204, 237, 238, 249
Bridegroom, 10, 47, 222, 228, 244, 245
Caiaphas, 161
Calf-Worship, 100
Calvary Chapel, 45
Chaldeans, 214, 217, 223, 245

281

Revelation

Cherubim, 60, 225
Codex Sinaiticus, 8, 66-70, 80
Codex Vaticanus, 8, 66-70, 80
Commercial Babylon, 5, 172, 195, 211, 214, 216, 218, 219, 221
Constantine, 28, 35, 36
Covenant, 7, 13, 20, 52, 53, 55-57, 59, 60, 74, 88, 128, 130, 133, 135, 148, 177, 183, 189, 225, 234, 246-248, 267, 268, 277
Cyrus, 43, 212
Dark Ages, 39
David, 26, 43, 44, 45, 63, 71, 102, 109, 143, 156, 177, 186, 225, 232, 233, 240, 241, 246-248, 262, 273, 279, 280
Day of Christ, 7, 20, 52, 53, 55, 88, 155
Day of the Lord, 7, 52, 53, 65, 67, 85, 87, 88, 92, 95, 108, 109, 113, 114, 120, 122, 123, 131, 135, 137, 170, 230, 231, 251, 254, 267-269
Deilos, 254
Demetrius, 154
Demons, 119, 120, 122, 124, 173, 196, 197, 212, 213, 238, 239
Devil, 27, 36, 37, 49, 61, 62, 84, 118, 119, 134, 143, 144, 145, 172, 204, 235, 237, 238, 249
Dogs, 260-262
Earthquake, 83, 84, 105, 118, 127, 130, 140, 145, 188, 190, 213, 214, 221, 232
Ecclesiasticism, 204
Ecumenical, 154
Edict of Milan, 36
Edom, 75, 148, 230
Egypt, 7, 32, 68, 69, 75, 108, 110, 112, 114, 122, 123, 134, 148, 153, 156-159, 164, 177, 179, 180, 182, 184, 185, 189, 205, 219, 242
Elders, 24, 32, 51, 59, 60, 63, 65, 66, 80, 102, 104, 123, 127, 128, 137, 140, 165, 176, 177, 183, 187, 225
Elijah, 11, 65, 109, 128-129, 135-137, 267
Emergent Church, 49, 154
Ephesus, 18, 23-27, 29, 45, 50, 52, 128
Epiphanes, Antiochus, 11, 75, 133, 154
Erasmus, 43
Eschatology, 49
Euphrates, 121, 185, 223
Ezekiel, 60, 92, 100, 101, 114, 138, 139, 144, 156-158, 181, 193, 194, 197, 200, 202, 218-220, 237, 238, 242, 247-249, 269, 270, 277
Foxes Book of Martyrs, 28
Fuller, David, 71, 279
Futurism, 12
Gnosticism, 68
Gog, 249
Gomorrah, 122, 167, 172, 212, 214
Graham, Billy 82
Great Tribulation, 38, 39, 56, 65, 76, 80, 81, 84, 92, 93, 95, 102, 103, 111, 121, 123, 128, 130, 131, 132, 146, 147, 148, 164, 183, 188, 215, 265-269
Greece, 151-153, 159

Index

Hades, 119, 240
Harrison, Norman, 96
Harvest, 169, 170-172, 186, 231, 233
Heads, 33, 51, 59, 86, 117, 121, 122, 142, 149-153, 158, 159, 162, 165, 177, 193, 194, 204, 220, 221
Herod, 37, 143, 235
High Priest, 27, 40, 64, 107, 256
Hislop, Alexander, 34, 195, 200, 279
Historicism, 12
Hitler, Adolf, 73, 96, 97, 147, 153, 163, 171
Holy Spirit, 10, 24, 29, 31, 37, 39, 42, 46, 49, 61, 102, 104, 105, 109, 135, 158, 162, 191, 228, 266
Horns, 63, 74, 121, 132, 142, 149-153, 159, 193, 194, 204-206, 219, 246
Intra-Seal, 6, 14, 83, 92-94, 96, 101, 103, 129, 164, 269, 280
Irenaeus, 56, 164
Isaiah, 17, 44, 45, 49, 57, 85, 88, 89, 92, 108, 112, 113, 118-120, 139, 144, 158, 162, 164, 166, 169, 171, 183-185, 189, 190, 193, 194, 199, 212-214, 216-218, 228-230, 233-235, 237, 238, 242-244, 250, 251, 257, 268, 269, 277
Iscariot, Judas, 11, 74, 158
Israel, 7, 12, 20, 30-33, 39, 50, 52, 53, 55-57, 66, 73, 74, 76, 85, 89, 90, 92, 93, 99-101, 104, 112, 126, 128-133, 136, 141, 142, 147, 156, 159, 162, 164, 170, 171, 177, 184, 186, 192, 219, 227-231, 233, 242-248, 255, 256, 268, 277
Jeremiah, 11, 50, 85, 110, 111, 167, 168, 195, 202, 212-216, 222, 223, 231, 245, 246
Jews, 13, 27, 33, 43, 49, 66, 76, 84, 85, 86, 92, 99, 100, 123, 128, 130-132, 134, 143, 146-148, 153, 154, 157, 161, 163, 171, 200, 216, 232, 233, 267, 273, 280
Jezebel, 38, 39, 111, 192, 197
Job, 10, 108, 142, 143, 181
Joel, 87, 88, 92, 109, 120, 123, 170, 231, 268, 269
John the Baptist, 135, 136, 162
John VIII, 208
John XII, 208
Josephus, Flavius, 93, 94, 200, 275, 280
Key of David, 43-45
King James Version, 3, 8, 12, 67-71, 267, 279
Kingdom Age, 5, 100, 128, 133, 171, 237, 238, 241, 242, 249
Lake of Fire, 29, 62, 97, 169, 176, 207, 234, 235, 249, 250, 254
Lamb, 7, 39, 63-66, 73, 80, 82-85, 89-91, 94, 102-104, 107, 140, 143, 145, 148, 149, 152, 159, 160, 162, 165, 166, 168, 170, 175, 183, 187, 188, 206, 226, 244, 255-257, 259, 267
Laodicea, 18, 25, 44, 46-50, 52, 56, 70, 81, 104, 173, 192, 266, 280
Locusts, 117, 120, 121, 137, 166, 238
Lot, 46, 54, 87, 172, 187, 188, 214
Luther, Martin, 39
Maccabees, 133
Magog, 249
Malachi, 11, 65, 109, 135-137, 250, 267
Marinus, 208
Mark of the Beast, 52, 56, 92-94, 123, 133, 155, 162-164, 167, 169, 171, 179, 180, 207, 234

Revelation

Marozia, 208
Marriage, 10, 35, 47, 87, 196, 226, 227, 228
Mary, 69, 141
Medes, 34, 151, 153,159, 195, 196, 205
Megiddo, 186
Messiah, 11, 13, 34, 50, 107, 128, 132, 135, 143, 153, 154, 167, 171, 176, 232, 233, 262, 273
Meta Tauta, 19, 51
Michael, 84, 118, 126, 143, 144
Midrash, 10, 11, 13, 154, 158-160, 234, 249
Mid-Tribulation, 6, 14, 67, 91, 92, 96, 97, 103, 164, 268
Moab, 31-33, 75, 148
Moon, 18, 83, 85-88, 92, 109, 110, 112-114, 118, 120, 141, 145, 170, 184, 190, 231, 256, 257, 268, 269
Mosque, 130
Most Holy Place, 11, 100, 103, 107, 177
Mountain, 54, 75, 83, 110, 119, 120, 139, 144, 148, 152, 166, 168, 170, 188, 190, 205, 221, 229, 231, 232, 235, 238, 244, 248, 255
Muslim, 43, 130
Mussolini, 163
Nebuchadnezzar, 93, 160, 163, 197, 198
Nephesh, 181
Nero, 28, 162, 192
Nicolaitanes, 23, 26, 27, 30, 31
Nimrod, 34, 153, 154, 183, 195, 196, 199-203, 207, 221, 229, 249, 276
Noah, 59, 60, 87, 93, 153, 154, 181, 199, 201-203, 207, 275, 276
Olive trees, 134
Orge, 7, 83, 89-92, 95, 96, 103, 106, 107, 109, 121, 122, 124, 140, 168, 221, 265, 266, 268-270
Orr, Edwin, 81, 82, 103, 280
Partial Rapture, 14, 45, 270
Paul, 20, 24, 26-29, 35, 37, 38, 43, 47, 52, 55, 62, 90, 93, 106, 107, 109, 163, 196, 227, 254, 255, 270
Pergamos, 18, 30, 31, 34-37, 45, 50, 52, 81, 104, 191, 192, 195, 196, 207, 266
Persians, 34, 151, 153,159, 195, 196, 205, 212
Pesher Midrash, 10, 154, 161
Peterson, 71
Pharaoh, 114, 123, 156-158, 180, 182
Philadelphia, 18, 43-46, 50, 81, 280
Pilate, 235
Poemicism, 12
Polycarp, 28, 56, 164
Pompeii, 157
Pope, 21, 39, 40, 111, 163, 192, 202, 208
Pope Benedict IX, 208
Pope Gregory, 41, 208
Pope Innocent III, 21, 208
Pope John Paul II, 163

284

Index

Pope Pius XXII, 163
Pope Sergius III, 208
Post-Tribulation, 6, 14, 90, 104, 106, 107, 164, 270
Prasch, Jacob, 10, 12, 34, 94, 129, 280
Pre-Nicaean, 28
Preterism, 12
Pre-Tribulation, 6, 13, 19, 20, 53-55, 57, 64, 65, 90, 265, 266
Pre-Wrath, 6, 14, 65, 67, 95, 96, 101, 103, 106, 109, 164, 269, 270, 280
Priest, 27, 33, 40, 52, 64, 88, 107, 139, 189, 234
Priesthood, 31, 40, 64, 192, 195, 258
Protestant Reformation, 39, 42, 191-193, 203
Purpose Driven, 49
Qatsaph, 89
Rabshakeh, 162, 277
Received Text, 7, 8, 66-68, 70, 71, 81, 103, 267
Reformation, 39, 42, 162, 191-193, 203, 208
Religious Babylon, 5, 110, 116, 191, 211
Resurrection, 29, 60, 70, 140, 192, 202, 239, 240, 241, 251
Revivals, 24, 82
Roman Catholic Church, 39, 42, 111, 163, 192, 194, 200, 203, 207, 208, 279
Roman Empire, 28, 35, 151, 152, 159, 192, 196, 205, 206
Rome, 19, 34, 40, 110, 111, 151, 153, 157, 159, 192, 196, 203-205
Rosenthal, Marvin, 65, 95, 280
Sardis, 18, 39, 41-47, 50, 52, 81, 104, 173, 192, 193, 266, 271
Satan, 27, 30, 38, 39, 41, 43, 45, 74, 84, 89, 97, 118, 122, 138, 142-147, 150, 153-155, 158-161, 173, 188, 195, 196, 201, 203, 204, 212, 237, 238, 249
Saul, 143
Semiramis, 200-203, 279, 280
Shinar, 35, 154, 183, 196-200, 212, 213, 221, 223, 275-277
Sixth Seal, 6, 14, 65, 67, 82-92, 94-96, 103, 106, 107, 109, 116, 118, 140, 145, 161, 190, 221, 268-270
Smith, Chuck, 81, 280
Smyrna, 18, 27-30, 81
Sodom, 46, 54, 122, 134, 167, 172, 187, 212, 214
Solomon, 10, 60, 177, 202
Spurgeon, 24, 173
Stars, 18, 19, 23, 41, 83-86, 88, 110, 112-114, 118, 120, 139, 141, 142, 144, 145, 147, 170, 180, 231, 237
Stepinac, 163
Sun, 18, 19, 33, 80, 83, 85-88, 92, 103, 104, 109, 110, 112-115, 117, 118, 120, 125, 141, 145, 170, 172, 183-185, 188, 190, 207, 231, 234, 256, 257, 259, 268, 269
Tammuz, 200-202
Temple, 11, 14, 31, 43, 50, 52, 55, 60, 74, 76, 80, 92-95, 100, 103, 104, 107, 127, 129, 130, 132, 133, 134, 135, 140, 155, 164, 169, 175, 176, 177, 179, 183, 185-188, 194, 202, 213, 214, 221, 233, 242, 256, 261, 268, 269
The Message, 71
Theodora, 208

Revelation

Throne, 16, 34, 36, 39, 40, 45, 47, 48, 51, 52, 59, 60, 63, 64, 66, 67, 80, 83, 102-105, 109, 118, 128, 137, 139, 142-145, 165, 176, 183, 187, 188, 189, 190, 195, 199-201, 213, 214, 221, 225, 226, 237, 239, 241, 246, 249, 250, 253, 259, 261, 266, 267
Thumos, 5, 7, 83, 89, 103, 104, 107, 109, 124, 126, 140, 146, 163, 166, 168, 169, 175, 176, 181, 185, 214, 265, 270
Thyatira, 18, 38-41, 45, 47, 50, 52, 81, 104, 110, 192, 196, 207, 266, 268, 271
Tree of Life, 23, 27, 259, 260
Tribulation, 12, 13, 14, 18, 27, 28, 38, 85, 86, 91, 240, 266, 268, 269, 270, 271
Tyre, 156
Tyrus, 138, 144, 156, 194, 200, 218-220, 237
Vatican, 8, 39, 66, 68, 110, 163, 191, 192
Virgins, 10, 14, 47, 104, 165, 166, 202, 208, 270
Witnesses, 5, 6, 65, 99, 109, 118, 121, 128, 129, 133, 134-140, 267, 268
Wormwood, 111
Zechariah, 34, 35, 130, 131, 134, 135, 154, 159, 160, 186, 190, 197, 212, 213, 215, 221, 232, 233, 238, 242
Zeus, 31
Zombie Apocalypse, 121

About the Author

ROBERT LEE DRUMHELLER was born at West Point, New York, on October 15, 1954. He is a licensed minister with the Full Gospel Assemblies, International. He has been teaching the Bible for over 25 years. He has served as an assistant pastor at Beth-Hebron in Crafton, Pennsylvania, for four years.

Robert was taught and held to the Pre-Tribulation view of the harpazo for many years. After hearing of alternate views of the harpazo, and after much research, he came to the conclusion that the Pre-Tribulation view lacked scriptural support. It was his desire to write and reveal to others the various views of the harpazo and to present the Scriptures that each side presents to demonstrate their viewpoint. The Scriptures that Robert presents for each of the various views should not be considered exhaustive as that would be beyond the scope of this book.

Robert is retired from secular work and is now devoting his time to the study of the Scriptures and to writing. He is currently a Cell Group leader, teaching the Bible.

Robert resides in Pittsburgh, Pennsylvania, with his wife Jadwiga.